D0893665

Shakespearean Power
and Punishment

Shakespearean Power and Punishment

A Volume of Essays

Edited by
Gillian Murray Kendall

Madison ● Teaneck
Fairleigh Dickinson University Press
London: Associated University Presses

Associated University Presses
440 Forsgate Drive
Cranbury, NJ 08512

Associated University Presses
16 Barter Street
London WC1A 2AH, England

Associated University Presses
P.O. Box 338, Port Credit
Mississauga, Ontario
Canada L5G 4L8

The paper used in this publication meets the requirements
of the American National Standard for Permanence of Paper
for Printed Library Materials Z39.48–1984.

Library of Congress Cataloging-in-Publication Data

Shakespearean power and punishment : a volume of essays / edited by
Gillian Murray Kendall.
  p. cm.
Includes bibliographical references (p.   ) and index.
ISBN 0-8386-3679-9 (alk. paper)
1. Shakespeare, William, 1564–1616—Political and social views.
2. Politics and literature—Great Britain—History—16th century.
3. Literature and state—Great Britain—History—16th century.
4. Shakespeare, William, 1564–1616. Measure for measure.
5. Literature and society—England—History—16th century. 6. Women
and literature—England—History—16th century. 7. Power (Social
sciences) in literature. 8. Punishment in literature. I. Kendall,
Gillian Murray, 1956– .
PR3017.S575 1998
822.3'3—dc21   96-50028
                                                                CIP

Contents

6 CONTENTS

Introduction

Gillian Murray Kendall

The following essays demonstrate how effectively different—indeed, seemingly contradictory—theoretical paradigms can work with Shakespeare's plays to excavate issues of power and punishment. Within these essays, readers will meet the old historicism and the new historicism, the work of Bakhtin and the work of de Sade, the principles of cultural poetics and of feminist materialism, Foucault's theories about power and punishment, and King James'. Each theoretical tool is sharp; each unearths different complexities of the intertwining power relations within Shakespeare's plays and, in a number of essays, those of his contemporaries.

From these approaches emerge not only answers, but key questions about Shakespearean power and punishment—questions that merit future exploration: Where, in these plays, does power lie? Are there inherent limits to the exercise of power? Are established power structures stable, or, as certain branches of new historicism might suggest, do processes of subversion and containment cause a constant metamorphosis of those structures?

In their examination of just such issues of power and punishment, these essays also begin to excavate the enormous number of questions that future explorations of Shakespearean power and punishment will need to address: What is the relationship between acts of power and punishment in Shakespeare's plays and historical enactments of power in the Renaissance? And what, finally, do the extremely varied approaches of these essays to a given topic have to say about the critical enterprise itself?

The Renaissance Culture of Power and Punishment

One central Renaissance concept frames the essays of this volume: From minor domestic disputes to mighty falls from the giddy heights of power, the Renaissance discourse of power and punishment was a highly public one. All acts of power had potential repercussions for the state (one might note James' interest in the status of domestic authority) making them public acts. Most acts of punishment, moreover, are enhanced (or even, one might say, made legitimate) by public display. And as Michel Foucault (often quoted by the contributors to this volume)[1] has noted, the material public suffering that was often a consequence of (in particular) the state's manipulations of power was in the Renaissance everywhere evident.

This was an age in which subjects (including, of course, overdaring playwrights) could be put on the scaffold ostensibly to display their utter powerlessness, and in which the exercise of power and punishment could be almost unimaginably cruel. The body of the subject itself became a locus for the discourse of power and punishment. The work of Stephen Orgel, Steven Mullaney, Stephen Greenblatt, Jonathan Dollimore, Leonard Tennenhouse, J. A. Sharpe, and Fran Dolan,[2] to name just a few, has, indeed, shown the scaffold functioning as a kind of theater meant to exhibit the power of the state over the body (and, as repentance speeches seem to show, over the mind) of the subject. But there is evidence, too, that the excesses of the state—as Elaine Scarry has suggested of the uses of torture in general[3]—show a fundamental weakness in that state. Like the excesses of revengers and murderers, spectacular state-orchestrated executions full of sound and fury could sometimes end by signifying nothing—or worse than nothing.

The spectacle of outdoor executions and mutilations was, moreover, never discrete from the literary products of the culture. Hangings and quarterings were an inspiration to the creators of broadside ballads, and, as Annabel Patterson has noted in *Censorship and Interpretation*,[4] a significant influence on the shape of literary forms. Simply to function as an author, to write, as Jonathan Goldberg states in *James 1*, is both to wield authority and, thereby, to risk attracting the censorious eye of authority:[5] Writers had not only the censor to fear, but the executioner. Stubbs lost a hand for authorial impertinence: Today it takes the case of Salman Rushdie for us to see feelingly to what extent literature can play a significant part in the dynamics and dialectics of power.

Shakespeare, like other playwrights, poets, and writers, had a stake in the discourse. As this volume demonstrates, the more we examine Shakespeare's plays, the more we realize that they wrestle with issues of power—the power of the playwright, of the text itself, and of characters who do battle with power structures, who, for example, flirt with the possibility that a member of the body politic might be able to attempt to act autonomously—to resist or, perhaps, to attempt to acquire the power held by the state.

Many of Shakespeare's plays portray characters who try to pull away from social constraint and to exercise their own kind of power. Whether through the use of disguise or magic or acting ability, these characters attempt to step outside of a role that might be seen as entirely socially articulated. In come cases, too, Shakespeare's plays demonstrate the willing submission of characters to such constraints—a submission that is itself sometimes a paradoxical acting out of power. The actions of these characters, however, is complicated by the fact that within the plays, as within the culture, the state never exists as a monolithic all-encompassing power structure. Tillyard's picture of the Elizabethan world picture[6] has, for some time, been demonstrated to be an inadequate window on Renaissance centers of power, but the extent to which that picture is distorted by competing voices/texts/performances has only begun to be explored.

In the worlds and subworlds of Shakespeare's plays, small loci of power are ever-present to stir up disturbing eddies and currents within structures of authority—structures that, often, would like to portray themselves as overarching. Valerie Wayne, in her collection *The Matter of Difference,*[7] uses feminist materialism (a reply to the divisions between the old new historicism and feminism) to show how complex power relations within a culture can be. And as Heather Dubrow writes in *The Historical Renaissance*[8] "we tend to concentrate too exclusively on centralized power." Dubrow notes the complicating presences of "a Catholic landowner" and "a wealthy widow in a Suffolk village." How, she writes, "did the presence of such alternative power bases complicate those at court and, indeed, complicate the very notion of power?" This is a question that, in part, these essays will address.

This does not mean that there is always agreement among the contributors to this volume as to whether or not the plays involved are tapping into Elizabethan/Jacobean orthodoxies about power and punishment or, to borrow a term from new historicist criticism, subverting those orthodoxies. As the following papers make clear, even the question of where power lies can be a knotty one. In the worlds Shakespeare presents, sometimes the seemingly powerless can control their worlds, while the powerful are sometimes hampered by their very authority. If there is one thing that the following essays demonstrate—whatever their critical approach—it is that Shakespearean power is never a permanent investiture in one being or one state. Power centers shift constantly, and power can prove suddenly elusive at moments when characters seem most in control. There is no possible way (nor, these essays collectively make clear, should one make the attempt) to define power monolithically. The center of power is always temporarily located, often in unlikely characters, and is frequently wielded at unlikely moments. Power can be a commodity to be bought, borrowed, lent, lost or usurped, and it can also be beyond commodification: a concept intangibly fluid, abstract and remote, and at the same time, subject to time and change, distortion and slippage.

The Essays

The essays in this volume divide themselves rather neatly, I think, into three major sections. The first group of essays discusses power and punishment as it relates to women in Shakespeare's plays; the second group centers on *Measure for Measure,* a play that recently has been brought into new prominence; and the third and final group extends the discussion of power to broader issues— for example, the tendency of power to undermine itself; the ruthlessness of the process of empowerment; the question of power and the playwright's relationship to the text. As, perhaps, befits the closing section of a book centered on Shakespeare's works, a number of these essays deal with *The Winter's Tale* and *The Tempest.*

Part I: Women and Shakespearean Power and Punishment

The papers in this section of the volume present an extended discourse on the ways in which women characters participate in the brokering of power and the meaning and meting out of punishment. While using very different approaches to this issue, all of these papers note the doubleness inherent in the representation of the female in Shakespeare's plays: Women, as objects of desire, as royalty, create anxiety in ways that, to a certain extent, would seem to give them power—to lift them out of the roles of powerlessness that social context would impose on them. Matching this imagery of women as figures of power, however, is a movement towards their constraint and eventual silencing. The very power that women wield in these plays, then, can be seen as a dramatic tool leading inevitably to a state of powerlessness when, with closure, anxiety must be assuaged.

Ann Rosalind Jones' essay, "Revenge Comedy: Writing, Law,

and the Punishing Heroine in *Twelfth Night, The Merry Wives of Windsor,* and *Swetnam the Woman-Hater,* deals with the power that comes to women (to Maria in *Twelfth Night* in particular) through movement in the public sphere—in Maria's case, as a writer and, according to Sir Toby's metaphors, a legal consultant. Jones notes, however, that Maria must, by play's end, return to a less dangerous (and anxiety provoking) sphere—the private sphere of spouse. Viola, too, is ordered back into the women's clothes that will, presumably, also remove her from the public sphere. The social conventions of marriage re-subordinate these characters to their social milieu. In *The Merry Wives of Windsor,* in contrast, power comes from within the middle-class domestic stations of the merry wives. Their weapons are laundry baskets and women's clothes; further, the more public humiliation of Falstaff must come with husbandly permissions, and the humiliation itself must reassert a discourse that valorizes traditional gender assumptions. In contrast to these plays, but as part of the discourse in which they partake, Jones discusses *Swetnam the Woman-Hater,* a play that undoes gender stereotypes and makes more apparent the containment of women provided by the closure of Shakespeare's plays, in which the power women wield is both beneficial and temporary—and beneficial because temporary.

Sexual jealousy motivates the (almost) stabbing of Imogen in *Cymbeline* and the wounding of Arethusa in *Philaster,* but by juxtaposing these two plays, Susanne Collier, in "Cutting to the Heart of the Matter: Stabbing the Woman in *Philaster* and *Cymbeline*", shows that what we are witnessing in these plays is a kind of ritual sacrifice in which power invested in royal women is undermined and transferred to male figures. Powerful women are suspect, not least because they are what Collier calls "opaque"—difficult or impossible to interpret beyond the surface. In a topical analysis calling up interesting new work on *Cymbeline,* Collier sets this opacity against James' use of the image of a transparent breast (an image that she notes crops up twice in *Philaster*): The rightful male heir may be read, but literal violence must be used to penetrate the heart of the female. Both of these plays, then, move towards the moment when royal women relinquish power. Imogen and Arethusa both lose thrones even as they gain husbands; Collier suggestively relates this to the movement of power from an Elizabethan court to that of the patriarchal "living nourse-father" of James.

But if Jones and Collier show how the anxieties raised by the powerful energy of some of Shakespeare's heroines is constrained (by marriage and/or by violence), Sara Eaton, in "'Content with

Art'?: Seeing the Emblematic Woman in *The Second Maiden's Tragedy* and *The Winter's Tale*" shows how the emblem tradition both reveals and then frames (and, in that sense, encloses) the power of women. The bodies of the Lady and of Hermione inspire actions that almost destroy kingdoms—and in that sense their bodies are objects of power and are, too, under intense scrutiny from the powerful. But in the course of these plays, their bodies are separated from their voices (Hermione speaks in Antigonus' dream; the Lady's ghost speaks), and when the women are reembodied, it is as emblems to be read—emblems that provide a reification of the power structures that frame them. Eaton's essay is not only a comment on the nature of power as it relates to women, but an analysis of the entire humanist endeavor to "read" and extract "truth"—in this case from what Collier would term the "opacity" of women.

Each of these essays moves us towards an understanding of women characters—an understanding that shows their power to be, most often, something fleeting, a sort of cultural bubbling up of characters who seem on the verge of escaping their cultural context. In that sense, the power wielded by these characters acts, too, as a plot-mover, as a tool of the playwright to generate anxiety that he must finally contain. Perhaps, then, not only playwright, but audience and theatrical convention as well, finally dictate the subjugation of these female figures of power, and their reintegration into the fabric of society.

Part II: Measure for Measure

Measure for Measure is a play that has recently achieved new prominence, not because of some sudden new insights into the problems of that problem play, but perhaps more because of a shift in interests. Whatever drawbacks critics may point to in new historicism (from which many early practitioners have since distanced themselves), the advent of such a critical school has served to focus attention on issues of power and subversion, rebellion and containment. And so it is not, perhaps, surprising that *Measure for Measure,* with its rebellious, libidinous citizens, its disguised Duke who engages in elaborate power plays, its discussions of law and of execution etiquette, has become a highly visible play.

While new historicism may have brought certain issues to our attention, the papers on *Measure for Measure* reveal radically the number of planes on which discussion of an overtly political phenomenon like power and punishment can take place. These essays show the wealth of approaches possible, and the way in which—perhaps because of the fluidity of drama in performance—different plays may be found nesting in the same text.

David McCandless' essay, "'I'll Pray to Increase your Bondage': Power and Punishment in *Measure for Measure*," locates the arena of power and punishment in the psyches of the characters, finding in Angelo (and, with various permutations, in others) desires to punish that, in their theoretical underpinnings, are not unrelated to the workings out of sadomasochistic pornography. In particular, McCandless sees Angelo as, in his public punishment of Claudio, engaging in a kind of flagellation of himself (or, rather, of his feminized sensual self) with Claudio as the stand-in for Angelo's libidinous flesh. In the same way, the Duke, in his desire to marry Isabella and possess her, may be seen to engage in a similar need to subjugate the feminine. McCandless discusses, too, how staging would enhance what the language of characters suggests.

Arthur L. Little, Jr., in his essay "Absolute Bodies, Absolute Laws: Staging Punishment in *Measure for Measure*," focuses on the Duke's attempt to gain psychological control of Vienna's citizenry. Little looks less, however, to Foucault's model and more to Bakhtin's paradigm of the classical and grotesque body. Little finds in the Duke the desire to become the one absolute body and absolute law in Vienna, and reveals Vienna to be a place of statues (and, of course, statutes)—where subjects conceive of their bodies as finished, complete, and therefore in competition with the Duke's absolutism. The Duke's subjects, moreover, have begun to imagine themselves as more than bodies, as possessing souls. By play's end, however, the Duke refocuses the gaze of his subjects onto himself as the only absolute body, and as one that possesses all the voices of Vienna—an idea that, Little notes, adds significance to Isabella's silence. Little suggests, however, that the playwright, in some sense, ultimately mocks even the Duke by demonstrating his absolute power to stage and script the Duke's actions. In other words, even the Duke is subject to the constraints of the world in which he lives and the psychic dramas that the world of Vienna produces. This important question about the playwright's relationship to the acts of power and punishment he stages is critical, and the subject of debate among the papers of the final section of this volume.

Robert N. Watson, in "The State of Life and the Power of Death: *Measure for Measure*", exposes much of the deep uneasiness that surrounds the standard state appeals that the Duke employs regarding procreation (as Benedick says, "the world must be peopled"), fame, and Christian piety. The Duke appears eager to use his power to promote lawful procreation and Christian attitudes towards death, but, according to Watson, this play threatens to expose piety, legitimacy and reputation as tools of the state in its own quest for immortality. The promise to the *individual* that immortality can be obtained through offspring, fame (reputation), or piety proves to be a hollow one. In the long run the state may get more citizens, and ones reconciled to their lot, but it is the state machinery that will ultimately survive, not individual human beings—not even the Duke. Lucio, as a voice of doubt, calls into question what characters (and audience) may want to believe about piety, reputation, and procreation, and he cannot finally be silenced, no matter how many penalties the state may threaten to impose on him.

While these essays allow us to view issues of power in *Measure for Measure* in very different ways, it is interesting that all three of them (like so much material dealing with power and punishment) focus on the body as signifier. For McCandless, the body as a site of punishment becomes the locus for sadopornographic display; for Little, the Duke attempts to show his power by marking other bodies as unfinished and grotesque, his own as classical; for Watson, the bodies in *Measure for Measure* ultimately reveal the constraints of biology—the force of survival that, embodied in the incorrigibly physical Barnardine, takes precedence over the desires of the individual and the state alike. These essays show how effectively one can interrogate the nature and function of power by interrogating the body.

Part III: The Limits to Power

Kathyrn Barbour's essay, "'Flout 'em and Scout 'em and Scout 'em and Flout 'em: Prospero's Power and Punishments in *The Tempest*," poses the difficult questions that Prospero must face: As a ruler, how can he be visible, seemingly benevolent, and retain power? Barbour shows Prospero's early blunders—his absence from the public gaze in Milan, his blindness to conspiracy—and she likens the island on which he finds himself to a laboratory where he can test out methods of political control. There, Prospero acquires the necessary skills of a political leader: He learns to use surveillance and (depending on the class of the potential offender) to administer physical and psychological punishment. His return to Milan, then, will be that of a politically astute, if slightly Machiavellian, prince, though Barbour hints that, without magic, Prospero's task in setting up a surveillance network in Milan may be difficult.

My own essay, "Overkill in Shakespeare," examines scenes of excess, scenes in which, for example, twenty mortal gashes are inflicted on a body when one would suffice. Like a number of essays in this volume, my piece attempts to show that the impulse to punish, when linked to a power that can inflict such punishment, often reveals limits to the body politic's ability to control and suppress the body natural. In examining three plays, *Measure for Measure, Macbeth,* and *The Winter's Tale,* the essay shows the ways in which the etiquette of execution can hamper the power of the state, the extreme punishments imposed on bodies can prove futile, and, in *The Winter's Tale,* the body originally destined for punishment can become an object of reverence.

The tasks of a political leader seeking control and of a playwright seeking control over his text are linked in Ronald R. Macdonald's essay, "The Unheimlich Maneuver: Antithetical Ways of Power in Shakespeare." Macdonald points out in many places the curious discrepancies between the power Prospero claims to have and the moments in which he seems mortal, unsure, absentminded. Like "Overkill in Shakespeare," this piece questions whether or not authority is always in some sense limited. The essay then goes further to ask whether or not the portrayal of those limitations in Shakespeare's plays shows a corresponding anxiety on the part of the playwright—who, at his desk, has absolute control, and who, once the play has been turned over to the players, becomes a marginal figure. Indeed, Macdonald posits the playwright as a kind of ghost figure, and invokes the legend that Shakespeare played the role of the ghost of Hamlet's father—as he notes, of course, the revenge tragedy that the ghost wants to see is very different from the one young Hamlet has in mind.

These concluding essays mark the enterprise of establishing power as fraught with contradictions and limitations. While other of the essays examine the marginal or marginalized, those whose power might more clearly seem weak or uncertain, these examine power at its most absolute. Yet it seems that while "absolute" may be the kind of power Prospero and Duke Vincentio and Macbeth and Leontes wish to wield, when stripped of rhetoric *about* their power these characters are revealed to exist in a slippery and unstable and contingent universe of power relations. Perhaps it is not surprising that we find, in Shakespeare's drama, that to rule a body politic—inevitably made up of individual bodies—is as tenuous a process as any playwright's attempt to maintain control over a play.

The papers in this volume invite us to ask a multitude of questions about Shakespearean power and punishment. Was Shakespeare a voice of orthodoxy, finally situating power in conventional places? Or do these plays constantly raise disturbing questions about the very places Shakespeare situates power? Do Shakespeare's plays contain characters who exhibit anxieties about autonomy and state control, about the ability to obtain power outside of their cultural context? These are not questions that any one essay or book can answer—nor are these the only questions that can be asked. But in reading and rereading the pieces contributed here, I cannot help but feel that the existence of Shakespeare's plays (as they unfold on stage) is based on disruptions of orthodox power or, conversely, on the disturbing consequences of employing that power. That is to say, just as Renaissance drama depends upon the deictic word to conjure up its characters and worlds, thus, inevitably, pointing to its own temporary power, so, too, Shakespeare must appropriate power in order to create his drama. Whether or not we and Shakespeare's characters are forever confined in the cloven pine of culture, whether the energy of Shakespeare's heroines is finally contained or whether the Duke of *Measure for Measure* and Prospero are characters who finally undermine or valorize the power of the state, Shakespeare's plays move forward only at moments of anxiety about power, at moments when the location and nature of power is in question. The plays can exist and avoid closure only so long as something is rotten in Denmark, so long as the fantastical Duke of dark corners lacks complete control, so long as Prospero's plot is made uneasy—even if only by his own machinations. Perhaps we should think less about closure; as these essays make clear, the moment of the play constantly interrogates the nature of power.

NOTES

1. See Michel Foucault, *Discipline and Punish: The Birth of the Prison*, tr. Alan Sheridan (New York: Vintage Books, 1979).
2. See Stephen Orgel, *The Illusion of Power: Political Theater in the English Renaissance* (Berkeley, University of California Press, 1975); Steven Mullaney, *The Place of the Stage* (Chicago: University of Chicago Press, 1988); Stephen Greenblatt, *Shakespearean Negotiations: The Circulation of Social Energy in Renaissance England* (Berkeley: University of California Press, 1988); Jonathan Dollimore and Alan Sinfield, eds., *Political Shakespeare* (Ithaca and London: Cornell University Press, 1985); J. A. Sharpe, "Last Dying Speeches", *Past and*

Present 107 (May, 1985), 144–67 and *Crime in Early Modern England 1550–1750* (London; New York: Longman, 1984); Frances E. Dolan, *Dangerous Familiars: Representations of Domestic Crime in England, 1550–1700* (Ithaca: Cornell University Press, 1994). See also Pieter Spierenburg, *The Spectacle of Suffering* (Cambridge: Cambridge University Press, 1984); Christopher Pye, *The Regal Phantasm* (London: Routledge, 1990); L. B. Smith, "English Treason Trials and Confessions in the Sixteenth Century", *Journal of the History of Ideas* 15 (1954), 471–98. All of these works discuss the state's use of the scaffold as a tool of power.

3. See Elaine Scarry, *The Body in Pain: The Making and Unmaking of the World* (New York: Oxford University Press, 1985).

4. Annabel M. Patterson, *Censorship and Interpretation: The Conditions of Writing and Reading in Early Modern England* (Madison, Wisconsin: University of Wisconsin Press, 1984).

5. Goldberg, Jonathan, *James I and the Politics of Literature: Jonson, Shakespeare, Donne, and their Contemporaries* (Baltimore: Johns Hopkins University Press, 1983).

6. E. M. W. Tillyard, *The Elizabethan World Picture* (New York: Macmillan, 1944).

7. Valerie Wayne, *The Matter of Difference: A Materialist Feminist Criticism of Shakespeare* (Ithaca New York: Cornell University Press, 1991).

8. Heather Dubrow and Richard Strier, eds., *The Historical Renaissance* (Chicago: University of Chicago Press, 1988). All quotations are from page 9.

Shakespearean Power
and Punishment

Part I
Women and Shakespearean Power and Punishment

Revenge Comedy: Writing, Law, and the Punishing Heroine in *Twelfth Night, The Merry Wives of Windsor,* and *Swetnam the Woman-Hater*

ANN ROSALIND JONES

ONE way that the culture of early modern Europe figured the spectacle of women punishing men was as comic inversion. In cartoons of the world turned upside down, Phyllis rides on Aristotle's back, the farmer's wife beats him with her distaff, a troop of women storms a city held by men. Folk rituals represented women on top to nonreading publics in charivaris and skimmington parades, while polemical pamphlets entertained the literate with the speeches of angry women putting misogynist men on trial.[1] Occasionally a broadside reported and pictured a woman who had, actually and locally, humiliated a powerful man; one instance, which crystallizes the conflicting hilarity and punitive violence such an incident provoked, is the title-page woodcut and the text of a 1595 pamphlet, "The Brideling, Sadling and Ryding, of a rich Churle in Hampshire, by the subtill practise of one Judeth Philips, . . . 1594."[2] But such comic inversions, appearing, among other places, in the plays of Shakespeare, handle female power in ways that suggest anxiety as much as amusement. In a period in which actual women were increasingly marginalized as workers and subordinated as wives,[3] scenes in which fictive women put men through public shaming rituals provoke questions about how social tensions might have been managed—contained, displaced, turned loose—in playhouse interventions in the Elizabethan and Jacobean gender war. I want to suggest the range of such possibilities by juxtaposing a pair of Shakespeare's comic punishing heroines, Maria in *Twelfth Night* and the country wives in *The Merry Wives of Windsor,* to the female chorus in the anonymous play *Swetnam the Woman-Hater Arraigned by Women,* performed in 1619. Two cultural territories, conceptually opposed yet increasingly inter-implicated in early modern England, connect the shifting represen-tations of gender conflict in these plays: the overlapping realms of oral and print culture, and the contested division of the private and public spheres—the household, the polis—into separate arenas for fantasy and action.

MARIA IN *TWELFTH NIGHT:* WHENCE "THE BEAGLE'S" POWER?

Maria punishes Malvolio by exposing him to public humiliation, in the form of the amused gaze of high and low members of the large household presided over by the countess Olivia. Rowe's 1709 "Dramatis personae" identifies Maria as a "waiting gentle-woman," that is, an unattached woman of upper-middling rank in attendance on a noblewoman. Similarly, Sir Toby Belch introduces her to Sir Andrew Aguecheek as "my lady's chambermaid."[4] These status terms are synonymous (in the 1590s, a chambermaid could be a lady-in-waiting as well as a female servant in an inn), yet they give the in-house gentlewoman an ambiguous position in relation to Malvolio. Maria's lines to Olivia suggest that she occupies the household as a "friend," housed and fed as a more or less class-equal companion rather than hired as a servant contracted for spe-cific wages. But Malvolio is employed as a paid retainer, Olivia's "steward." The play keeps open the possibility of an alliance be-tween Maria and Sir Toby Belch, a kinsman to the aristocratic Olivia, whereas Malvolio's fantasy of claiming Olivia as a wife, which he affirms by invoking a parallel case ("The Lady of the Strachy married the yeoman of the wardrobe," 2.5.39–40) elicits outrage from the knights spying on him.

Nonetheless, Malvolio is first represented as having considerable power in the household. In the scene of nocturnal revelry that he interrupts (2.3), he threatens Maria with Olivia's displeasure by blaming her for Sir Toby and Sir Andrew's uproarious singing: "Mistress Mary, if you prized my lady's favour at anything more than contempt, you would not give means for this uncivil rule; she shall know of it, by this hand" (120–23). Such a menace to woman/woman patronage gives social meaning as well as comic energy to Maria's plot against Malvolio. She repeats Olivia's moral judgment of Malvolio as "sick with self-love" (1.5.89), but she also points out the self-interest that determines his behavior: "The devil a

Puritan that he is, or anything constantly, but a time-pleaser"
(2.3.146–47)—a man ready to say or do whatever is required to
make his way in the world. So her plot against Malvolio is a revenge
plot, to remove her rival from Olivia's favor by maneuvering him
into upstart behavior and a costume the lady-in-waiting knows will
turn her mistress against the steward: "yellow stockings, and 'tis
a colour she abhors, and cross-gartered, a fashion she detests"
(2.5.190–200). What for Toby and Andrew Aguecheek is a domestic
prank, a drunkards' lark, "a device to dream on," is for Maria a
strategy to preserve what we would now call her job security.

In another crucial way, too, the play locates Maria as a player
in the public world: Her literacy makes possible her staging of
Malvolio's humiliation. She can read and she can write—not an
automatic pairing of skills for Renaissance women. Conjectures
about the literacy of Renaissance women are various and inconclusive, but Margaret Spufford has demonstrated that women who
could sign their names were fewer than those who could read.[5]
What's more, Maria can forge: By imitating Olivia's handwriting,
she acquires an epistolary power that she uses to defeat her rival.
By composing a letter in which she copies what Malvolio will take
for Olivia's "very C's, her U's, and her T's" and by using Olivia's
seal, her "Lucrece," to complete the deception, Maria manipulates
aristocratic orthography to make Malvolio fantasize himself as the
hero, like a farcical Tarquin, of the sexual conquest of a woman
high above him in the social hierarchy.

Maria's (and Olivia's) handwriting would presumably have been
the Italic mode, recommended for women in England because it
required less concentration to learn than, for example, chancery
script. But as Jonathan Goldberg points out in his study of handwriting theory and practice in the Renaissance, *Writing Matter,* a
widening contradiction became evident in attitudes toward
women's handwriting during the 1590s. While male pedagogues
argued that training in handwriting would consolidate women's enclosure in the private sphere (like needlework, handwriting could
train them in domestic obedience), the French-Scottish Huguenot
Esther Inglis, presenting her calligraphic books to royal and aristocratic patrons, likened herself to an Amazon queen on account of
the "defiant bravery" of her pen.[6] Maria as writer is less defiant
but more cunning. She produces, as she says, an "obscure epistle
of love," in which she uses enigmatic rhymes and the riddle of the
initials "M. O. A. I." to entrap Malvolio as desiring reader. The
forgery, the phrasing, and the apparently accidental dropping of
the letter set him up as the interpreter of a text designed to elicit

a predictably self-aggrandizing construal from an upstart whom its writer knows all too well. This play reassigns the writerly persuasion reserved for publicly trained men in early modern England to a privately employed woman.

Besides writing the script that prompts Malvolio to action, Maria directs a series of scenes in which other characters push his humiliation further. She ensures Olivia's mockery of him by acting as a *nuncio,* declaring before his entrance that "he is sure possessed" (3.4.9), and she leads Sir Toby into the role of exorcist. He addresses Malvolio by drawing upon a discourse that combines theological cliché with concern for public safety: "How do you, Malvolio? . . . What, man, defy the devil! Consider, he's an enemy to mankind." In fact, Sir Toby claims two kinds of authority: A shift from ecclesiastic to legal language occurs in his plan to keep Malvolio in a dark room as a madman. Toby says to Maria: "we may carry it thus for our pleasure, and his penance, till our very pastime, tired out of breath, prompt us to have mercy upon him: at which time we will bring the device to the bar, and crown thee for a finder of madmen" (3.4.138–42). Like Maria's handwriting, Toby's metaphor positions her in the public world, now as a legal consultant, an inspector of lunatics. The "finder" of lunatics was an actual position, an enforcer of the writ *De lunatico inquirendo* (*TN,* note to 3.4.142, 100).

However fanciful Toby's conceit of Maria as public prosecutor may be, it is, in fact, her public shaming of Malvolio that prompts Olivia's remark at the end of the play: "He hath been most notoriously abused" (5.1.378). Olivia may well be parodying Malvolio here rather than sympathizing with him; as the Arden editors point out, he has used the word "notorious" to complain of his treatment three times in the play (at 4.2.90, 5.1.328, and 342). At the time, moreover, "notoriously" could simply mean "in public fashion, as a matter of common knowledge" (*Oxford English Dictionary*). But that commonness of knowledge is exactly what pains Malvolio: His courtship of Olivia has been exposed as the bid for social power so clearly revealed in the soliloquy in which he imagines using his new "place" as a height from which to abuse Sir Toby (2.5.55–78). It could even be said that by making Malvolio's private desires a topic for public derision, Maria effeminizes him: Like a "common" whore, he is condemned for a transgression that combines the private and the public, the sexual and the social.[7]

Malvolio's final humiliation, read as the scapegoating scene generic to festive comedy, is also, significantly, a humiliation invented and staged by a woman: Maria puts Malvolio on trial. In the carnival world of the play, a reversal of gender roles is to be expected. But Maria is not allowed to circulate permanently as a free-floating judge, outside male control. Her role as righter of class disorder is only temporary, and Shakespeare assigns the use of legal language to the male characters who surround her rather than Maria herself. What makes her "device" permissible, representable without too much danger to conventions of gender, is that it convinces Sir Toby to marry her, that is, to replace her in a social system ordered according to masculine privilege. However disorderly Olivia's kinsman may be, he is an aristocrat and a man. Although Toby's delighted comment on Maria's wit inverts conventional marriage contracts ("I could marry this wench for this device . . . And ask no other dowry but such another jest" 2.5.182–85), his admiration goes hand in hand with his conviction that "the wench" is slavishly devoted to him. His description of her to Andrew Aguecheek suggests that her reinforcement of his self-love endears her to him as much as her wit: "She's a beagle, true-bred, and one that adores me" (2.3.179–80).

Indeed, the slippery connotations of the terms of affection applied to Maria by various characters suggest how deeply suspicion of witty women permeated Elizabethan language. Feste, praising Maria for an "apt" bit of repartee, encourages her to use her intelligence to make Toby stay sober: "if Sir Toby would leave drinking, thou wert as witty a piece of Eve's flesh as any in Illyria" (1.5.27). Taken simply, the synecdoche "a piece of Eve's flesh" simply means "woman"; but its connotation of dangerous female wiliness, like Sir Toby's later "thou most excellent devil of wit!" (2.5.207), belongs to the discourse of misogyny. Similarly, Sir Toby's "Good night, Penthesilea" (2.4.177) raises the specter, however mock heroic, of Amazonian victories over men as a sex (a specter that was, in fact, enabling rather than comic to Ester Inglis). Toby's diminutives, predictably, put Maria into a more manageable size and species: She is "the little villain" (2.5.13), "the youngest wren of nine" (3.2.64). And when he calls her "my metal of India" (2.5.14), he uses the vocabulary of woman as treasure and territory. This is a vocabulary shared by John Donne, apostrophizing his mistress in "The Sun Rising" as "both the Indias, of spice and mine," and by Falstaff in *The Merry Wives of Windsor,* to whose "she is a region in Guiana, all gold and bounty" I will return.[8]

Twelfth Night, then, mobilizes women as "gull-catchers" and suitors on their own account. But at its conclusion, Orsino orders Viola to resume her women's "habits" and Fabian speaks for Maria, concealing her part in the game and assigning it to Toby, probably because as Olivia's kinsman Toby is less in danger of her wrath.[9] "The little villain" disappears under masculine protection. In spite of the play with dominance and submission at the end of Act 2, when Toby asks Maria, "Will thou set thy foot o' my neck?" and offers to become her "bond-slave," the symmetrical coupling with which the comedy ends places all of its heroines under male jurisdiction. Can Maria direct the play only insofar as it can finally contain her?

PAGE AND FORD IN THE MERRY WIVES OF WINDSOR:
MISTRESSES OF BOURGEOIS VIRTUE

In *The Merry Wives of Windsor,* the number of heroines and the punishments they mete out are doubled. Falstaff, in fact, is triply humiliated, twice in the private household of Mistress Ford and once in the folk pageant played out by the entire cast in the Windsor woods. This multiplication of comic humiliations has a counterpart in the occasionally abstract quality of the play's language, the tendency of its men and women to assess each other not as individuals but as members of a gender or class category. The positioning of characters in opposing factions links the comedy to contemporary pamphlet wars and to the Swetnam play, which directly invoke public discourses and public arenas to generalize the battle between the sexes. But in this play, in contrast to *Twelfth Night,* the temporary power of women to expose and humiliate a man is predicated on their class-celebratory corroboration of proper gender arrangements. As models for women of their station, Shakespeare's merry wives do more than to orchestrate a power reversal amidst the festive disorder of a large, aristocratic household. Instead, the playwright assigns them the role of turning their codirected plot to torment Falstaff into a larger drama that transforms the mischief of female tricksters into a Windsor-wide celebration of the chastely respectable middle-class woman.[10]

Falstaff's punishable act in the play, as many critics point out, combines sexual and financial transgression. He courts two married women in hopes of extracting their husbands' cash from them, gleefully imagining Mistress Page as "a region in Guiana, all gold and bounty" and exulting that both wives "shall be my East and West Indies, and I will trade to them both" (1.3.65–68).[11] The knight, as London opportunist-entrepreneur, hopes to deceive two country women and to poach on two husbands' territories.[12] What traps him immediately, however, is what might be called his hyper-literacy: by writing exactly the same conventionally amorous letter to Mistresses Page and Ford, he provokes Mistress Page into denouncing him as a publishing scoundrel. Comparing the seducer of women to the printer of books, she links Falstaff's power over the printed word to the sexual power she intends to resist. Her metaphor of Falstaff as heavier than Mt. Pelion plays upon the gendered vocabulary of printing, according to which the male-run press operated from above upon a "bed" in which female "forms" had been "laid down" by men working with individual letters:[13]

> I warrant he hath a thousand of these letters, writ with blank space for different names—. . . and these are of the second edition. He will print them, out of doubt; for he cares not what he puts into the press, when he would put us two. I had rather be a giantess, and lie under Mount Pelion. (2.1.71–77)

Falstaff's attempt to manipulate the wives by putting them into the category of identically impressionable readers prompts them to categorize him in an even more hostile way: They imagine an attack on him as an attack on the entire sex to which he belongs, legitimated by the official legal apparatus. Reading his letter, Mistress Page exclaims, "O wicked, wicked world . . . ! Why, I'll exhibit a bill in Parliament for the putting down of men" (1.1.20–29). Later, recalling his entrapment in Mistress Ford's laundry basket, she uses the same generalizing vocabulary: "Hang him, dishonest rascal! I would all of the same strain were in the same distress" (3.3.171–2). And as she and Mistress Ford plan the nocturnal pageant in which he will be pinched and singed by children disguised as fairies, Shakespeare assigns her a couplet that represents Falstaff as an example to others of his kind: "Against such lewdsters and their lechery / Those that betray them do no treachery" (5.3.21–2).

Stylistically, the axiomatic ring of the couplet suggests that this final punishment calls for more justification than the laundry-basketing and crossdressing the wives first impose on Falstaff. Why should this be so? The wives themselves make a distinction between private and public justice. The dirty laundry and fat woman's costume in which Falstaff takes refuge are humiliating precisely because they belong to the domestic realm of women's work and adornment. As judges—although only in this private sphere—the wives declare themselves content with the sentences they have meted out. Mistress Ford asks Mistress Page, "What think you: may we with the warrant of womanhood and the witness of a good conscience, pursue him with any further revenge?" The legal vocabulary is extended in Mistress Page's lenient response: "The spirit of wantonness is sure scared out of him; if the devil have him not in fee-simple, with fine and recovery, he will never, I think, in the way of waste attempt us again" (4.2.193–199). For a private offense, private justice. Although Shakespeare assigns his two women characters legal language and represents them using it with considerable precision here, he limits the discourse to the playful, private sphere of a female tête-à-tête.

But Falstaff's offense has also been an assault on town dwellers who he assumes will be too simple to defend themselves, and this rural (more properly, suburban) class requires revenge of a more public kind. So the wives invoke their husbands' authority for the outdoor ritual that will be performed by their fellow Windsorites. Mistress Page renounces judicial power, saying that the wives will not declare a final sentence against Falstaff but only carry out their husbands' will: "If they can find in their hearts the poor unvirtuous fat knight shall be any further afflicted, we too will still be the ministers" (4.2.203–5). Mistress Ford's prediction suggests that husbandly revenge, the townspeople's judgment against London chicanery, and dramatic necessity all reinforce one other: "I'll warrant they'll have him publicly shamed; and methinks there would be no period to the jest should he not be publicly shamed."

Master Ford's willingness to see Falstaff tormented in public is predictable, according to the logic of cuckoldry: he has been obsessed throughout the first four acts of the play with what he thinks is his own humiliation as a betrayed husband. Ford suffers more than Falstaff, at least mentally, once he is convinced that his wife is setting up rendezvous with the "damned Epicurean rascal" (2.2.276). Through Ford, the type of the jealous husband, Shakespeare draws the hostile generalizing formulas of gender polemic into the comedy. In the first soliloquy he writes for Ford, the husband denounces his wife as an example of all women's duplicity in a typical misogynist leap from "she" to "they," from what he thinks his wife is doing to the claim that all women do the same:

Would any man have thought this? See the hell of having a false woman: my bed shall be abused, my coffers ransacked, my reputation gnawn at. . . . I will rather trust a Fleming with my butter, Parson Hugh the Welshman with my cheese, an Irishman with my aqua-vitae bottle, or a thief to walk my ambling gelding, than my wife with herself. Then she plots, then she ruminates, then she devises; and what they think in their hearts they may effect, they will break their hearts but they will effect. (2.2.280–97)

Although the play eventually discredits such assumptions about women (though not about Welshmen and horse thieves), it gives full energy to Ford's enunciation of them. Indeed, it is by quoting a supposed rant of Ford's that Mistress Page terrifies Falstaff into dressing as Mrs. Ford's "maid's aunt, the fat woman of Brainford." The audience does not need to hear Ford saying what Mistress Page attributes to him because the predictability of misogynist discourse allows her to invent spontaneously a convincing outburst for the angry husband:[14]

> your husband is in his old lines again: he so takes on yonder with my husband: so rails against all married mankind; so curses all Eve's daughters, of what complexion soever; and so buffets himself on the forehead, crying, "Peer out, peer out!", that any madness I ever yet beheld seems but tameness, civility and patience to this his distemper he is in now. (4.2.17–24)

Yet the play treats even Ford's final conversion comically. When he assures his wife, "I rather will suspect the sun with cold / Than thee with wantonness; now doth thy honour stand / In him that was of late an heretic, / As firm as faith," Page warns him against excess of any kind, including total faith in female virtue: "Tis well, tis well; no more. Be not as extreme in submission / As in offense" (4.4.7–12). A middle ground like Page's is free of the totalizing positions that ground misogyny and its opposite: exceptionally, he neither damns nor idealizes women.

Curiously, however, the pageant with which the play ends does both. According to the plot of the comedy, this is a show designed to put Falstaff on trial. Its "Song" targets him as an example to be avoided and a body to be punished: "Fie on sinful fantasy, / Fie on lust and luxury! / . . . Pinch him fairies, mutually; / Pinch him for his villainy" (5.5.94–101). If, as has been conjectured, Shakespeare wrote the forest scene for the 1597 celebration of a feast of the Garter, his audience was Elizabeth as well as her courtiers.[15] Hence the compliment, in the fairies' masque, to "Our radiant Queen" (5.5.47) and the command to sweep and decorate Windsor Castle to make it "in state as wholesome as in state 'tis fit, / Worthy the owner, and the owner it" (60–61). But the queen's unique radiance is contrasted, in Pistol's verse, to the "sluts and sluttery" she hates (47): the royal lady's purity is defined against the sloppy housekeeping of bad maids. Evans, dressed as "a Welsh fairy,"

expands the attack on the depravity of average women by sending
another fairy to give sound sleep to "a maid / That ere she sleep
has thrice her prayers said" but adding: "But those as sleep and
think not on their sins / Pinch them, arms, legs, backs, shoulders,
sides, and shins" (50–55).

What is the relevance of such a command? The country wives
have proved that they are free of "sins to think on." Indeed, as the
masque ends, Page's wife addresses a triumphant gender and class
challenge to the would-be trickster from the city: "Now, good Sir
John, how like you Windsor wives?" (107). What's more, Mistress
Page and Mistress Ford have declared their virtue outright in the
previous act, contradicting the assumption, endemic to conduct
books and misogynist satire, that a woman seen to enjoy herself
in public was certain to be immoral in private. Because this attitude
is articulated in Falstaff's interpretation of Mistress Ford's hospi-
tality ("she discourses, she carves, she gives the leer of invitation,"
1.3.41–42), it is understandable that Shakespeare gives the wives
an emphatic pair of couplets in which to refute it:

> We'll leave a proof, by that which we will do
> Wives may be merry and yet honest too.
> We do not act that often jest and laugh;
> 'Tis old but true: 'Still swine eats all the draff.'
>
> (4.2.95–98)

Nonetheless, the masque invokes traditional magic against bad
women: The festive folk vocabulary reproduces suspicions that the
wives have been at pains to dispel. This is a comedy in which
women expose the enemies of their sex—the jealous husband and
the venal lecher—to laughter. But the wives are themselves controlled by a discourse of female cleanliness and marital chastity
that never becomes an object of mockery.[16] By revealing Falstaff's
plot to her husband, Mistress Ford proves herself "the honest
woman, the modest wife, the virtuous creature" he accuses her of
not being in Act 4 (2.118–20). The play's celebration of its heroines'
temporary power as directors of the plot and playful users of legal
vocabulary does not extend to destabilizing the model according
to which Elizabethan gender ideology defined proper feminine
behavior.

SWETNAM AND THE JACOBEAN PAMPHLET WARS: WOMEN AS JUDGES AND EXECUTIONERS

If Shakespeare's punishing heroines are read through the lens of
pamphlets by men and women published in the decades following

Twelfth Night and *The Merry Wives of Windsor,* writing and printing stand out clearly as material conduits for polemical critique of male/female relations. Legal metaphors and fictions through which women put men on trial continue into Jacobean texts, where they become more vivid and more violent. One example is *Swetnam the Woman-Hater Arraigned by Women,* a play performed at the Red Bull in 1619. No author is named in the printed script; critics have conjectured that it was written by Thomas Heywood, probably with collaborators.[17] The villain of the piece, Swetnam or "Misogunes," is based on the historical Joseph Swetnam, the writer of *The Araignement of Lewd, Idle, Froward and Unconstant Women,* a pamphlet first published in 1615 and frequently thereafter. Swetnam also published a guide to fencing, an aspect of the historical model comically attacked in the play, in which he is exposed as an inept swordsman. More emphatically than *The Merry Wives of Windsor,* this play works generically, structurally, and satirically to discredit the enemy of women. The legal framing of courtroom scenes in which women interrogate Swetnam and the physical violence the play figures in its anonymous heroines' attacks on him are evidence that its writer(s) were responding (and perhaps adding fuel) to a fiercely heated gender debate.

Swetnam's genre, tragicomedy, calls for a plot that puts women attacked by men at greater risk than they run in comedy. The story brings Swetnam, driven out of England by the rage his pamphlet has aroused, to Sicily, where the princess Leonida has been accused of unchastity for her secret meetings with Lisandro, the prince of Naples. Leonida's brother, Lorenzo, returning to Sicily in disguise, undertakes to defend his sister at a trial where, disguised as the Amazon Atalanta, he confronts Swetnam in a "publike disputation" over which sex is guilty in an affair such as Leonida's and Lisandro's (3.2). Because the party judged to deserve greater blame will be executed, the play presents Swetnam's antiwoman arguments as potentially lethal to Leonida; she is condemned to die by male judges and jurymen, who give the victory to the misogynist. Only after arranging a false execution for Leonida and preventing Lisandro from committing suicide does Lorenzo/Atalanta reveal himself and save the lovers. No festive conventions protect Leonida against Swetnam's claims. Instead, all the big guns of romance are required to save her: Lorenzo's intricate plot, his physical heroism, and his production of a masque in which "Repentance" converts the king who has condemned the lovers.

Structurally, the play counters the gender debate won by Swetnam with a second trial in which the women of Sicily seize the roles of judges and jury. His humiliation begins when Atalanta exposes the love letter he has written her as proof of the insincerity of his misogyny; women eavesdropping on the scene rush out to pinch him and stab him with pins. This treatment recalls Malvolio and Falstaff as objects of female ridicule and targets of women's weapons (laundry baskets, old clothes), but gender reversals in the tragicomedy are considerably less playful. The stabbing with pins sets Swetnam up as a male victim of the technique by which female suspects were examined for witchcraft, and the play differs from Shakespeare's comedies in the ferocity of the women's attack. They imagine a series of other possibilities, including tearing Swetnam's "limmes in pieces, joynt from joynt" and piercing him with "Bodkings" (5.2.159–63). This play also provides an elaborate legal setting for the women's refutation of Swetnam. The fourth act stages their revenge as a full, formal hearing, implying that the gender debate cannot be dealt with through individual solutions but requires public resolution. Swetnam is condemned as "Guiltie, guiltie, guiltie. / Guiltie of Woman-slander, and defamation" (5.2.289–90). His pamphlet is adduced as evidence, and he is sentenced to be muzzled, led through public squares, tied to a post "In every street i' the Citie" to be baited by women, whipped throughout the land, and finally shipped into exile "amongst the Infidels" (5.2.338). Rather than a comic enactment of private revenge, this decree is a startlingly systematic blueprint—though not yet the enacted spectacle—for antimisogynist discipline and punishment.

As satiric challenge to the commonplaces of misogyny, *Swetnam the Woman-Hater* plays off a set of contemporary sources: three pamphlets published against Swetnam under women's names in 1617.[18] The pseudonymous Ester Sowernam called the second half of her *Ester hath hang'd Haman* "The Arraignment of Josep Swetnam . . . and under his person . . . of all idle, franticke, forward and lewd men," a title that obviously provided the governing idea for the play. The title of Rachel Speght's *Mousel [Muzzle] for Melastomas* is the source of the first element of Swetnam's sentence. And one threat posed in Constantia Munda's "Worming of a Mad Dog" is the basis of Swetnam's punishment as well as of the two-trial pattern of the play: "we will baite thee at thine owne stake, and beat thee at thine owne game." The playwright, then, appropriates ideas and phrasing from a recent printing-press war, and he constructs Swetnam not as an idiosyncratic "overweener" in class terms, as Malvolio and Falstaff are, but as an institutionalized gender bully, the linchpin of a trial that Atalanta/Lorenzo exposes as structurally unfair because it permits only one sex to speak.

The play undoes gender models in other ways, too. Lorenzo deliberately undermines the authority of his father, King Atticus; the son's plot convinces the king to regret his harsh decision and to feel relief rather than anger when he discovers that it has not been carried out, so that the happy ending of the play, the marriage of Leonida and Lisandro, supports their illicit love over the paternal decree. If this ending belongs to romantic comedy, it is nonetheless made possible by Lorenzo's disguise as a woman, which, in contrast to Falstaff's, is not a temporary comic mishap but a sustained strategy central to his success. By cross-dressing as Atalanta, he claims rhetorical authority in the courtroom through his status as an Amazon (unmarried and foreign, he is allowed to speak, where Leonida cannot). And at the end of the play, the contrast between his feminine disguise and his masculine expertise in fencing allows him to surprise Swetnam into revealing his inadequacy as swordsman and pamphleteer alike.[19]

Above all, *Swetnam* mobilizes an anonymous chorus of angry women to determine its villain's sentence. No status as merry yet virtuous wives, named Mistress in relation to a Master Ford or Page, is affirmed by the mass *ad hominem* of women rising up against Swetnam as the representative of ideas publicly circulated against their sex. Two "Old Women," categorized neither as maids nor wives, pronounce the final judgment on Swetnam. And the woman-hater's servant exposes him not as a comic scapegoat who consolidates the marriages of his betters but as a writer whose theory has undermined matrimony as an institution: "He put his Booke i' the Press, and publisht it, / And made a thousand men and wives fall out" (5.3.319–20). In contrast to Shakespeare's fleeting conceits, the legal language of the public sphere becomes the central issue in this tragicomedy. It derives from and plays back into a world of published texts and sustained polemics among them, and it mobilizes the discourse of law as a vocabulary and practice appropriated by women not only metaphorically but politically.

I've traced out these contrasts not to make an anachronistic argument that *Twelfth Night* and *The Merry Wives of Windsor* should have dramatized a 1617 pamphlet "flyting." Still less, however, am I claiming that the Bard could prophesy what was to come in the gender war. My co-reading of three texts that belong to an innovative genre best called revenge comedy is intended to reveal a canon-aerating difference among them. Women's power in the Shakespearean texts works in the interests of social order; the takeover of printed polemic and legal discourse by historical and fictive women in the Swetnam controversy refuses that order. *Swetnam the Woman-Hater* is a mold-breaking play. Its use of prose polemic to rework dramatic conventions and its legitimizing representation of women as a unified group in protest jolt its eponymous "hero" into a newly typical and therefore politically significant status. What next? What new trials, in the press and onstage, awaited the early modern misogynist?

NOTES

1. For a richly detailed analysis of women punishing men in popular ritual, see Natalie Zemon Davis, "Women on Top," in *Society and Culture in Early Modern France* (Stanford: Stanford University Press, 1975), 124–51. For analysis of female violence against men in English pamphlet debates and on the stage, see Simon Shepherd, *Amazons and Warrior Women* (Brighton: Harvester, 1981); *The Women's Sharp Revenge: Five Women's Pamphlets of the Renaissance* (New York: St. Martin's Press, 1985); and Linda Woodbridge, *Women and the English Renaissance* (Urbana: University of Illinois, 1984), chaps. 8, 10 and 12.

2. See Stephen Foley, "Falstaff in Love and Other Stories." *Exemplaria* 1:2 (1989), 226.

3. For the classic argument for the economic disempowerment of women throughout the Renaissance, see Alice Clark, *The Working Lives of Women in the Seventeenth Century* (London: Routledge and Sons, 1919; reprint, Routledge and Kegan Paul, 1982). Her argument is confirmed by Susan Cahn, *Industry of Devotion: The Transformation of Women's Work in England, 1500–1660* (New York: Columbia University Press, 1987). See also Davis, "Women in the Crafts in Sixteenth-Century Lyon," in *Women and Work in Preindustrial Europe*, ed. Barbara Hanawalt (Bloomington: Indiana University Press, 1986), and Martha Howell, "Women, the Family Economy, and the Structures of Market Production in Cities of Northern Europe during the Late Middle Ages," in *Women and Work.* For increasing constraints on women in marriage, see Constance Jordan, *Renaissance Feminism: Literary Texts and Political Models* (Ithaca: Cornell University Press, 1990) and Cahn.

4. This and subsequent quotations from *Twelfth Night* are taken from William Shakespeare, *Twelfth Night,* J. M. Lothian and T. W. Craik, eds., Arden (London: Methuen, 1975).

5. Margaret Spufford, *Small Books and Pleasant Histories: Popular Fiction and its Readership in Seventeenth-Century England* (Cambridge: Cambridge University Press, 1981), 21–22.

6. Jonathan Goldberg, *Writing Matter: From the Hands of the English Renaissance* (Stanford: Stanford University Press, 1990), 135–55, 149.

7. In an interesting Lacanian reading of Maria's letter as an endlessly circulating signifier, Barbara Freedman links the letter to the floating identities of the principle characters in the play. See *Staging the Gaze: Postmodernism, Psychoanalysis, and Shakespearean Comedy* (Ithaca: Cornell University Press, 1991), 217–18. Lacan's interpretation of the purloined letter in Poe's story is relevant to my analysis, too, to the extent that Lacan stresses the unfixed quality of the letter-as-phallus in Poe's text. In Shakespeare's play, similarly, whoever controls

the letter, of whatever sex—in this case, Maria—occupies at least temporarily the phallic position by controlling how others in the intersubjective network will be seen.

8. For an extended analysis of territorial metaphor applied to women in Elizabethan and Jacobean texts, see Patricia Parker, "Rhetorics of Property: Exploration, Inventory, Blazon," in *Literary Fat Ladies: Rhetoric, Gender, Property* (New York: Methuen, 1987), 125–54.

9. Critics have concurred in the misattribution of the letter-plot, and the motives for it, to male characters. Lothian and Craik read the device as Sir Toby's triumph over Malvolio, with no reference to Maria (*TN*, Iviii n4), and W. S. Walker argued that her line on Malvolio as "a kind of Puritan" properly belongs to Sir Andrew (*TN*, note to 2.3.139, 52).

10. This assessment of the play is shared by two critics whose essays on the play I admire. Carol Thomas Neely concludes, "the play can incorporate . . . witty and manipulative married women who control all the men . . . because all [its] motifs function to protect the crucial possessions of the middle rank—money, land, and marital chastity." "Constructing Female Sexuality in the Renaissance: Stratford, London, Windsor, Vienna," in *Feminism and Psychoanalysis,* ed. Richard Feldstein and Judith Roof (Ithaca: Cornell University Press, 1990), 218. Sandra Clark emphasizes more than Neely the subversive teamwork of the wives but draws similar conclusions. See "'Wives may be merry and yet honest too': women and wit in *The Merry Wives of Windsor* and some other plays," in *"Fanned and Winnowed Opinions": Shakespearean Essays Presented to Harold Jenkins,* ed. John Mahon and Thomas Pendleton (London: Methuen, 1987), 249–67. Barbara Freedman offers a psychoanalytic conjecture about the gender affect of the play: Falstaff's role as buffoon, which the audience both criticizes and relishes, mobilizes the clown's traditional function "of playing on fears of and hostility towards women," a role Ford shares when he attacks Falstaff disguised as "mother Prat." "Falstaff's Punishment," *Shakespeare Studies* 14 (1981): 170.

11. This and subsequent citations from *The Merry Wives of Windsor* are taken from William Shakespeare, *The Merry Wives of Windsor,* H. J. Oliver, ed., Arden (London: Methuen, 1971).

12. Three critics have recently refined the consensus about the territorial and class conflict between Falstaff and the Windsor husbands. G. K. Hunter argues against a simple categorization of the play as citizen comedy by pointing out that Falstaff as courtly seducer is never taken seriously by anyone but himself. See "Bourgeois Comedy: Shakespeare and Dekker," in *Shakespeare and his Contemporaries: Essays in Comparison,* ed. E. A. J. Honigmann (Manchester: Manchester University Press, 1986), 10. Peter Erickson argues that the romantic hero, Fenton, by deceiving both wives in order to marry Anne Page, "enacts the rehabilitation and vindication of true aristocracy," which he sees further affirmed in the garter pageantry of the last act. "The Order of the Garter, the cult of Elizabeth, and class-gender tension in *The Merry Wives of Windsor,*" in *Shakespeare Reproduced: The Text in History and Ideology,* ed. Jean Howard and Marion O'Connor (New York: Methuen, 1987), 124. But Stephen Foley suggests that Shakespeare, by drawing on anecdotes about actual women's trickery for the forest scene, allies himself with the wives against royal power by using the kind of female unruliness sensationally represented in popular pamphlets to destabilize the Garter ceremony's compliments to the court. See "Falstaff in Love and Other Stories," 240–1.

13. Margreta de Grazia, "The Matter of Printing: Technologies of Mechanical

and Sexual Reproduction in Early Modern England" (MLA paper, San Francisco, 1991).

14. For a related comment on the "irrational fear of women as 'they'" in this speech, see Nancy Cotton, "Castrating (W)itches" Impotence and Magic in *The Merry Wives of Windsor," Shakespeare Quarterly* 38, no. 3 (1987): 323.

15. For a discussion of the Garter ceremony as occasion for the play, see Oliver, ed. *The Merry Wives,* 45–49.

16. Erickson states the point very firmly: "Both for the culture and for this play, chastity is the central term through which male leverage over women is effected. It designates the one condition on which women are allowed to exercise power. Chastity provides the conceptual and emotional basis for the cult of Elizabeth, and the wives are made compulsively to stress their honesty as the source of their license." "The Order of the Garter," 134.

17. Coryl Crandall, ed., Introduction to *Swetnam the Woman-hater: The Controversy and the Play* (Purdue, Illinois: Purdue University Studies, 1969).

18. For an edition of these pamphlets and good notes, see Shepherd, *The Women's Sharp Revenge;* for commentary see Betty Travitsky, "The Lady Doth Protest: Protest in the Popular Writings of Renaissance Englishwomen," *ELR* 14 (Autumn 1985): 255–83; Woodbridge, 85ff., and Ann Rosalind Jones, "Counterattacks on the 'Bayter of Women,'" in *The Renaissance Englishwoman in Print: Counterbalancing the Canon,* ed. Anne Haselkorn and Betty Travitsky (Amherst: University of Massachusetts, 1990), 45–62.

19. I am grateful to members of my 1992 Folger seminar on the gender polemic in Europe, however, especially Susan Anderson, for pointing out that the play assigns eloquence and effective action to Lorenzo in ways that contradict its emphasis elsewhere on female agency.

Cutting to the Heart of the Matter: Stabbing the Woman in *Philaster* and *Cymbeline*

Susanne Collier

THE woodcut gracing the title page of the first quarto *Phylaster* must have appealed to a popular audience in 1620–21 with its lurid depiction of the subtitle, *Love Lyes a Bleeding*. It signals action with Philaster sneaking off into the bushes on the right; at left, it conveys violence in the dark gash of blood staining the Princess' breast; it suggests sex in the illustration of her exposed nipples and also, perhaps, in the central figure of the "Cuntrie Gentellman" with his upright sword. There is even a sense of the scene's comic possibilities in the insouciance with which the beruffed and feathered country gentleman reclines, oblivious to the injured woman on the left. It is a remarkably concise rendering of the climactic scene of the play—Arethusa's survival of a chest wound from her murderous lover because of the melodramatic intervention of a bewildered countryman.[1] The woodcut and its inspiration, "Love Lies a Bleeding," refer specifically to Arethusa's role as the victim of her lover's mistaken passion; in that sense, her stabbing is the central action of the play. Similarly Imogen, pictured in an engraving, prefigures in 1786 her enormous popularity with nineteenth-century audiences as she decorously gestures with one arm to her well-draped bosom (although we do catch a glimpse of tantalizing ankle) as she offers the hilt of the sword to a horrified Pisanio. Her desperate expression and Pisanio's unsteady footing offer the possibility that the sword, which points directly at the area of her groin, might hit a different mansion of her love. Nevertheless, the caption repeating her invitation for him to stab her heart underscores her meekness and submission. Indeed, one of the many similarities between *Philaster* and *Cymbeline* is the earnest desire with which each of these slandered women meets her unjust punishment by the direction of her chosen husband.[2] Further, the simi-

39

The woodcut on the title page of the first quarto of *Phylaster*, reproduced from the original in the Henry E. Huntington Library and Art Gallery.

larity of these characters' entire situations is part of one of the most intriguing of the insoluble Shakespearean mysteries. Without arriving at consensus, critics have disputed the precedence of either *Cymbeline* or *Philaster* for decades.[3] In my view, however, chronological primacy is not so important to establish as is the potential significance of the fact that two discrete public plays with marked similarities in language, situation, and plot were staged in such close proximity, geographically and temporally, that for subsequent readers their origins have effectively merged into a single point in time. Dating most probably from the same year, 1609 or 1610, we are confronted with two plays written for the same elite company and the same audience[4] in which a princess and heir to the throne, after defying her father to choose her own husband, is slanderously reported as sexually unfaithful and is then murderously assaulted by the chosen husband (or his agent), only for him to discover her true fidelity. The critical questions, therefore, are these: what broader political issues of Jacobean court and theater may we see articulated within this contrapuntal presenta-

CYMBELINE.

—— take it, and hit
the inward mansion of my love, my heart.

Act 3   Scene 4.

Imogen offers the hilt of the sword to a horrified Pisanio, London, 1786.

tion of the spectacle of punishment—within scenes in which a royal female of slandered sexuality is threatened with death by stabbing through the heart? And what does the seemingly inscrutable, opaque nature of these women (as far as their chosen husbands are concerned) reveal about women as part of a political world?[5]

Certainly the plot material of sexual jealousy was familiar to audiences of the King's Men. Obviously *Othello, The Merry Wives of Windsor,* and *The Winter's Tale* all profile the pathological anxiety of a powerful or prominent male who fears his wife has cuckolded him. In *Cymbeline* and *Philaster,* however, both Imogen and Arethusa are the heirs to a throne. Thus, I would argue, by depicting the future queen's two bodies—as the physical locus of desire as well as an embodiment of the political state—the potential uses of her sexuality diffuse the location of fidelity from the merely domestic to social and political sites of power and punishment.[6] The issue of her punishment oscillates from a cuckold's revenge upon his seemingly unfaithful wife to a traitorous attack upon the nation. In the interpretive space between these two poles, I read conflicting anxieties exercised by the use of authority upon women's multivalent identities—stabbing the woman can be seen as an attempt to eradicate female powers, both physically and politically. In both *Cymbeline* and *Philaster,* attacks on princess-brides result in two effects: First, the woman is removed from the exercise of political power; second and equally important, the woman forgives and accepts her repentant husband so gratefully that even comic credulity is stretched. The display of these two relocations of the female reinforce a cultural discourse in which representatives of a patriarchy, when threatened by an inscrutable, seemingly opaque female of power, can stab first and repent at leisure.

Why do Imogen and Arethusa get attacked and why do the playwrights choose the mode of stabbing? I argue that they are attacked because the truth of their sexual identities is incomprehensible both to their male intimates and to a dominant male culture threatened by its dependence upon the princesses' potential political power. Further, I suggest that the playwrights' staging the use of a knife to cut into a woman's heart expresses a peculiarly Jacobean anxiety with the intersection of gender, truth, and power.

If we can read these displays of violence against women as an attempt by the "rightfully" dominant man to discern, contain, or control woman's multivalent identities, then the question of women's overlapping or shifting roles ought to concern us. How are these female characters presented? How are they interpreted or read? Certainly the audience is privileged with the truth of each princess' fidelity, but in both plays that truth about her sexuality is completely incomprehensible to her husband; instead, we see him rely upon the false information a male companion swears to be true. By simultaneously creating two different truths about the women—the fidelity an audience knows and the slanderous "true story" of cuckoldry that animates each husband—the playwrights create conflicting and overlapping females and explore a male incapacity to read women correctly.

Ostensibly the moment of the cuckold's revenge, Imogen's stabbing scene in *Cymbeline* is the central scene in the central act of the play. By letter, the banished Posthumus has ordered his servant Pisanio to exact "revenge" for "grief": "if thy faith be not tainted with the breach of hers; let thine own hands take away her life" (3.4.26–28); Pisanio is further ordered to send proof that Imogen has been stabbed. Although no actual blood is drawn, Pisanio indicates that Imogen is figuratively wounded by Posthumus's sentences: "What shall I need to draw my sword: the paper / Hath cut her throat already. No, tis slander / Whose edge is sharper than the sword" (3.4.33–35). Later, Imogen refers to the mortal "tent" that Posthumus's accusation has dealt to her (3. 4. 114–17). Thus, although the potential stabber balks at his task, the blow is given by proxy, and Shakespeare presents a princess who welcomes her punishment as martyrdom and, indeed, encourages her surrogate murderer: "Look, I draw the sword myself, take it, and hit / The innocent mansion of my love, my heart" (3. 4. 67–69). In *Cymbeline,* what starts as a contract killing is subtly transmuted into ritual sacrifice. A metaphoric coup de grace, "a feodary for this act" (3. 2. 21), the letter cuts her throat, while Imogen's lines depict her heart as an emptied house offered for open inspection by an obedient, sacrificial lamb bleating for its own slaughter. "Prithee, dispatch, / The lamb entreats the butcher. Where's thy knife?" (3. 4. 97–99).

While Imogen's looked-for martyrdom is the centered moment of Shakespeare's play, in *Philaster,* the act of stabbing Arethusa (for her supposed infidelity with the page, Bellario) is the dramatic climax of Act 4, and the scene's importance is reflected in the play's subtitle, "Love Lies a-Bleeding." It is also perhaps the best comic moment in *Philaster.* The scene is set in the forest, where Philaster enters to discover the page supporting a swooning Arethusa. His passion overcomes him and he draws his sword. In character with many cuckolds, Philaster excuses his "male" rival, Bellario, who then exits.[7] Philaster first asks Arethusa to use the sword to kill him, but, when she refuses, he tries to execute her with it. Simultaneously the "good" second quarto's stage directions call for the entrance of the Country Fellow, who exclaims in laudable though unsophisticated horror at the violent act: "Hold, dastard, strike a woman?"

> Philaster:
>   Leave us, good friend.
> Arethusa:
>   What ill-bred man art thou, to intrude
>   thyself
>   Upon our private sports, our recreations?
> Country Fellow:
>   God 'uds me, I understand you not; but I know
>   the rogue has hurt you.
>
> (4. 5. 89–93)

I imagine the comic implications work very well in performance, a bumbling bumpkin wading in to save a damsel in distress, only to have her turn on him haughtily for interrupting her "private sports." But equally insistent is the obvious psychoanalytical interpretation of the stabbing as a sexual act: a couple's private sport and recreation. The portrayal of the affianced husband punishing his bride for supposed sexual misconduct symbolically enacts the loathed act, including her fierce desire for the final thrust. In anthropological terms, the mythic association of death with the sexual act reinscribes the male as the priestly authority and the woman as the virgin, sacrificial offering to the gods. As in *Cymbeline,* the dramatists inscribe the princess as a willing martyr to male authority: Philaster, rightful heir to his kingdom, saves his people from corruption by spilling virgin blood. By staging the two stabbing scenes with overtones of ritual sacrifice, intertextual resonances of the salvation of society are superimposed upon the punishment of a domestic offense. Although the propitiation of the gods by Arethusa's sacrifice is further implied by Philaster's instant excuse of Bellario's supposed sexual role as the cuckolder ("I blame not thee / Bellario; thou hast done but that which gods / Would have transformed themselves to do" [4. 5. 57–59), nevertheless, the glibness of these words equally bears out the assumption that cuckoldry creates a bond among men as the dupes of women's betrayal (Kahn, 144). Similarly, although Posthumus revels in salacious horror at his mind's-eye picture of yellow Iachimo mounting Imogen, his revenge is directed solely at her and what she represents as his wife and his country's heir. Once Iachimo wins the wager, Posthumus not only tries to kill Imogen in "revenge," but he also fulfills his promise to the Italian to be "no further your enemy" (1. 5. 156). Indeed, in *Cymbeline* the bond between the two men, cuckold and cuckolder, is strengthened to the extent that Posthumus initially arrives traitorously in Britain to fight for the Italian nobles.

It is ironic, given that the ultimate result of these plays is to reduce women to political powerlessness, that consequent to the purposed stabbings of their wives, both Posthumus and Philaster temporarily lose their own identities in terms of familial and patriotic allegiance. Posthumus disguises not only his nationality but also, later, his nobility as a fighting Leonati by adopting the attire of a British peasant. The princely Philaster is reduced to a hunted animal and concocts an alibi for being weakened and bleeding while creeping into the bushes in order to escape arrest. As Coppélia Kahn reminds us, the apprehension of the loss of masculine name and honor felt by a cuckold dehumanizes him into a beast: simultaneously murderous and ridiculous (127). It is symptomatic of this degradation that traditional critics displayed their dislike for the characters of Posthumus and Philaster by branding them as being unworthy of the nobility.[8] Perhaps the heroes' paradoxical bestiality accounts for some of the historic unease with these plays: Tragicomedy as a genre is an uneasy mixture of the noble and the ignoble, the amusing and the life-threatening. Nevertheless, the husbands' derogation into a metaphoric, tragicomic mixed breed of bestial-nobility is further complicated by a diminution of masculinity. For the self-confessed cuckold, it has been suggested, his masculine identity has been threatened, and he can be seen as womanish.[9] In effect, I would argue, he becomes an androgynous figure: a compromised male who explains his identity as a fallen human exclusively in terms of the assimilation of vicious female characteristics. Posthumus's furious soliloquy at the conclusion of Act 2 dwells upon his mixed gender:

> Could I find out
> The woman's part in me—for there's no motion
> That tends to vice in man, but I affirm
> It is the woman's part: flattering, hers; deceiving, hers;
> Lust and rank thoughts, hers, hers; revenges, hers;
> Ambitions, covetings, change of prides, disdain,
> Nice longing, slanders, mutability;
> All faults that name, nay that hell knows, why hers
> In part or all: but rather all.
>
> (2. 4. 171–80)

The anxiety expressed here is equally misanthropic and mysogyni-
stic: ascribing human frailty to "the woman's part" and restating
traditional blame of Eve for original sin.[10] Nevertheless, Posthumus's lines refer to the essential sinfulness of all mortal human
identity, male and female, and it is in this context of mingled identity that Shakespeare stages Posthumus's later repentance in Act 5,
as the embracing of his membership in the commonality of sinners:

> You married ones,
> If each of you should take this course, how many
> Must murder wives much better than themselves
> For wrying but a little. O Pisanio,
> Every servant does not all commands:
> No bond but to do just ones. Gods, if you
> Should have ta'en vengeance on my faults, I never
> Had liv'd to put on this: so had you saved
> The noble Imogen, to repent and struck
> Me, wretch, more worth your vengeance. . . .
> For thee, O Imogen, even for whom my life
> Is, every breath, a death: and unknown,
> Pitied nor hated, to the face of peril
> Myself I'll dedicate.
>
> (5. 1. 1–29)

As Ann Thompson has pointed out, Posthumus is unique among
Shakespeare's jealous husbands in forgiving Imogen for her supposed sin.[11] Further, his consequent forgiveness in the soliloquy
seems to underscore Posthumus's acceptance of his woman's part,
by its position before the exposition of Imogen's innocence. The
comic resolution thus now appears dependent upon a husband
coming to terms with his assimilation of female characteristics.

Recognition of Posthumus's androgynous identity, however, problematizes the clear-cut distinction between the "rightly" vengeful
cuckold and the "justly" punished wife, just as it problematizes
the broader political implications of the play. If in his makeup as
a sinful human being he can be seen as ineluctably female, he also
must participate in the female part of the sexual sin. Once the
female has been sacrificed, the righteous justicer assumes her guilt:
as he has shed her blood, he takes on her qualities. In the light of
this assumption of the "guilty" female role, Philaster's melodramatic documentation of his passions in his stabbing scene takes
on a more interesting possibility. Philaster's entrance into the forest
is timed so that he should observe Bellario holding Arethusa, without realizing that her womanly weakness has simply caused her to

faint. Misconstruing the sight, Philaster declaims the conflicting emotions that govern him:

> I am to blame to be so much in rage.
> I'll tell her cooly when and where I heard
> This killing truth. I will be temperate
> In speaking and as just in hearing, [Sees them]
> O monstrous! Tempt me not you gods! Good gods,
> Tempt not a frail man! What's he that has a heart
> But he must ease it here. . . .
>   I have done;
> Forgive my passion. Not the calmed sea,
> When Aeolus locks up his windy brood,
> Is less disturbed than I. I'll make you know't.
> Dear Arethusa, do but take this sword [Offers his sword]
> And search how temperate a heart I have;
>
>   (4. 5. 18–46)

The repetition in the concluding line of the passage of the word "temperate" to describe the heart he wishes her to search surgically could carry more complicated overtones than the character's obvious ambition to moderate his passions: The *Oxford English Dictionary* construes the root word "temper" as "the mingling and combining of elements in due proportion."[12] Would it strain credibility too far to read Philaster's confusion over whether to kill Arethusa or to be killed by her as a tempering of his masculine and his feminine qualities, each dictating an opposing role in the climactic act? To put it another way, is he unsure whether he is right to offer his own life or to sacrifice the lamb he loves?

If one can accept these enactments of a man's stabbing a woman to be partially diffused by the perception of his feminine part, is there a corresponding masculinization of the woman that mediates these scenes of violence? As we have seen, both women eagerly embrace the offered martyrdom as innocent sacrifices and, once death is denied them, they accept an invitation to play masculine roles. However, although Imogen dresses as the page, Fidele, immediately after her "stabbing" scene, and although the King gives Arethusa the role of sentencing judge, the play texts do not support a persuasive case for either woman's assumption of a male identity that effectively counterpoises her husband's inward assumption of the female. Indeed, the assumption of both the page's identity and that of the judge are the most superficial of outward disguises. Even as Imogen says she is "almost a man already," Pisanio counters her with the ironic statement "First, make yourself but like one"

(3. 4. 166–67) nicely foreshadowing her immediate observation, "I see a man's life is a tedious one" (3. 6. 1), as she makes her first entrance in man's apparel and shortly before she turns to cookery. Similarly Arethusa no sooner appears as judge than she declares that she will discard her judicial robes immediately:

> And I (the woefull'st maid that ever was,
> Forced by my hands to bring my lord to death)
> Do by the honour of a virgin swear
> To tell no hours beyond it
>
> (5. 1. 21–24)

Both heroines are seen donning male identities as a result of their husbands' murderous assaults, only to disavow immediately such potentially powerful masculinity. Indeed, by the plays' conclusions, a rejection of masculine roles reinforces both plays' political situations, which dictate that a newly acknowledged, rightful, male heir will supplant each princess's claim to the throne.[13] As Cymbeline is careful to point out, Imogen loses a kingdom through the recovery of her long-lost brothers, while Arethusa's claim to the throne of Sicily becomes both understood and undercut by Philaster's prior patrilinear claim. Each of them has the body of a weak and feeble woman, but neither of them has the heart of a king.

If the princesses are derogated to patient, sacrificial victims, and the cuckolds temporarily lose their manly identities and assimilate lost feminine qualities, what topicalities can we propose about stabbing powerful women as a means to male empowerment in James's reign? As Leonard Tennenhouse has demonstrated in *Power on Display,* during Elizabeth's reign romantic comedies dramatize the courtships of female heirs and stage desire for political power under a "virgin queen" as erotic desire. During James's reign, however, tragicomic romances depict the triumph of a patriarchal royal family whose dynastic succession is secured by the female heir marrying the one suitor whose bloodline can restore patrilinear descent of the throne.[14] Indeed, as Ann Thompson has concluded, modern responses to *Cymbeline* may be uneasy at the play's "insistence on defining royal power as male . . . in the post-Elizabethan period" (86). Thus, if Elizabethan and Jacobean drama configures the aristocratic body as central to the display of power, the scenes of corporal punishment in *Philaster* and *Cymbeline* also stage what Tennenhouse describes as "a political crisis which must be understood and resolved in sexual terms" (19). The depiction of Posthumus' and Philaster's attacks upon their princess-brides recreates in microcosm a Stuartian process of the "proper" distribution of monarchical power. As princesses and women, Imogen and Arethusa represent a power vacuum waiting to be filled by the right master. Anxiety for king and kingdom is created by the potential misuses of their sexual identity and, once compromised, their identities as women with political power are transferred.

Inscribing punishment for putative sexual use on the bodies of the women in these plays then must be seen in political terms. Each of the plays opens with a statement of its central concern, a king's political need to arrange the dynastic marriage of his female heir. In both plays, the female heir's sexual truth is slandered and must be proved, and in that process of proving her sexual truth, the female heir is replaced after recognition that the rightful heir to the throne is really a male. James, as a self-styled husband and "living nourse-father" figure, assimilated and transformed Elizabeth's metaphoric identity as England's chaste wife into a new and triumphant metaphor of husbandly authority. And these plays present the spectacle of husbandly authority as it confronts the sexual/political nature of a princess-wife's power—here, by attempting to shed her royal blood certainly, these plays depict the divinely sanctioned sacrifice of power to a rightful male heir by means of the husband's "duty" to stab his wife. Thus, James and his public intercourse of political and marital unions replaced the discourse of an unmarried, "unstabbed" princess. But six or seven years after Elizabeth's death, what interrogation of Jacobean power politics, apart from the obvious Freudian interpretation of stabbing, makes the cutting open of a woman's heart a spectacle that these particular plays should stage in such dramaturgically prominent positions?

Cymbeline, certainly, has recently attracted several fascinating topical readings. David Bergeron, Jonathan Goldberg, and Leah Marcus have all approached Shakespeare's play from a central trope: reading and writing characters as public texts. Leah Marcus, for example, in her *Puzzling Shakespeare,* argues that Shakespeare's use of plot materials in *Cymbeline* demands a topical, political reading specifically because of the repeated emphasis on riddling texts that both characters and audience find themselves interpreting.[15] Similarly both David Bergeron and Jonathan Goldberg have concentrated upon James's use of himself as a text published and open to interpretation yet, at the same time, as a king, mysterious and inscrutable.[16] "In *Cymbeline,* Shakespeare explores . . . the critical matter of interpretation of texts" (Bergeron,

Images 35). This recent emphasis on James's authorship and authority, his presenting himself as a text to be read (not to mention
his penchant for supplying his own correct reading), and what critics see the Jacobean drama contributing to these readings of
person-texts becomes central to reading the characters of disem-
powered women.

I would like to explore further the issue of inscrutability by arguing, as I have suggested earlier, that textual opacity is gendered
in these two plays. Imogen is not the only powerful woman in
Cymbeline—and a brief glance at Shakespeare's characterization
of Cymbeline's unnamed Queen can amplify a reading of women's
power and the political imperative to remove that power. The first
anagnorisis of the many that crowd *Cymbeline*'s last scene is the
Doctor's revelation that the Queen abhorred Cymbeline and only
loved his power (5. 5. 37–40). At the conclusion of her "confession"
the King's speech explicitly refers to his inability to read her
character:

> Mine eyes
> Were not in fault, for she was beautiful:
> Mine ears that heard her flattery, nor my heart
> That thought her like her seeming. It had been vicious
> To have mistrusted her.
>
> (5. 5. 62–66)

It is his ultimate perplexity that makes the line, "Who is't can read
a woman?" (5. 5. 48) a persistent memory for a reader of both
plays; based upon this line, Bergeron has argued that Cymbeline's
Queen remained an opaque text: half of a ruler's contradictory
identity as both an opaque and a transparent text. Not only in the
Queen, however, is opacity roundly condemned. In both *Cymbeline*
and *Philaster,* the problem of misreading or being unable truly to
read a character drives the potential tragedies, and in both plays
the opaque texts undecipherable to powerful male characters are
women. In these plays female gender and sexual capacity are seen
to invite misreadings. The kings in each play believe unquestion-
ingly the falsehoods that the Queen and Megra create, and that
belief is curiously grounded in the fact that both these women are
sexually experienced. Implicit in Shakespeare's Queen is that her
power over Cymbeline, and by extension Britain, results from her
seduction of him through her beauty and flattery. With rather more
panache, Beaumont and Fletcher place Megra's slander of Arethusa at the exact moment in which Megra has been exposed as a

whore. Within the space of twenty-six lines, the crowd of courtiers
and the king are transformed from proving Megra to be sexually
"false" to believing the "truth" she tells. In each play, the vulnerability of the chaste princesses to misinterpretation by the least
trustworthy of slanderers is made more acute by the ease with
which irredeemably wicked, sexually active, female characters are
shown to manipulate public policy. To any audience, clearly, neither the kings nor the nobility can read correctly the virtue or truth
of the women who might control, or who do control the political
destinies of the kingdom through the use of their sexuality.

That courtier characters are particularly subject to this reading
disorder is a point made all the more forcefully by both plays'
juxtaposition of commoners and servants, such as the Country
Fellow in *Philaster,* whose very ignorance of courtiers and their
discourse arrests the stabbing: "I know not your rhetoric, but I
can lay it on you if you touch the woman" (4. 5. 98). Similarly,
whereas Cymbeline is unable to read his Queen, throughout the
play Shakespeare interpolates asides from the Doctor, and to a
lesser extent Pisanio, that illustrate that they have no trouble in
discerning and attempting to thwart her evil nature. In the plays'
conclusions, the playwrights foreground and underscore the fact
that the court characters are unable to read the true natures of
female characters by adding extra anagnorises in which startled
courtiers recognize those women disguised as servants. Metaphorically and actually disguised, the princess-brides are crafted to embody the problem of seeing and believing the truth and, for the
sake of the kingdom, the truth that must be read correctly is their
sexual truth: marital fidelity.

While useful new historicist readings of *Cymbeline* have invigor-
ated critical dialogue on that play, the discourse of truth employed
in *Philaster* that I feel particularly invites a topical reading has
been relatively unexplored. Despite some attempts to equate James
with the King,[17] it is surprising that none of the critics who have
searched for topical allusions has yet noticed that one of James's
repeated tropes of reading, his image of a transparent crystal
breast, is used twice in *Philaster,* first by the courtier, Dion:[18]

> Every man in this age has not a soul of crystal, for
> all men to read their actions through; men's hearts and
> faces are so far asunder that they hold no
> intelligence.
>
> (1. 1. 247–50)

Dion's subsequent role in the play makes it ironic that he should use James's rather self-righteous phrase to lament the corruption of the age in general. Dion's political ambitions to replace the King with Philaster are foregrounded: Believing Megra (as does the whole court), Dion reinforces the slander of Arethusa by the lie that he caught the princess *in flagrante delicto,* specifically to galvanize Philaster's opposition to the King (2. 4. 128–92; 3. 1. 62–135). Beaumont and Fletcher nicely problematize the political situation of *Philaster* through this characterization of Dion. As chief supporter of Philaster's undoubted right to the throne of Sicily and speaking lines that lament the inscrutability of a court by using James's own image of virtuous transparency, he then participates in and consciously perpetuates the slanderous clouding of Arethusa's reputation in order to achieve his own patriotic, political aims.

The second appearance of James's image of the transparent heart is more specifically associated with the court's perception of Arethusa as opaque. After the staging of a confrontation with Philaster, in which his reliance upon reading her truth is ironically pronounced in his misreading of her sexual fidelity, Arethusa's soliloquy repeats the crystal image:

Philaster: Some far place,
                 Where never womankind durst set her foot
                 For bursting with her poisons, must I seek,
                 And live to curse you:
                 There dig a cave, and preach to birds and beasts
                 What woman is and help to save them from you;
                 . . . how that foolish man,
                 That reads the story of a woman's face
                 And dies believing it, is lost for ever;
                 How all the good you have is but a shadow,
                 I' th' morning with you, and at night behind you
                 Past and forgotten . . .
                 How you are, being taken all together,
                 A mere confusion, and being so dead a chaos,
                 That love cannot distinguish. These sad texts
                 Til my last hour I am bound to utter of you. . . . [Exit]

Arethusa: . . . What way have I deserved this? Make my breast
                 Transparent as pure crystal, that the world,
                 Jealous of me, may see the foulest thought
                 My heart holds. Where shall a woman turn her eyes
                 To find out constancy?

                                                              (3. 2. 121–48)

At this point, the stage directions call for the entrance of the page, Bellario, on whom Arethusa unjustly vents her wrath for being a false, dissembling traitor. Bellario then exits, also looking for a place to die. Of course, the crowning irony of this juxtaposition of disgruntled readers is that we ultimately discover that Bellario is a woman, Dion's daughter in disguise, and thus her sexual identity is actually false, albeit in pursuit of chaste affection. By implicating the audience as well as the characters in misreading Bellario/ Euphrasia, this seemingly straightforward encounter reinforces the play's dominant myth that women are opaque and that their internal, sexual truth cannot be read. With society thus bankrupt of truth, each of the three characters abandons court and kingdom in search of another world in which to die.

The issue of discovering the truth of women's sexuality thus becomes vital to the survival of the society, and violence is the literal solution to the problem of seeing into the heart. When he is finally convinced of Arethusa's infidelity, Philaster's enraged interrogation of the suspected correspondent, Bellario, suggests that knowing the truth involves amateur surgery:

> Tell me thy thoughts; for I will know the least
> That dwells within thee, or will rip thy heart
> To know it; I will see thy thoughts as plain
> As I do now thy face
>
> (3. 1. 235–38)

Cutting to the heart of a woman, symbolically and physically, is the answer these plays pose to the problem of knowing the truth. Upon the seemingly unknowable truth of royal female sexuality rests the union and future of the entire society and nation. In fictive courts, both Beaumont and Fletcher and Shakespeare explore the collapse of the symbolic into the real by staging attempts to cut to the heart of female mystery.

A topical reading of this dramatization could be that the playwrights of the King's Men stage shows of the potential tragedy that is the consequence of opacity—if only, like James, every woman had a crystal window into her heart the world would be a better place—but the plays seem curiously resistant to such an unproblematized reading. While both Posthumus and Philaster recognize and repent the futility of their violent attempts to read and write sexual truth on the bodies of their wives, private reconciliations and renewed avowals of love between the couples are essentially inadequate from the political standpoint of the plays' corporate conclusions. Indeed, the dramaturgy of both fifth acts establishes a demand for a public text of sexual fidelity, which must be produced and interpreted by the court before marriage and royal succession can be established. As Leah Marcus has shown, *Cymbeline*'s final scene bristles with the interpretation of riddling texts as well as the correction of misinterpretations (*Cymbeline*, 138). In addition, I would argue that *Philaster* ultimately achieves a comic conclusion by rereading a woman: Bellario's revelation that she is actually Euphrasia, the daughter of Dion, finally clears up Arethusa's misunderstood sexuality. Once Arethusa's truth has been proven by default, Megra, the false woman, is immediately banished from court and the King is free to ratify both Philaster's marriage and his rights to succession.

Tragedy has been miraculously transmuted to comedy, certainly, but in such a way that the slickness of the final outcome is at odds with the convoluted and highly artificial dramaturgy of the final scene. The comic ending is manipulated by surmounting the seeming indecipherability of women's hearts. Instead of by reading Imogen's heart, her fidelity, and the succession of Britain, are restored by means of a risible series of revelations: Iachimo's confession allows for a public recognition of her fidelity to Posthumus, while Belarius' confession and his ocular proof of the princes' lineage removes Imogen from direct succession and from royal disapproval of her marriage to a commoner. Imogen does not reinstate herself; her position as princess and wife is redefined by the recognition of the identities of the other characters. Arethusa, similarly, although she enters the final scene as the bride of a forgiving Philaster, is called into question a second time by Megra's renewed accusations of infidelity and is yet again required to prove her truth. The seemingly redundant repetition of Arethusa's powerlessness to publish her true chastity and the consequent threat to the succession reinforces the play's message of the seeming impossibility of deciphering female truth. Both princesses finally are only recognized by default and by their relationships to others' true identities. In these Jacobean plays, ultimately, powerful women still cannot be deciphered, but they can be, and are, redefined and relocated outside the center of political power.

If, however, dramatists of the King's Men so inscribe the central problem of reading a woman's truth in a discourse so specifically identified with James's own self-imaging, then the central problem of epistemology remains uneasily gendered. While royal mystery was, in conjunction with royal transparency, an equally useful rhetorical figure, to juxtapose James's deliberately conflicting images of himself as simultaneously mysterious and transparent with dramatic situations in which royal women are written as opaque texts reinscribes the plays' topicality with a curiously androgynous quality. Like the fictional husbands in *Philaster* and *Cymbeline,* if opacity is gendered, does not James's combination of opacity and transparency participate in female opacity as well as in male transparency?

Roughly three years before *Philaster* and *Cymbeline,* Jonson's *Hymenei* exalted union above singleness on the occasion of the ill-fated marriage between Frances Howard and the Earl of Essex.[19] The masque concluded with a female Angel, manifesting ultimate truth, who descended "in a second thunder," attired in a mirror whereby "you may see her heart shine through her breast" (line 809). The Angel comes to end an argument between Truth, who advocates the virtues of marriage, and her look-alike, Opinion, who defends virginity. Naturally, in a wedding masque, the Angel exposes Opinion's virginity as a fraudulent identity but moreover, in conclusion, transfers all symbolic attributes of ultimate Truth, including the mirror and a true heart, to James, "the royal judge of our contention":

> Lastly this heart, with which all hearts be true;
> And truth in him make treason ever rue.
>
> (lines 856–57)

In 1606 *Hymenei,* perhaps the archetypal wedding masque celebrating the Jacobean ideal of union, staged the bestowal of Truth and all her symbols onto James. By the time the King's Men staged their complementary tragicomedies, the symbols of feminine truth and their conjunction with James have come to celebrate the uneasiness of feminine truth in dynastic unions.

NOTES

1. Although the first quarto's woodcut labels him a "Cuntrie Gentellman," its stage directions describe him as a "Country Gallant"; in the second quarto, however, he is a "Country Fellow." Most modern editors agree with Robert K. Turner Jr., who maintains that the second quarto is far superior to the first and further that authoritative modifications were made in Q2 to emphasize the pastoral distinction between the country and the court. See *Philaster* in vol. 1 of *The Dramatic Works in the Beaumont and Fletcher Canon,* ed. Fredson Bowers (Cambridge: Cambridge University Press, 1966).

All quotations from *Philaster* are taken from Andrew Gurr's Revels edition (Manchester: Manchester University Press, 1969); all quotations from *Cymbeline* are taken from J. M. Nosworthy's New Arden edition (London: Methuen, 1955).

2. Although I refer to Philaster as Arethusa's husband throughout, their marriage is not actually solemnized until Act 5; her chastity is emphasized throughout the play.

3. Earlier in this century, the disputed issue of Shakespeare's putative artistic dominance over Beaumont and Fletcher was characterized by the conflicting titles of two influential books: Ashley Thorndike's *The Influence of Beaumont and Fletcher on Shakespeare* (1901. Reprint, New York: Russell and Russell, 1965) and *The Debt to Shakespeare in the Beaumont and Fletcher Plays* by Daniel Morley McKeithan (1938. Reprint, New York: AMS Press, 1970). More recent critics whose work are indispensable to consideration of Beaumont and Fletcher are Eugene Waith's *The Pattern of Tragicomedy in Beaumont and Fletcher* (New Haven: Yale University Press, 1952) and Lee Bliss's work, especially "Three Plays in One: Shakespeare and *Philaster*" in *Medieval and Renaissance Drama in England* 3, 1986), 129–47; and her *Francis Beaumont* (Boston: Twayne, 1987).

4. Gurr argues that both plays were Globe plays, 44.

5. See *Myth, Emblem and Music in Shakespeare's Cymbeline* (Newark: Delaware University Press, 1992), in which Peggy Munoz Simonds argues that Shakespeare evokes "the medieval iconographic figure of the 'driven soul' as a 'harried stag' depicted in Emblem 47 of Hadrianus Junius in Imogen's hunting metaphor of herself as "th' elected deer" (151–54). She also connects Imogen's self-description, as the innocent lamb inviting slaughter from the proud lion, to the "Trimphe de humilitie" depicted by Gilles Corrozet in *Hecatomigraphe* (296–98).

6. See Linda Woodbridge's "Palisading the Elizabethan Body Politic," *Texas Studies in Literature and Language,* 33 (1991) 327–54, in which she argues that Imogen symbolizes the island of Britain, and that the thwarting of repeated attempts to invade her physically throughout the play are symptomatic of a new Jacobean ideology that downplays the threat of foreign invasion.

7. Coppélia Kahn treats Posthumus among other Shakespearean cuckolds in the fifth chapter of *Man's Estate: Masculine Identity in Shakespeare* (Berkeley and London: University of California Press, 1981); she articulates the puzzling disproportion between the "everlasting shame of the cuckold as victim and the mere disapproval directed at the cuckolder" (121–22).

8. Traditional critics magisterially condemned Philaster's ungentle violation of the code of noble behavior. A particularly nice example of this was phrased by Harold S. Wilson in *"Philaster* and *Cymbeline," English Institute Essays* (New York: Columbia University Press, 1952), who declares the stabbing of Arethusa to be "the most astonishing lapse in any hero of Jacobean romance" (159). He is also quoted by Dora Jean Ashe in her Regents' Renaissance Drama edition of the play (Lincoln: University of Nebraska Press, 1974). In assigning Philaster to the bottom of the nobility, Wilson does not mention the dramatists' earlier device of making Perigot stab faithful Amoret on two separate occasions in *The Faithful Shepherdess;* I avoid that incident myself, since it is outside the scope of my thesis.

Similarly, W. W. Appleton discusses both the potentially tragic consequences of applying lofty moral absolutes to human relationships in *Beaumont and Fletcher: A Critical Study* (London: Allen and Unwin, 1956), 19.

9. Madelon Gohlke, "'I woo'd thee with my sword': Shakespeare's Tragic Paradigms," in *Representing Shakespeare: New Psychoanalytic Essays* (Baltimore: Johns Hopkins University Press, 1980).

10. Lisa Jardine, in *Still Harping on Daughters* (New York: Columbia University Press, 1989), analyzes the ambiguous desires connoted by playing "the

woman's part," but her argument that the dependent roles of boy player and woman create a textured eroticism is more complex than mine, in that I have not broached the power politics of boy actors.

11. Page 82 of "Person and Office: The Case of Imogen, Princess of Britain," in *Literature and Nationalism,* eds. Vincent Newey and Ann Thompson (Liverpool: Liverpool University Press, 1991), 76–87. Thompson argues persuasively that this speech is part of a series of references to Posthumus' fundamentally inferior social position in relation to Imogen.

12. Philip J. Finklepearl, in *Court and Country Politics in the Plays of Beaumont and Fletcher* (Princeton: Princeton University Press, 1990), argues that *Philaster,* like *A Maid's Tragedy* and *A King and No King,* is primarily concerned with the effects of princely intemperance and irrationality. Christening *Philaster* a "comedy of blood," Finklepearl contends that the multiple blood images throughout the play undercut a courtly ideal that "bloodletting is the sport of princes" and shows the danger to the state from "heated blood" rebelling against reason.

13. Ann Thompson has also argued the importance of Imogen's "inevitable" displacement: "What auditor or reader is so naive as not to realize that if missing children are mentioned in the first scene of the play they will be found before the last one? We know, before we even meet her, that Imogen is scheduled to be superseded by her brothers." "Person and Office," 79.

14. *Power on Display: The Politics of Shakespeare's Genres* (London: Methuen, 1986). Tennenhouse links Shakespeare's romances specifically to absent monarch plays and to city comedy by arguing that all three genres attempt "to authorize patriarchalism over and against paternalism" (171), which leads his argument more towards analysis of Cymbeline's conflicting behavior as both father of a grotesque "natural" family and as the patriarch of Britain.

15. *Puzzling Shakespeare: Local Reading and Its Discontents* (Berkeley and London: University of California Press, 1989). Leah Marcus's chapter on *Cymbeline* first appeared in 1988 in "*Cymbeline* and the Unease of Topicality," in *Historical Renaissance,* eds. Heather Dubrow and Richard Strier (Chicago: University of Chicago Press, 1988), 134–168.

16. Jonathan Goldberg's *James I and the Politics of Literature* (Baltimore: Johns Hopkins University Press, 1983) gives the most valuable articulation of the uses, conscious and unselfconscious, of James's presentation of himself as a text.
In "Images of Rule in *Cymbeline,*" *Journal of Contemporary Dramatic Theory and Criticism,* 2 (1987), 31–41, David Bergeron focuses exclusively on *Cymbeline,* acknowledging that he is specifically taking up Goldberg's brief glimpse at the play, which concludes *James I.* It appears that "Images of Rule" is Bergeron's most recent thinking on Shakespeare's play, postdating *Shakespeare's Romances and the Royal Family* (Lawrence: University of Kansas Press, 1985).

17. Some critics have attempted to identify the King with James, particularly at the moment in Act 4 when the impotent King querulously enquires why, since a monarch is a god whose breath commands the winds and calms the seas, his courtiers cannot find his escaped daughter:

> Alas, what are we kings?
> Why do you gods place us above the rest,
> To be served, flattered, and adored till we
> Believe we hold within our hands your thunder,
> And when we come to try the power we have,
> There's not a leaf shakes at our threatenings?

(4. 4. 53–58)

See M. G. M. Adkins, "The Citizens in *Philaster:* Their Function and Significance," *Studies in Philology,* 43 (1946), 203–12. Nevertheless, the notion of satiric caricature seems unlikely to be consistent with a Jacobean drama that was explicitly identified with royal patronage and display. See also Peter Davison, "The Serious Concerns of *Philaster,*" *English Literary History,* 30 (1963), 1–16.

18. James's speeches are quoted below from Charles Howard McIlwain, ed. *The Political Works of James I* (1918. Reprint, New York: Russell and Russell, 1965).

James's speech of 1605:

> And for my part I would wish with those ancient philosophers, that there were a christall window in my brest, wherein all my people might see the secretest thoughts of my heart. (285)

James's speech of 1607:

> But in the general Vnion you must observe two things: for I will discover my thoughts plainly unto you: I study cleareness, not eloquence, And therefore with the olde Philosophers, I would heartily wish my brest were a transparent glasse for you all to see through, that you might looke into my heart, and then would you be satisfied of my meaning. (292)

James's speech of 1609/10:

> As ye have made mee a faire Present indeed in presenting your thankes and loving dueties unto mee; So have I now called you here, to recompence you again with a great and a rare Present, which is a faire and a Christall Mirror; not such a mirror wherein you may see your owne faces, or shadowes; but such a mirror, or Christall, as through the transparentnesse thereof you may see the heart of your King. The Philosophers wish, that every manys breast were a Christall, were through his heart might be seene, is vulgarly knowne, and I touched it in one of my former speeches unto you: But though that were impossible in the generall, yet will I now performe this for my part, that as it is a trew Axiome in Divinitie, that *Cor Regis* is *in manu domini,* so wil I now set *Cor Regis* in *oculii populi.* (306)

19. All quotations from *Hymenei* are taken from *Ben Jonson: Selected Masques,* ed. Stephen Orgel (New Haven and London: Yale University Press, 1970).

"Content with art"?: Seeing the Emblematic Woman in *The Second Maiden's Tragedy* and *The Winter's Tale*

SARA EATON

CESARE Ripa writes of Poesia thus in his gloss on her figure in *Iconologia,* printed in Milan in 1602:

> Poeisa: Young, beautiful, clothed in a celestial hue. On her raiment there will be many stars; she will be crowned with the laurel; let her also show bare breasts full of milk and a visage inflamed and pensive, with three winged cherubim fluttering about her; let one be handing her the lyre and the plectrum, another the flageolet, and a third the trumpet. . . . She is pictured as young and beautiful, for every man, no matter how rude, is allured by her sweetness and attracted by her force. She is crowned with laurel, which is evergreen, and fears not the striking of the celestial lightening, for Poesy makes men immortal and ensures them against the blows of time, which usually reduces everything to oblivion. The garment with its stars represents divinity, consonant with poetry's reputed heavenly origin. The breasts, turgid with milk, show the fecundity of conceits and inventions which are the soul of poetry. Her countenance is pensive and yet inflamed, for the poet's soul is brimming with spontaneous impulses, akin to a fury.[1]

Ripa's representation of Poesy shows up again in Davenant's *Temple of Love,* illustrating the widespread borrowing across Europe of images and interpretations that accompanied the production of the enormously popular emblem books. In vogue for approximately two hundred years, their popularity and their influence were widespread, and they served as a source for "conceits and inventions" in poetry, prose, frontispieces, portrait painting, tapestries, embroidery, and jewelry. As Alison Saunders suggests in the title of her book, *The Sixteenth Century French Emblem Book: A Decorative and Useful Genre,*[2] emblems functioned to replicate understandings of the Horatian dictum: Intended for both decoration and use, they were meant to entertain and to instruct.

Emblems served first the interests of humanists: Andrea Alciati's *Emblematum liber,* published in 1531, for example, was constructed as a mental linguistic puzzle. The motto or "word" complemented the engraving or woodcut and brief poetic explication, and the whole challenged the reader's interpretive abilities and knowledge concerning the relationship between *res* and *verba.* In their use of Latin, Greek, and the vernacular, and their borrowings from Ovid, Seneca, Horace, and Petrarch, to name the most popular sources, these emblem books reflect the humanist agendas for literacy and art in early modern Europe. Consequently, the books' progressively more sophisticated production allows us to trace the popularization of printed material, and their progressively increased attention to the didactic functions of the "text" allows us to trace concerns about signification and interpretation, about understanding the "speaking picture" correctly, in a world where emblem books frequently served as propaganda in the religious wars.[3] An example is Jan van der Noot's *A Theatre for Worldlings,* published in Dutch, French, and English by 1569, and credited with introducing the Petrarchan sonnet to these three languages,[4] both Clemont Marot and Spenser translating versions of Petrarch's sonnets as elucidations of the emblems. Michael Bath, in his analysis of the various editions of this work, comments that Spenser's edition "includes and reconciles the emblematic impulse of humanist poetics, the medieval topos of the poet as seer or dreamer, and the Puritan claim to revelation."[5]

The "emblematic impulse of humanist poetics," the positioning of the author and reader/viewer *vis à vis* textual iconography, and claims of "revelation" provide a general perspective for what I will suggest concerning the treatment of emblematic women on the stage, particularly the Lady in *The Second Maiden's Tragedy* and Hermione in *The Winter's Tale.* They were meant to be read as "speaking pictures," as emblems, and as such comment on the politics of humanists poetics, on complex exchanges of power perceived as interpretation. But first, I'd like to return to my first example of Poesia as a way of focusing on the gender issues embedded in these aesthetics. Ripa's description of Poetry emphasizes that she is an eroticized, "pensive," and "inflamed" nursing mother, "akin to a fury," that is, potentially unruly, and that secondly, her attributes signify a masculine experience of poetic inspiration and revelation. If, as the Muse, the image is feminized and internalized on the imaginative level of inspiration, that femininity is in turn

The Triumph of Venus, fifteenth-century Italian painted salver, by permission of the Musée du Louvre, Paris. Photo by Lauros-Giraudon.

masculinized in terms of authorial (re)production, making men immortal, full of fecund conceits, soul, and fury.

These mental movements from outside, from viewing the image, to inside, to allegorical interpretation and production, characterize humanist poetics and have been critiqued by others as the politics of display,[6] affording the viewer a "visual pleasure," in this case a sexualized and highly eroticized one. "Visual pleasure," a term borrowed from recent feminist film criticism,[7] may seem an ahistorical perspective, but it is one the period seemed cognizant of. In fact, art emphasizing the poetics and politics of sexual display was hardy new in early modern Europe. In *The Triumph of Venus,* dating from the early fifteenth century, thin streams of gold originate either in Venus's pudenda or in the eyes of her observers, and her pose replicates a popular religious subject—Mary's ascension into Heaven. The viewer of this picture is asked to see and worship the source of erotic love, participate as an observer, so to speak, at the same time that he or she would presumably recognize the

"The Knight and the Beggar-Wench" (a ballad), most likely printed in the 1620s.

Lady bitten by a snake, a woodcut from *A Theatre for Worldlings,* **published around 1559.**

artist's witty comment on the similarities between secular and religious love.[8] In an example from a ballad printed two hundred years later, most likely printed in the 1620s, intentionality is visualized as point-of-view; we see the narrator-as-voyeur positioned in a tree, watching the entwined couples below, his own outstretched arms indicative of his response to what he sees and sings. Lennard Davis remarks that scenes like this recreate a "primal scene fantasy" for reading, "a voyeurism which decreased the perceptual distance between the reader/narrator and the event, including the reader as a subject within the text".[9]

A similar observation concerning perceptual and subjective distance can be made from Van der Noot's illustration of temporality and the inevitability of death published around 1559, which in one frame illustrates the young, Eve-like, bare-breasted woman in the foreground shown in the background bitten by a serpent and blasted ("like a gathered flower," Bath remarks.[10]) If temporality (before and after) is enclosed in a single frame here, so are religious and sexual views, requiring the viewer to shift perspectives and recognize a complex of cultural associations presented simultaneously in the doubled icon, a point I shall return to in relation to the Lady in *The Second Maiden's Tragedy* and to Hermione. In this emblem and in the plays I will discuss, the young woman is perceived as both alive and dead, pure and blasted, embodying many of the stereotypes about beautiful women common to the period, but serving to illustrate an abstract concept about the nature of the world.

If the icon can be in two places at once, so to speak, the narrator and the reader/viewer usually are tempted to assume a unified "view." In the example of "The crost Couple," the audience is positioned for "visual pleasures" much like the narrator in the background. No longer a whole body, here only a face, the onlooker in the background sees (and presumably reacts) but does not participate with gestures in the scene depicted in the foreground. A character serves as a surrogate for the reader or audience, supplying both gestures and text to the visual, theatrically framed, emblematic whole. An apt textual example, one which adds a more violent component to this analysis of sexualized aesthetics, can be found in Barnaby Rich's *Farewell to Militarie Profession;* the third story, "Of Nicander and Lucilla," tells of how Lucilla's well-born but destitute mother is forced to sell her daughter's virginity to the son of the Duke of Ferrara so that she can provide her with a dowry.[11] The mother tells the rapist, "Tomorowe mornyng therefore will I rise and leaue her alone in that Chamber, and will set

"The crost Couple, OR A good Misfortune."

open the streate dorre, so as you shall not neede but to pushe at it, and the chamber dore likewise".[12] When the rapist has entered the house and Lucilla's chamber, the narrative provides this description:

> It was the Moneth of Julie, whiche season in that Countrie it is extreame hotte: by reason whereof Lucilla tumblyng from one side of the bedde vnto the other, had rolled of all the clothes wherewith she had been couered: so as she had lefte her self all naked, and in that sorte he found her, with Coralles about her necke and her armes, whiche with the difference of their ruddie couler did sette out and beautifie greatly the excellent fairnesse of her white bodie. She laie aslepe vpon her backe, with her handes cast ouer her hedde, (as for the moste parte yong women are wont to dooe): so that forthwith the yong Prince discouered her fro[m] toppe to toe. . . .[13]

The reader is aligned with the narrator and the rapist to view the sleeping victim. Her body literally framed by the entrance to her chamber door, her bed, and bed clothes, she is offered as an *objet d'art* for our perusal as well as the rapist's, at the same time that she is described as an innocent but passive accomplice to our glance ("as her hands cast ouer her hedde [as for the moste parte yong women are wont to dooe]").

The audience is thus implicated in scopophilia because it is positioned to view as an enthusiastic participant the icon in the text.[14] Stephanie Jed, in her discussion of how the figure of Lucrece elicited likewise compromised interpretations for fifteenth-century Florentine humanists, generalizes to argue that humanist habits of reading and writing were "inscribed in a language that invites sexual violence. . . . [T]he chaste thinking figured in the reading and writing practices of the humanists generates an eagerness to hear this tale over and over again, an eagerness which is, however, covered over by a certain solemnity and detachment from the rape".[15] In a sense, the capacity for "solemn" or transcendent experience of the text is facilitated by its inscription in an "eager" eroticized and potentially violent language.[16] By the late sixteenth century in England, this enclosure of "eagerness" in "detachment," or of delight in instruction, is common, as are attacks by iconoclasts who are especially sensitive to the delights images could inspire. Ben Jonson, for an example of "detachment," in his *Discoveries,* claimed that "*Poetry* and *Picture* are Arts of a like nature; and both are *busie* about imitation. It was excellently said of *Plutarch, Poetry* was a speaking picture, and *Picture* a mute Poesie. For they both invent, *faine,* and devise many things, and accommodate all they invent to the use, and service of nature. . . . They both beholde pleasure, and profit, as their common Object. . . . *Whosoever* loves not *Picture,* is injurious to Truth: and all the wisdome of *Poetry*".[17] Viewing leads to wisdom and truth. On the other hand, as one Elizabethan homilist "eagerly" put it, "Doth not the worde of GOD call idolatrie spirituall fornication: Doth it not call a gylte or painted idole or image, a Strumpet with a painted face".[18]

The homilist's sexualized and suspicious account *and* Jonson's abstract, objectified view is how "speaking pictures" are frequently imagined in the period, as a kind of mental "fornication" and pursuit of "wisdom," and even Jonson's detached and neutered discussion in the *Discoveries* is not typical of his dramatic practice. Because of this tendency to discuss aesthetic issues as gendered issues, and gendered issues as aesthetic issues, representations of women serve as iconic devices that reflect this emblematic tradition and question how meaning and knowledge are made and what kinds of pleasures and punishments viewing women affords. This is especially true in the theater, the site of steadily increasing iconoclastic attacks, where various perspectives on the powers and failures of interpretation could be offered the audience simultaneously through the language and gestures of a play.

Peter Daly has written of how the dumb show, a common Senecan device in Renaissance plays, is also a borrowing from the emblem-book tradition, and others have commented on isolated visual devices—the use of Gloriana's skull in *The Revenger's Tragedy,* for instance.[19] But other more fully integrated dramatic scenes, especially those that focus audience attention on women, can be better understood if we apply lessons of viewing in a potentially violent and sexualized emblematic tradition. For example, when Vittoria is arraigned in *The White Devil* for adultery, she says that "beauty, and gay clothes, a merry heart, / And a good stomach to a feast, are all / All the poor crimes that you can charge me with" (3.2.208–10).[20] This vision of a merry widow, however, is reversed in the Overburian character sketch of a whore her ex-brother-in-law, Monticelso, "paints" for the court, which culminates in this "picture":

They are worse
Worse than dead bodies which are begged at the gallows,
And wrought by surgeons, to teach man
Wherein he is imperfect. What's a whore!
She's like the guilty counterfeited coin

Which, whosoe'er first stamps it,brings in trouble
All that receive it.

(3.2.77–101)

Monticelso's hyperbolic rant is in contrast to Vittoria's physicality and dramatic facts. The audience, like her judges, is unsure of how guilty she is.

In this scene and throughout *The White Devil,* Vittoria is capable of being perceived as either "merry" or "counterfeit," as either innocent or guilty. Rendered somewhat like Van der Noot's woman blasted by a snake, her visual physical presence on stage is in this scene doubled, and she is both explained and contested by the conflicting rhetorics that describe her. At the end of this scene, when she is sentenced to live in a house of "convertites," presumably a halfway house for whores, she acknowledges her linguistic, emblematic "conversion": she says, "Since you cannot take my life for deeds, / Take it for words" (3.2.282–83). As a visible character and by her own comments, she functions reflexively as a character inside and outside of the "picture" meant to contain her, making the masculine gestures of the play, if not her own, accessible to interpretation by an audience positioned to see differences between "words" and "deeds."

Vittoria's attempts to escape the linguistic frame holding her are repeated by others, by the Duchess in *The Duchess of Malfi* and by Juliet in the balcony scene in *Romeo and Juliet,* for example. Women who accept "framing" also abound, notably in the extraordinary apostrophe given by her uncle to Lavinia in *Titus Andronicus* when she first appears on stage following her rape and mutilation. Physical and linguistic displays of violence are part of the emblematic dramatic frame, as Jed's generalizations suggest. But perhaps the most significant examples of seeing emblematic women as part of an aesthetic agenda inspiring potentially violent eroticized readings, useful in creating an allegory for men's "solemn" experience of "truth" or life as they would know it, are the statuesque treatments of the Lady in *The Second Maiden's Tragedy* and Hermione in *The Winter's Tale.* First disembodied and then reembodied, transformed by the rhetoric that finally frames or inscribes them, what the Lady accomplishes by dying, Hermione does by living.[21] What they produce are visions of social order and reifications of the power to interpret them.

The Second Maiden's Tragedy, attributed to Thomas Middleton, focuses explicitly on sexualized politics. The Lady's body is synonymous with the kingdom in this play, and it is a territory besieged by the principal male characters. The Tyrant and Govianus, the protagonist and dethroned king, define their sense of political worth sexually, in terms of an idealized possession of the Lady; they agree, as Govianus puts it, that "the loss of her sits closer to my heart / Than that of kingdom or the whorish pomp / Of this world's titles" (1.1.56–61).[22] The action of the play and the fate of the kingdom evolve out of the two men's struggle to physically possess her.

Up until the third act, Govianus and the Lady evade the Tyrant's attempts to possess her by employing witty rhetoric. They trick the Tyrant into letting them share Govianus' imprisonment; they persuade her father, sent to pander her, to confess his lapse of honor and to help them. Then the Tyrant, revealed as dim-witted in sexual language games and socially identified as the game's loser, resorts to physical violence: He decides to abduct the Lady and rape her. The Lady, telling Govianus that the Tyrant's "lust may part me from thee, but death, never; / Thou canst not lose me there, for dying, / Thou dost enjoy me still" (3.1.143–46), also chooses to abandon rhetoric and kill herself, announcing:

> I have prepared myself for rest and silence
> And took my leave of words. I am like one
> Removing from her house, that locks up all,
> And rather than she would displace her goods,
> Makes shift with anything for the time she stays.
> Then look not for more speech.
>
> (3.133–38)

If the Lady seems firmly embodied here—even willfully so, since Govianus faints at the critical moment, and she commits suicide— the play subsequently demonstrates how male desire is divisive enough not only to divide the kingdom but also to separate her speaking voice from the "house" she would "lock" it in. Her assurances to Govianus signal the play's disintegration into fetishism, necrophilia, and garbled metaphysics as it continues to explore the men's fascination with her body.[23]

The idea that he possesses the chaste memory of the Lady is at first enough for Govianus. As he says in the soliloquy following her suicide:

> Faith, she told me
> Her everlasting sleep would bring me joy,
> Yet I was still unwilling to believe her,
> Her life was so sweet to me. . . .

> Come, thou treasure of mankind,
> To him that knows what virtuous woman is
> And can discreetly love her. The whole world
> Yields not a jewel like her; ransack rocks
> And caves beneath the deep. O thou fair spring
> Of honest and religious desires,
> Fountain of weeping honour, I will kiss thee
> After death's marble lip. Thou'rt cold enough
> To lie entombed now by my father's side.
>
> (3.232–35, 244–52)

However, the Lady, chastely "cold enough," soon reappears on stage, "all in white, stuck with jewels, and a great crucifix on her breast" according to the stage directions in Act 4, to tell Govianus, praying at her tomb, "Behold, I'm gone; / My body taken up" (4.4.61–62). Idealized, bejeweled, and literally disembodied, this image of the Lady is the personification of Govianus' metaphors; her body, the referent for the pronoun "I," has been taken to court by the Tyrant where "he folds me with his arms and often sets / A sinful kiss upon my senseless lips" (4.4.71–72).

The Lady's ghost functions as a Lucrece, goading Govianus to revenge this dishonor upon a body she no longer inhabits, but only Govianus and the audience hear and see her spectral presence until the final scene. Middleton replicates conditions for "reading" emblematically not only by doubling the Lady's character, but also by aligning the audience's view of her with the hero's. He heightens these conditions by combining the effects of time with violence and scopophilia. The Tyrant sees "nothing to be mended" (5.2.27) at first in a body that horrifies his court when he installs it on a throne. But, her body begins to molder, and the Tyrant decides "it is no shame for thee, most silent mistress, / To stand in need of art" (5.2.41–42). He hires a disguised Govianus to apply paint to "hide death upon her face, / That now looks fearfully on us, and but strive / To give our eye delight" (5.2.81–83). The shame the Tyrant alludes to reflects his culture's widespread ambivalence about how "painting," a term applied to cosmetics, the visual arts, and rhetorical ornamentation, could "give the eye delight." As Lucy Gent has explained in her work on the relationship between literature and the visible arts in early modern England, "The eye has to accept deceptions to record accurately what it sees, just as the eye can only depict an unfallen, purely natural world by recourse to 'Nice Art'".[24] Similar understandings inform Puttenham's definitions of rhetorical ornamentations in the *Arte*, Gent argues, when he writes that *figures* "deceive the eare and also

the minde, drawing it from plainesse and simplicitie to a certain
doublenesse, whereby our talk is the more guilefull and abusing".[25]

Though unaware of the Lady's ghostly speaking presence, the
Tyrant is sensitive to the Lady's potential "certain doublenesse,"
a doubleness Govianus and the audience see as an enactment of
the "speaking picture's" power to unnaturally "give the eye delight." The Tyrant wants her to mime art so as to *seem* natural.
Painting her to appear natural, however, is to appropriate her representation of life for himself—to create as art the ways in which
the Lady seems to be alive in his imagination. Once painted, her
body becomes the vehicle for his expressions of an imagined sexual
loss and his faith in her rejuvenation:

> But alas,
> 'Tis as unpossible for living fire
> To take hold there,
> As for dead ashes to burn back again
> Into those hard, tough, bodies whence they fell.
> Life is removed from her now, as the warmth
> Of the bright sun from us when it makes winter
> And kills with unkind coldness. So is't yonder;
> An everlasting frost hangs now upon her.
> As in such a season men will force
> A heat into their bloods with exercise,
> In spite of extreme weather, so shall we
> By art force beauty on yon lady's face
> Though death sit frowning on't a storm of hail
> To beat it off. Our pleasure shall prevail. . . .
> O, she lives again!
> She'll presently speak to me.
>
> (5.2.96–112, 115–15)

Not a jewel to him, the Tyrant uses nature's metaphors to read the
Lady's body once she is "painted." In this passage, he attempts to
reestablish the link between language and an iconic body through
art, a link forged by his belief in her dissemblance of life, in her
representational possibilities. If the Lady can look as if she were
alive, ironically, as if she could *speak,* then "his arms and lips /
Shall labour life into her" (5.2.118–19).

What is "bejeweled" for Govianus is "natural" for the Tyrant.
Seemingly in opposition, their metaphors are two sides of the same
coin, or body, the two men mirroring what Peter Stallybrass has
described as the articulations of the class aspirant in this period.
Stallybrass argues that the class aspirant's "conceptualization of

woman will . . . be radically unstable; she will be perceived as oscillating between the enclosed body (the purity of the elite to which he aspires) and the open body (or else how could he attain her?), between being 'too coy' and 'too common'".[26] The Lady's forms accommodate both visions. Her split linguistic and physical properties reveal how much she defines herself as the men do, her "coy" spiritual imperatives to Govianus directing his attention, and ours, towards her "common" disintegrating body to the same extent that the Tyrant's words and actions articulate their mutual idealized desires for possession.[27] Thus, her doubleness is mimetic in function. She mimes how speech and the speaker can be split when the terms of possession, as well as interpretation, are violently contested.

The Lady's doubled body is first the site for a continual reproduction of violence and contested power as well as contested meanings. When the Tyrant is moved by her simulation of life to kiss her, she "kills with unkind coldness": Her lips have been painted with poison by Govianus. Then, "in the same form" as her body according to the stage direction, the ghostly Lady returns to escort herself to the tomb. Govianus, again made king by a court repulsed by both men's actions, also reproduces the Tyrant's actions when he crowns the body queen:

> The first and last that ever we make ours,
> Her constancy strikes so much firmness in us.
> That honour done, let her be solemnly borne
> Unto the house of peace from whence she came
> As queen of silence.
>
> (5.2.200–205)

The resolution of the play's action depends on the Lady's return to the tomb, to silence, in all of her metamorphic forms. The end of the play valorizes her silence—she becomes queen—for as a speaker, alive and dead, she has been the source of violent dramatic reactions. Her silence signals and enables the play's movement toward closure. From this point of view, the Lady as a speaking character has been responsible for creating the deadly sexual chaos that results in the Tyrant's death and in Govianus' restoration as king. Her kingdom, the "house of peace," the tomb, is one the other characters have urged her towards from the beginning. Peace in this kingdom occurs when its queen is silent, "constant," interred imagistically, and the characters can "rest content with art" (5.2.33). If the Lady demonstrates her willingness to be buried within social and artistic constructs that define her imagistically as a property, that fethishize and manipulate the uses of her body as though she were neither living nor dead, both "coy" and "common," the action of the play demonstrates the political necessity for this kind of thinking. The Tyrant loses his credibility, his kingdom, and his life when he would restore her natural body. Govianus regains his throne by means of her death, making her the "jewel" in his crown.

The Lady moves from one "house" to another, from a living center-stage position to an entombed one located, by the end, offstage. Conversely, her acquiescence in her iconic idealization results in an exchange of meanings concerning her "nature" as the Tyrant expresses them and her "cold," bejewelled representation as art. Her final configuration as a sterile and abstracted representation of a queen, a return to an idealized position in Govianus' imagination, is celebrated. As Govianus said, "Faith, she told me / Her everlasting sleep would bring me joy." The image of her that brings joy is in counterpoint to her painted, disintegrating body. The chaste body eliciting joy can only be imagined; the body eliciting the drama's sexual violence is buried. The Lady's voice, which would deny any actions but the imagined uses of her body, dies with her.

As Leonard Barkan has pointed out, the idea that "living" women can become statuary, and vice versa, has its sources in Ovid's Pygmalion and in Petrarch. The convention can signify "a mutual triumph of nature and art": "From antiquity onwards that transformation has been at once a triumph of nature, in the appearance of flexibility, liveliness, and love out of hard stone, and a triumph of art in that it has celebrated the genius of the sculptor in capturing an essence and equalling or even perfecting God's creation".[28] Barkan repeats here the early humanist's desire for transcendent aesthetic experience. But the dramatists in early modern England do not forget that the representation "created" out of the sculptor's "genius" is an attempt to replace one sort of woman with another. As Barkan puts it, "Pygmalion creates a statue-woman both because he sees woman as stony and because he believes he can create an ideal in sculpture that does not exist in real life".[29] The Tyrant and Govianus reflect both of Pygmalion's perceptions of women, and the play portrays the hazards of "equalling or even perfecting God's creation" unless that creation is viewed as an object, as an artifact signifying its corrupted manmade status to its viewers.

The Second Maiden's Tragedy replicates the tensions inherent

in reading emblematically by locating the site of those tensions in
the Lady's "doubleness" in time, and by positioning the audience
to attend to the consequences of "visual pleasures." Leontes begins *The Winter's Tale* reflecting Pygmalion's perceptions of
women, but because the play is a romance, it must necessarily
shift our attention away from the corrupted female body towards
an idealized one.[30] In both plays, however, the dramatic effect of
a silent and emblematic female statue is created from her movement from one metaphorical position to another, so that ideas
about "art" and "nature" can conjoin with the violent sexual rhetoric surrounding the female body to signify its fallen nature.

Like the Lady in her assertion of wit and will, Hermione's ability
to engage in witty sexual innuendos stimulates Leontes' violent
expressions of intended sexual revenge. Even though Polixenes
claims in Act 1 that only Leontes' tongue can move him to stay,
it is Hermione's that does so. Hermione's response to Leontes'
praise of her speech—"I have spoke to th' purpose twice: / The
one forever earned a royal husband; th'other, for some while a
friend" (1.2.106–8)—[31] is the occasion for Leontes' first jealous
outburst, some of which stems from Hermione's presumptuous
and effective use of a courtier's witticism implying that Polixenes'
friendship has sexual meanings for herself, and some of which is
a response to her intrusion into what others have characterized a
homoerotic or homosocial relationship between the two men.[32]
Thus, in spite of her physical appearance—the late stages of pregnancy—Hermione's potentially unruly speech inserts her between
the two men as a "common" and contested sexual possession, and
the play begins with a demonstration of how words *may* correlate
with deeds.

Leontes embodies this struggle for logocentric connections,
miming the motions of reading emblematically. He builds a solipsis-
tic linguistic world of "cogitations" (1.2.271), of tautologies, based
on a sexually active female body, needing only to see Hermione
with Polixenes to create an adulterous scene "whose issue will
hiss" his conclusions:

> And many a man there is, even at this present,
> Now, while I speak this, holds his wife by th'arm,
> And little thinks she has been sluiced in's absence,
> And his pond fished by his next neighbor, by
> Sir Smile, his neighbor, nay there's comfort in't,
> While other men have gates, and those gates opened,
> As mine, against their will. . . .

> Be it concluded,
> No barricado for a belly. Know't
> It will let in and out the enemy,
> With bag and baggage. Many thousand on's
> Have the disease, and feel't not.
>
> (1.2.190–98, 203–7)[33]

Similar in impulse to how Govianus and the Tyrant construct an image of what will "give the eye delight," Leontes eagerly ponders over what he cannot "feel" and can imagine only as metaphors. The result is that "My wife is nothing, nor nothing have these nothings, / If this be nothing" (1.2.295–96). He validates in metaphor what he imagines as failures of feminine flesh, collapsing Hermione's sexuality, her physicality, and his thoughts into "nothing," a sexually ambiguous term for everything he feels and imagines.[34]

His court, his wife, and his friends all think him crazed, responding much like the court in *The Second Maiden's Tragedy* to the Tyrant's actions. Like the Tyrant, Leontes aggressively asserts the veracity of his perceptions: "You smell this business with a sense as cold / As is a dead man's nose; but I do see't and feel't, / As you feel doing thus; and see withal / The instruments that feel" (2.1.152–55). And, like the Tyrant, Leontes responds to social isolation with violence. The Signet edition of the play glosses the action for this passage to suggest that Leontes strikes himself or Antigonus, whom he is addressing. Either action makes sense, for Leontes—in this scene, in his banishment of Antigonus and Perdita, and in the trial scene—acts out through violence his desire for correlations between thought, language, and the body and his attempts to find a way back into the community that should validate but denies him the truth of his perceptions.

When Hermione tries to separate herself from Leontes' rhetorical indictments—"You speak a language that I understand not. / My life stands in the level of your dreams, / Which I'll lay down"— Leontes responds, "Your actions are my dreams" (3.2.78–80). She attempts to find a distinction in his "dreams" between what he says and what she does, and Leontes denies that possibility. He creates an interpreter's nightmare. The victim of his scopophilia, Hermione's only recourse is to return as an image of Truth and Wisdom (to recall Jonson's goals for "speaking pictures"), as something other than "nothing." The rest of the play moves to restore a physical world, a world of constant bodies and consistent gesture compatible with the rhetorical one of dreamt sexual anxiety and

revenge established in the first three acts, a world in which
Leontes' dreams are informed by Hermione's actions.[35]

While the deaths following the Oracle's pronouncement are for
Leontes the first reassurance he has that words are connected to
concrete actions, his next sixteen years are "shame perpetual"
(3.2.235), which he imagines as a sexual loss reminiscent of both
the Tyrant's and Govianus' metaphors: "I might have looked upon
my queen's full eyes, / Have taken treasure from her lips—. . . .
No more such wives, therefore no wife" (5.1.53–54, 56). As with
them, the imagined "treasure" of the perfected female body is perceived in the context of its absence.[36]

If Leontes, like the Tyrant and Govianus, interprets Hermione's
death as the loss of her body, he also has her surrogate voice of
recrimination and revenge, Paulina, at his side, and she, like the
Lady's ghost, serves as one of the "interpreters of [Leontes'] be-
hindhand slackness" (5.1.150–51). Paulina's voice, as an extension
of Hermoine's, keeps the image of Hermione before Leontes' eyes
and in his thoughts, shrieking "Remember mine" (5.1.67) when he
thinks of remarriage. Thus, Hermione's and Leontes' constancy is
articulated by Paulina[37] and she, by creating a "certain doubleness," again like the Lady's ghost, manipulates the action of
the play through her speech: It is she who interprets Leontes' high
praise of Perdita as potentially sexual (and, we know, incestuous),
who remembers and repeats the earlier violent rhetoric of sexual
possessiveness and revenge, and who moves the play towards a
reconciliation by creating a "winter of unkind coldness" in which
Hermione becomes a "queen of silence."

Barkan argues that "the silence at the end of the play in which
the couple can meet as statue and speechless viewer purifies the
disasters of speech",[38] but if so, it is because we, like Leontes and
the Tyrant, are willingly "mocked with art" (5.3.68).[39] We read her
emblematically and view a "coy" and "common" likeness marred
by time, much like the Lady, Hermione's age conflicting with her
iconic perfections, those perfections themselves undercut by her
"maker," Julio Romano, the well-known illustrator for the notoriously pornographic *I Modi*.[40] Inspired, Leontes moves to kiss her,
and Paulina remonstrates: "The ruddiness upon her lip is wet; /
You'll mar it if you kiss it; stain your own with oily painting"
(5.3.81–83).[41] If, like the Tyrant, Leontes imagines he can force life
and breath into Hermione to make her more than his dream, Paulina's jarring commentary points out that Leontes' physical gestures are "visual pleasures" inspired by his interpretation of the
representation. She is painted to resemble what Leontes has lost,

including time. Unlike the Tyrant, but like Govianus, Leontes grows content with art: "What you can make her do, / I am content to look on; what to speak, / I am content to hear; for 'tis as easy / To make her speak, as move" (5.3.91–94). Though he responds to the same interpreted gestures that enraged him in Act 1, Leontes is content with the representation of Hermione that mimes his sexual loss, the reconciliation scene restoring his "faith" (5.3.95) in a logocentric world where all—or anything—that he wants to believe about female sexuality is true.

Like the Lady, who defines herself in terms of male desires, Hermione functions as a physical representation of Leontes' rhetoric since she continuously seems to be how he would imagine her. She is "coy" and "common," perfect and flawed. Perceived as powerful agents achieving transformation because they inspire acts of sexual revenge, the Lady and Hermione act as icons initiating these desires. They are objects of interpretation. Similarly, Hermione and Paulina are enclosed within "houses," literally and figuratively, and finally silenced by (re)marriage and art. Both Hermione and the Lady end their plays vindicated and valorized for their silence, for their refusal to be other than what they seem, emblems for a community dominated by male perceptions of what constitutes the experience of women.[42] In the ways these female characters embody and mime sexual loss for the male characters, returning in silence to the grave or public life and becoming artful, they "cease to conceal a menace to the public order," to use Peggy Kamuf's distinctions. The menace they conceal is female sexuality as the male characters perceive it. As Kamuf puts it, "what is displayed here—put on show, brought to the surface—is, indeed, the mechanisms of social legitimacy: the inspections of a woman's interior, that hidden contradictory space where things may not be as they appear".[43] The Lady's return to her tomb and Hermione's reunion with Leontes suggest that "social legitimacy" has been restored because they have encouraged an "inspection" of their bodies as representational art. Leontes and Govianus both "grow content with art," with the representations of female sexuality they would believe are as they appear, and peace returns to their kingdoms.

But again, what Hermione and the Lady have mimed is sexual loss and the corruption of the body in art and in time. They have acted out physically what reading emblematically implies, miming the disjunctures between language and gesture, between imagined experience and actuality. They become silent in their own bodies and acquire supplementary "voices" to re-create and express their physicality in the metaphoric abstractions that would characterize them as art. Paulina's voice urges remembrance of Hermione's body just as the Lady relays the Tyrant's illicit uses of hers to Govianus. In this way, they become images of something other than "nothing," images that include recognition that "nothing" has been lost that can't be recovered through exchanges of metaphoric meanings. As Leontes says, "O royal piece! / There's magic in thy majesty, which has / My evils conjured to remembrance" (5.3.38–40).

The imagistic female body, then, dramatically operates to recall what is missing in the exchange of one vision of feminity for another more perfect one. The Lady refuses to copulate with Govianus and the Tyrant, but she says that her chastity in death makes for an eternal union with Govianus *in his mind*. Physical union is exchanged for the imagined memory of its imagined possibility. The Tyrant reverses this process in his thinking of her body and exposes her decaying body as the referent for this language. These exchanges work towards a deadly deferment of both men's pleasure with the Lady's body, a pleasure that finally coincides with her entombed position offstage.

The Winter's Tale, too, exchanges physical representations for the imagined loss of the remembered body, but this play's action also defers to remembered representations in language. Hermione's Ovidian pose is the culmination of similar scenes in which observations acquire validity because they are expressed as remembered gesture. Leontes' confusion about this connection between what is seen and what seeing can mean leads to Hermione's initial disappearance.[44] In true emblematic fashion, the narration of Hermione and Leontes' embrace occurs even while the audience watches. And, Leontes also defers in his last speech, when he announces that all will "demand and answer to his part" (5.3.152–54) offstage. The dramatic space in which this exchange could occur, since the play is over, must be in the audience's minds. We are left imagining, like Leontes and Govianus, a world in which reconciliation and sexual reunion are possible.

The one important generic difference between *The Second Maiden's Tragedy* and *The Winter's Tale* may be Govianus' and the Lady's final enclosed and tragic positions inside their dramatic structure as compared to *The Winter's Tale*'s characters' movement outside it into the audience's imagination. The female characters in both plays are the site of what is perceived as the experience of "nothing"—or the experience of art as nothing. The dramatic motion of both plays is to locate that site elsewhere, offstage, through a process of deferments, so that the memories of nothing are memorable. We, like the characters, are encouraged to grow content with that art. But if both plays demonstrate that the loss of the physical body can be re-created as art by exchanging the corrupted physical body for the imagined memory of it, both plays also note that the degree of physical corruption increases relative to the attempts to replace it with artifice: The Lady decays and Hermione ages. Both plays, then, argue that to grow content with art is to accept that the art's referent, the "lost" feminine body, can never be fully recovered except as an illusory image that mimes its own loss.

These two plays especially mimic and comment on the humanist tradition of reading emblematically in early modern England. The plays' uses of "visual pleasures" reflect the culture's understandings of the ways in which interpretation could be manipulated and knowledge conveyed and why, increasingly, these images signify a dependence on, and suspicion of, the visualized world, the world of appearances.[45] As Thomas Wright explains it, in *The Passions of the Minde in Generall* (London, 1604):

> Wise men are most moued with sound reasons, and lesse with passions: contraiwise the common people or men not of deepe iudgement, are more persuaded with passions in the speakers; the reason is, because as we haue two senses of discipline especially, the eyes & the ears: reason entreth the eares; the passion wherewith the oratour is affected passeth the eyes, for in his face we discover it, and in other gestures: the eyes are more certain messengers and lesse to be doubted . . . but those passions we see, nature imprinteth them deeper in our hearts.[46]

Reasons are heard, Wright suggests, but persuasion, the moving of passions "lesse to be doubted," is a visual experience. John Ford, in his work *Honor Triumphant: of the Peeres Challenge,* argues that iconic representations of women are especially moving in this regard:

> Being overcome with the affection of some excellently deserving beauty, with admiration of the singular perfection thereof, with what curious workmanship it is framed, with what glorye of majesty it is endowed, it is an immediate occasion, to bring [male observers] in serious conceit of weighing the wonders of the heavens in compacting such admirable quintessence in so precious a form, by which they will deeply acknowledge the weaknesse of their owne nature in comparison of beauty.[47]

The Lady and Hermione persuasively perform just such a delight in instruction, moving the audience to an acknowledgment of eroticized and violent human weaknesses transcended by beauty, or more specifically, art.

And there may be even less transcendent emblematic meanings available. In their vision of social order at each play's end, the Lady's and Hermione's "doubleness" embody for the audience the familiar contemporary understandings of the Queen's two bodies, one the representation of the natural body, the other what Nigel Llewellyn calls the Monumental body, its political representation.[48] Llewellyn discusses how "in an elusive and mysterious way the post-Reformation Monumental Body replaced the deceased 'Natural' Body with an ideal 'Political' Body. Symbolic values traditionally attached to the 'Natural' Body such as pollution, decay, individuation, and separation were replaced by monuments which emphasized the living 'political' significance of regeneration, the solid, socialization, and continuity".[49] Most royal funerals visualized these two bodies for mourners, and from the 1580s on, the "characteristic woodenness and idiosyncratic sense of proportion so disliked by connoisseurs" reflects "the clear distinction between a legal effigy, which replaced its subject as part of a civil honouring, and a scandalous image which was an art object replicating nature and rivalling the creativity of God".[50] Not surprisingly, given England's iconoclastic practices, these Monumental Bodies were frequently attacked and defaced, but Llewellyn suggests further that these monuments reflect the health of the state, "a way of establishing political continuity".[51] Shortly before these plays were produced, both Mary Stuart's and Elizabeth's elaborate Monumental tombs had been completed, helping James to "construct a political legitimacy with a continuous history."[52]

James's need for visualized "legitimacy" coincided with and perhaps created the conditions for what John N. King terms a "sentimental idealization of the late queen"[53], which can be documented in plays, masques, and histories. King suggests that "Jacobean politics provided a motive for the anachronistic revival of the cult of Elizabeth as a model ruler whose perpetual virginity symbolized political integrity, Protestant ideology, and a militantly interventionist policy against Spain. Because these values were increasingly found wanting at the court of England's Scottish king, Protestant militants praised the late queen in order to attack Jacobean pacificism."[54] As Roy Strong has noted, Elizabeth's portraits and impresas enjoyed widespread continued popularity because they exposed a gap between the "poetic dream of the peace and justice of the empire embodied in the state portraits of the Queen and the grim realities of the political scene."[55] If, as Queenly icons representing the lost Elizabeth, the Lady and Hermione function nostalgically to recall the politically chaste "dreams" of the old order, the desire for its return, and its irretrievable loss, they also expose the violent "grim realities" of both Elizabeth's and James's courts, where courtiers jockeyed with rulers for favor and power, mimicking the actions of Govianus, the Tyrant, Leontes, and Polixines as "class aspirants," to recall Stallybrass's terminology. And, because what these "speaking pictures" mean can only, finally, be possessed or known as representations of oscillating and deferred desires that mime their own loss, as art, they represent all the social and political powers and perils inherent in what gives the eye delight.

NOTES

1. Cesare Ripa, *Iconologia,* (Milan, 1602): 215, quoted in Robert Clements, trans., *Picta Poesis: Literary and Humanist Theory in Renaissance Emblem Books* (Rome: Edizioni Di Storia E Letteratura, 1960), 34.

2. Alison Saunders, *The Sixteenth Century French Emblem Book: A Decorative and Useful Genre,* Travaux d'Humanisme et Renaissance CCXXIV (Geneve: Librairie Droz, 1988).

3. For more detailed recent discussions (from a variety of perspectives) of the relationship between humanist agendas for learning and Reformation and Counter-Reformation politics, see Phyllis Mack Crewe, *Calvinist Preaching and Iconoclasm in the Netherlands, 1554–1596* (Cambridge: Cambridge University Press, 1978); Jonathan Goldberg, *Writing Matter: From the Hands of the English Renaissance* (Stanford: Stanford University Press, 1990); Karl Josef Holtgen, *Aspects of the Emblem: Studies in the English Emblem Tradition and the European Context* (Kassel, Germany: Edition Reichenberger, 1986); the collection *Word and Visual Imagination: Studies in the Interaction of English Literature and the Visual Arts,* ed. Karl Josef Holtgen, Peter M. Daly, and Wolgang Lottes (Nürnberg: Erlanger, 1988); John N. King, *Tudor Royal Iconography: Literature and Art in an Age of Religious Crisis* (Princeton: Princeton University Press, 1989); Carole Levin, "Power, Politics, and Sexuality: Images of Elizabeth I," in *The Politics of Gender in Early Modern Europe,* Sixteenth Century Essays & Studies, ed. Jean R. Brink, Allison P. Coudert, and Maryann Horowitz, XII (Kirksville: Sixteenth Century Journal Publishers, 1989): 95–110; Margaret Miles, *Image as Insight: Visual Understanding in Western Christianity and Secular Culture* (Boston: Beacon Press, 1985); and Annabel Patterson, *Censorship and Interpretation: The Conditions of Reading and Writing in Early Modern England* (Madison: Wisconsin University Press, 1984).

4. Michael Bath, "Verse Form and Pictorial Space in Van der Noot's "Theatre for Worldlings," in *Word and Visual Imagination,* 73–105.

5. Ibid., 87.

6. For detailings of the humanist mechanics for the production of meaning, see Rosamond Tuve, *Elizabethan and Metaphysical Imagery* (Chicago: Chicago University Press, 1947); O. B. Hardison, *The Enduring Monument: A Study of the Idea of Praise in Renaissance Literary Theory and Practice* (Chapel Hill:

North Carolina University Press, 1962); and Stanley Fish, *Self-Consuming Arti- facts: The Experience of Seventeenth Century Literature* (Berkeley: California University Press, 1972). For recent critiques, see David Bergeron, *Shakespeare's Romances and the Royal Family* (Lawrence: Kansas University Press, 1985); Jonathan Goldberg, *James I and the Politics of Literature: Jonson, Shakespeare, Donne, and their Contemporaries* (Baltimore: Johns Hopkins University Press, 1983); and Leonard Tennenhouse, *Power on Display: The Politics of Shake- speare's Genres* (New York: Methuen, 1986), among others.

7. See, in particular, Laura Mulvey's "Visual Pleasure and Narrative Cin- ema," reprinted in her *Visual and Other Pleasurers* (Bloomington: Indiana Uni- versity Press, 1989).

8. For an extended discussion of this point, see Alcuin Blamires, "The 'Reli- gion of Love' in Chaucer's *Troilus and Criseyde*, and Medieval Visual Art in *Word and Visual Imagination*, 11–32.

9. Lennard J. Davis, *Factual Fictions: The Origins of the English Novel* (New York: Columbia University Press, 1983), 63.

10. Michael Bath, 74.

11. I am grateful to Constance Relihan, who first pointed out this passage to me.

12. Barnaby Rich, *Rich His Farewell to Militarie Profession*, 1581, ed. T. M. Cranfill (Austin: Texas University Press, 1959), 97.

13. Ibid., 98.

14. Much criticism, and feminist criticism beginning with Judith Fetterley's work on the resisting reader, has analyzed how authors of prose works align readers with narrators to view the work. Less work of this kind has been done in theater criticism, primarily because drama critics tend to remember the exigen- cies of performance when making their arguments. In this essay, I focus on scenes that ask for or call into question the audience's and characters' focus on the female figure.

15. Stephanie Jed, *Chaste Thinking: The Rape of Lucretia and the Birth of Humanism* (Bloomington, Indiana University Press, 1989), 7–8.

16. For a similar discussion concerning how violence is encoded in acts of reading and writing, see Jonathan Goldberg, *Writing Matter*.

17. Ben Jonson, vol. 8 of *Discoveries*, 609–10, quoted in Ernest B. Gilman, *Iconoclasm and Poetry in the English Reformation* (Chicago: Chicago University Press, 1986), 50.

18. Gilman, 179.

19. Peter Daly, *Literature in the Light of the Emblem: Structural Parallels between the Emblem and Literature in the Sixteenth and Seventeenth Centuries* (Toronto: Toronto University Press, 1973).

20. This and subsequent quotations from *The White Devil* are taken from John Webster, *The White Devil* in *Drama of the English Renaissance, II*, ed. Russell A. Fraser and Norman Rabkin (New York: Macmillan, 1976).

21. *The Second Maiden's Tragedy* and *The Winter's Tale* most likely appeared on the stage within six months of each other. E. K. Chambers dates the first performance of *The Second Maiden's Tragedy* 11 October 1611. The Variorum edition of *The Winter's Tale* argues its performance date through consensus; most bibliographers date the play's production in 1611. The first known reference to the play is in Simon Foreman's diary entry of 15 May 1611. Frank Kermode, the editor of the Signet edition, suggests the ending of the play might have been altered after Foreman saw it, since his diary does not mention the statue scene. W. W. Greg, in his edition of the First Folio, suggests that the most likely occasion

for altering the ending would have been its performance at Princess Elizabeth's wedding in 1612–13 (417). Recently, Eric Rasmussen has argued that Shakespeare revised *The Second Maiden's Tragedy* for production by the King's Men; a subsequent exchange on this issue between MacD. P. Jackson and Rasmussen was inconclusive. See Rasmussen's "Shakespeare's Hand in *The Second Maiden's Tragedy,*" *Shakespeare Quarterly* 40, (1989): 1–26 and Jackson's "The Additions to *The Second Maiden's Tragedy:* Shakespeare or Middleton?," *Shakespeare Quarterly* 41, (1990): 401–7. My argument is not an attempt to suggest that one play influenced the other; the similarities between the two are striking enough to warrant comment.

22. This and subsequent quotations from *The Second Maiden's Tragedy* are taken from Thomas Middleton, *The Second Maiden's Tragedy,* ed. Anne Lancashire (Baltimore: Johns Hopkins, 1978).

23. For an alternative humanist reading of the play, see Anne Lancashire's introduction to this edition of the play, in which she argues for an explicitly Christian interpretation: The Lady leads Govianus into spirituality and grace.

24. Lucy Gent, *Picture and Poetry 1560–1620: Relations between Literature and the Visual Arts in the English Renaissance* (Leamington Spa: James Hall, 1981), 54.

25. Ibid., 49.

26. Peter Stallybrass, "Patriarchal Territories: The Body Enclosed," in *Rewriting the Renaissance: the Discourses of Sexual Difference in Early Modern Europe,* ed. Margaret W. Fergusen, Maureen Quilligan, and Nancy Vickers (Chicago: Chicago University Press, 1986), 123–42.

27. Stallybrass sees a similar configuration between Iago and Othello in *Othello.* His arguments have influenced mine, especially his assertion that "there can be no simple opposition between language and body because the body maps out the cultural terrain and is in turn mapped out by it." Ibid., 138.

28. Leonard Barkan, "Living Sculptures and *The Winter's Tale,*" *ELH* 48 (1981): 639–67.

29. Ibid., 644.

30. Stephen J. Miko comments that pastoral "patterns are very familiar and comforting. They encourage us, as does most pastoral literature, both to admire the dreams acted out (low and high may come together, true virtue may emerge, one's true place may be secured or found) and to consider that they are dreams." *"Winter's Tale," SEL* 29 (1989): 265.

31. This and subsequent quotations from *The Winter's Tale* are taken from *The Complete Signet Classic Shakespeare,* ed. Sylvan Barnet (New York: Harcourt Brace Jovanovich, 1972).

32. The generally disastrous consequences of such an intrusion have been discussed by Eve Sedgewick, *Between Men: English Literature and Male Homosocial Desire* (New York: Columbia University Press, 1985); C. L. Barber, "'Thou that beg'st him that did thee beget': Transformation in *Pericles* and *The Winter's Tale,*" *Shakespeare Survey* 22 (1969): 56–67; Richard Wheeler, *Development and the Problem Comedies: Turn and Counter Turn* (Berkeley: California University Press, 1981); and Peter Erickson, *Patriarchal Structures in Shakespeare's Drama* (Berkeley: California University Press, 1985), who analyze in detail the homoerotic aspects of Leontes and Polixenes' friendship. Rene Girard argues that "Leontes has been using his wife as a go-between with another man. Reflecting on this fact, he sees himself as a mimetic model quite different from the one he wanted to be, an involuntary Pandarus, driving his wife into the arms of his friend,

driving his friend into the arms of his wife." "The Crime and Conversion of Leontes in *The Winter's Tale,*" *Religion and Literature* 22 (1990): 196. Girard continues, "Polixenes' unfair singling out of woman [as the source of evil in the world in this scene] is prophetic not only of Leontes' injustice against Hermione but of his own injustice against Perdita in the second half of the play. Leontes and Polixenes are very much alike; they deserve one another more than they realize" (206).

33. One source for the pond metaphor here may be Martial's Epigram, which describes Lydia who "is as widely developed as the rump of a bronze equestrian statue"; after a series of metaphoric statements that expand on the "nature" of her expansive rump, the epigram ends with "This woman I am said to have embraced in a marine fishpond; I don't know; I think I embraced the fishpond itself." *Sex and Literature: The Classic Experience of the Sexual Impulse 2* (London: Calder and Boyars, 1973), XI.21. But where Martial metaphorically re-creates his own sexual experience, Leontes tries to approximate another's, and in the play it is Antigonus who frequently uses equestrian imagery to depict his wife and daughters.

34. "Nothing" was a slang term for "vulva, rounded during coitus," according to E. A. M. Colman, and is thus designated an origin for Leontes' imaginings. See *The Dramatic Uses of Bawdy in Shakespeare* (London: Longman, 1974).

35. As Girard notes, "In the world of Leontes, already, the greatest shame is *to be taken in by representation*", 209; "a liberated Leontes should experience *real presence after all,* and indeed, he does . . . with a little delay" 218.

36. For a more detailed discussion of the problems of presence in the play, see Howard Felperin, "'Tongue-tied our queen?': the deconstruction of presence in *The Winter's Tale,*" in *Shakespeare and the Question of Theory,* ed. Patricia Parker and Geoffrey Hartman (New York: Methuen, 1985).

27. In a general discussion of how the play positions two views of Ovid in Autolycus and Paulina, Mary Ellen Lamb argues that Paulina functions as the artist here and is a "human enactment of divine will." "Ovid and *The Winter's Tale:* Conflicting Views toward Art," in *Shakespeare and Dramatic Tradition,* ed. W. R. Elton and William B. Long (Newark: Delaware University Press, 1989), 72.

38. Leonard Barkan, 659.

39. Many critics have focused on the end of the play as a transcendent statement conflating the meanings of art and life, what L. G. Salingar termed "the relationship, at once likeness and difference, between the experience of real life and the experience of art." "Time and Art in Shakespeare's Romances," *Renaissance Drama* 9 (1966): 30. Miko writes that "the last scene indeed shows us art under the aspect of regeneration, and that regeneration is a function of Time and Nature, beyond human manipulation" 273. Inga-Stina Ewbank suggests that "rather than a myth of immortality, then, this play is a probing into the human condition, and—as a whole as well as in details—it looks at what this means and does to man." "Triumph of Time in *The Winter's Tale,*" *Review of English Literature* 5 (1964): 99. Theresa M. Krier comments that "Hermione's wrinkles remind us, in the midst of this breathtaking and hushed suspense, of the enormous waste and ruin, of the deaths of Mamillius and Antigonus and the ship's passengers, of Leontes and Hermione's years apart. There is loss for which there can never be abundant recompense, but there is succor as well." "The Triumph of Time: Paradox in *The Winter's Tale,*" *Centennial Review* 26 (1982): 352. R. R. Hellenga says "the happiness we share with Leontes as the statue begins to move derives entirely from the fact that an impossible desire has been satisfied," while Lamb

argues that "we may hold in suspension our double perception of the statue scene as miracle and fraud," a view most compatible with my own. See Hellenga, "The Scandal of *The Winter's Tale*," *English Studies* 57 (1976): 18 and Lamb "Ovid and *The Winter's Tale*," 82.

40. Andrew Gurr makes this connection and conjectures that Inigo Jones and Florio, both known to have copies of *I Modi*, may have shared the work with Shakespeare. In addition, he claims that "if [Shakespeare] had read Vasari, as it is claimed he had, in the chapter on Marcantio Raimondi, who engraved Romano's pictures for the *Sonnetti*, he would have got the full story of how Aretino's postures originated from Julio Roman's drawings," and he suggests an intended pun when Leontes first sees the statue and says, "Her natural posture!" (5.2.23). *I Modi* was also known as "Arentino's Postures." "The Many-Headed Audience," *Essays in Theatre* 1 (1982): 58.

41. Given the number of plays that resolve when poisoned lips are kissed, this line must have elicited a more uncanny response in Shakespeare's audience than it does in our time. B. J. Sokol argues that English taste in how statues appeared (painted, as was English custom, or plain, as was the Continental fashion) changed, and "by 1608 or 1609 certain Jacobean aesthetes held painted statues in contempt, and their views are reflected in contemporary plays by Jonson and Shakespeare." "Painted Statues: Ben Jonson and Shakespeare," *Journal of Warburg and Courtauld Institutes* 52 (1989), 250.

42. Susan Dwyer Amussen's study concerning women's responses to defamation as well as Anthony Fletcher and John Stevenson's assertion that "supervision at home, and if necessary, . . . intervention and correction by the community in which she lived" supply another historical background for this kind of enclosure. See Amussen, *An Ordered Society: Gender and Class in Early Modern England* (Oxford: Basil Blackwell, 1988), and Anthony Fletcher and John Stevenson, ed., *Order and Disorder in Early Modern England* (Cambridge: Cambridge University Press, 1985), 11.

43. Peggy Kamuf, *Fictions of Feminine Desire: Disclosures of Heloise* (Lincoln: Nebraska University Press, 1982), 106.

44. Perdita's potential sexual relationship with Florizel has this quality when the Shepherd tells Polixenes, "If young [Florizel] / Do light upon her, she shall bring him that / Which he not dreams of" (4.4.179–80). Girard points out that Perdita and Florizel's hand-holding scenes mimetically repeat the earlier scene when Hermione held Polixenes' hand (209). Similarly, the young lovers' reunion and reconciliation with Polixenes and Leontes is a gesture played off-stage and recalled as high drama by the court.

45. As E. H. Gombrich explains it: "The artist as a maker of such visual images leads away from truth and feeds on delusion . . . True knowledge only results from the third and highest process [the first being sense perception, the second, reason], that of intellectual intuition of ideas or essences." "Icones Symbolicae: The Visual Image in Neo-Platonic Thought," *Journal of Warberg and Courtauld Institutes* 11 (1948): 170. Stephen Greenblatt, concurring, suggests that artifacts like these mime "the representational power of art, its central role in man's apprehension and control of reality, even as [they] insist, with uncanny persuasiveness, on the fictional character of that entire so-called reality and the art that pretends to represent it." *Renaissance Self-Fashioning: From More to Shakespeare* (Chicago: Chicago University Press, 1980), 21. But our modern and post-modern readings are not "new" understandings; as Nicholas Breton, Shakespeare and Middleton's contemporary, put it—"But how wise is the man that hath his wits so cozened,

to take one thing for another. They be lunatic, or in love, that worship such idols."
See *Praise of Virtuous Ladies and Gentlewomen,* London 1606, ed. Sir Egerton
Brydges (Kent: Press of Lee Priory by Johnson and Warwick, 1815).

46. Thomas Wright, *The Passions of the Minde in Generall* (London: 1604),
174–75.

47. John Ford, *Honor Triumphant: or Peeres Challenge,* London, 1606. Shakespeare Society of London Publications 10, no 19. (Nendeln, Liechtenstein: Kraus
Reprint LTD, 1966), 29.

48. Philippa Berry suggests that "Elizabeth as queen had a triple rather than
a dual aspect, like the triune God of Christian theology," and that "Elizabeth's
rule figured *the feminine in a mystical or symbolic relationship with itself.*" See *Of
Chastity and Power: Elizabethan Literature and the Unmarried Queen* (London:
Routledge, 1989). I would add to her claim, "as perceived by others."

49. Nigel Llewellyn, "The Royal Body: Monuments to the Dead, For the Living," in *Renaissance Bodies: The Human Figure in English Culture c. 1540–1660,*
ed. Lucy Gent and Nigel Llewellyn (London: Reaktion, 1990), 222.

50. Ibid., 223.

51. Ibid., 224.

52. Ibid., 228.

53. John N. King, "Queen Elizabeth I: Representations of the Virgin Queen,"
Renaissance Quarterly XLIII, (1990): 66.

54. Ibid., 67.

55. Roy Strong, *Gloriana, The Portraits of Queen Elizabeth I* (London: Thames
and Hudson: 1987), 43.

Part II
Measure for Measure

"I'll Pray to Increase Your Bondage": Power and Punishment in *Measure for Measure*

David McCandless

THE first and most striking instance of power and punishment in Shakespeare's *Measure for Measure* is also the play's true beginning: At Angelo's command, Claudio is publicly disgraced, enchained, and paraded through the streets to prison. The preceding action—the Duke's inexplicable departure and hasty deputizing of Angelo, Lucio's scurrilous badinage about venereal disease—amounts to a prologue. The punishment of Claudio, which manifests Angelo's "mortal" power, is the incident upon which the play's entire action turns. It seems to me absolutely crucial that this scene be staged in such a way as to heighten Claudio's humiliation: Lucio and his scruffy cohorts disport themselves in some sort of tavern/gaming den/house of ill repute. They and other customers are hastily diverted from their disreputable amusements by a steadily increasing rumble portending the arrival of a rowdy crowd. Suddenly they find themselves spectators to a shocking event: the public shaming of their friend Claudio.

This directorial choice necessitates excising or transposing the dialogue between Pompey and Overdone, but, to my mind, the resultant theatrical effect more than justifies the revision. Indeed, the director ought, I think, to go further: Claudio is not only in chains but very nearly naked, as part of a ritual of mortification, which sharpens his shame and imparts particular urgency to his protest to the Provost, "why dost thou show me thus to th' world?" (1.2.116). An unruly throng accompanies him, some of them jeering and savoring his torment. From a second-level balcony, Lord Angelo himself watches Claudio's degradation with discernible satisfaction. The image ought to convey the extent to which Angelo succeeds in making a spectacle of Claudio, putting his mortified, fetishized body on public display, reducing him to the personification of an errant flesh that must be extravagantly punished, submitting him to a sadistic, voyeuristic gaze.[1]

I would like, in this essay, to assay the sadopornographic nature of the punishments in *Measure for Measure,* examining the process by which the play's central characters attempt to master sexuality by punishing representatives of their rejected sexual selves. This process parallels the aggressive displacement necessary to sadism as Gilles Deleuze defines it: The empowered superego's persecution of feminized images of the rejected ego.[2] Deleuze's account of sadism, in turn, coalesces with the feminist reading of pornography as a sadistic mode of representation through which men indulge fantasies of mastering women who embody their own discarded fleshly selves.[3] Thus, in *Measure for Measure* Angelo enjoys a brief reign of authority during which he dominates a series of feminized surrogates forced to accept the status of his own mortified flesh: Claudio, Isabella, and Mariana. The final scene reveals, however, that Angelo has unknowingly functioned as the Duke's feminized surrogate, suffering a kind of public emasculation for falling prey to the female sexuality that the Duke, in his own strange way, aims to regulate.

The imagined staging of Claudio's punishment, then, works to foreground the play's sadopornographic drama. Claudio's tormentor, Angelo, cannot, strictly speaking, be called a sadist, primarily because, once incited by lust, he lacks the sadist's passionlessness: "the true sadist is self-controlled to the point of apathy. . . . Sade deplores the pornographer's 'enthusiasm.'"[4] By Sade's standard, Angelo seems primarily a pornographer who enacts his fantasy of mastering a helpless "feminine" figure.[5] That the "feminine" figure is initially a man only underlines his status as the pornographer's chastened double. Indeed, the persecuted Claudio could be said to function as a kind of male intermediary between Angelo and the person who comes ultimately to occupy the position of degraded "feminine" double: Isabella. The cataclysmic lust that Angelo unleashes against her proves that his severe, desexualized persona is a self-suppressing fiction. The sexual insurrection that he undertakes to defeat arises not simply in Vienna but within his own psyche. In mortifying Claudio, he not only punishes a criminal but pummels the principal adversary in his own *psychomachia,* forcing Claudio to play the villainous Flesh. He chastens Claudio's body in place of his own. He makes Claudio bear the cross of sexual guilt.

The sadopornographic spectacle of Claudio's degradation has ample historical sanction. In an influential essay, Carolyn Brown traces the play's excoriative imagery to the monastical practice of flagellation, which was celebrated as the most efficacious agency of penitence, breeding in anchorites a capacity for deriving pleasure from the infliction or reception of pain.[6] As Brown points out, while monks and nuns frequently flayed themselves in private for bodily trespasses, they also regularly submitted to public beatings from their superiors that, as Brown says, "promoted both active sadism in the flogger and vicarious sadism in the spectators"—turning the punishment of sinning flesh into public spectacle.[7]

Perhaps even more to the point, Shakespeare's society seems to have elevated sadism to a juridical principle. The exorbitant abuse of lawbreakers was a popular form of public entertainment. Chastised criminals were regularly submitted to a voyeuristic, sadistic public gaze. A Londoner on his daily rounds could amuse himself with a chained robber hanging in a gibbet, "a petty thief in the pillory, a scold in the ducking stool, a murderer drawn to the gallows on a hurdle."[8] Executions, sometimes featuring grisly torture, were likewise turned into public spectacles. Foucault's description of such dramas as rituals for repairing a metaphorically shattered sovereignty seem as apposite to Shakespeare's England as to the seventeenth-century France that he surveys.[9] As Foucault suggests, "the punishment is carried out in such a way as to give a spectacle not of measure, but of imbalance and excess; in this liturgy of punishment, there must be an emphatic affirmation of power and its intrinsic superiority."[10] Angelo's public degradation of Claudio becomes the visible sign of the "excess" of executing a man for enjoying conjugal relations with his common-law wife. The absence of "measure" in Angelo's sentence is particularly telling, given the play's title, and recasts the Duke's threatened retribution at the end as "excess for excess."

In the sense that Claudio represents Angelo's fleshly double, he must be punished for doing willingly what Angelo abhors and can only be hoodwinked into doing: having sexual relations with the woman he has sworn to marry. On the surface, Angelo's dismissal of Mariana for reasons of "levity" seems simply a moralistic cover for a cold financial maneuver—deserting a dowerless, hence undesirable, woman. On the other hand, Angelo's charge that his fiancée is unchaste may have a kind of psychological validity: Since he does not desire her or cannot permit himself to desire her, her unabashed and unextinguishable desire for him must seem frighteningly wanton and excessive. Thus, her loss of dowry frees him

from marriage, from a perilous deliverance to a potentially devouring female sexuality. In short, in breaking his betrothal to
Mariana, he averts emasculation.

Claudio, however, who reciprocates and fulfills Juliet's desire,
who allows himself to become entangled with female sexuality,
does not avert it—at least does not in Angelo's eyes. So, in this
imagined staging, Angelo turns Claudio's emasculation into a piece
of street theater, a fetishistic sadopornographic spectacle, savoring
the power of punishing a feminized weakling. Claudio in chains,
seminaked, paraded through the streets, is Claudio unmanned,
forced to submit to the feminization of his body.

This image of youth and beauty degraded, of the body shamed,
calls to mind the brutalized martyrs of early religious iconography
(perhaps including Christ himself) as well as the chained and
lashed goddesses of contemporary pornography.[11] It may also call
to mind the degraded god of Euripides' *The Bacchae*, Dionysos,
who, disguised as a mysterious, polymorphous-perverse stranger,
is likewise placed in chains and paraded through the city and forced
to submit to the chastisements of the Angelo-like governor Pentheus, who ridicules his effeminacy. Pentheus' pose as omnipotent
male authority, however, proves as shaky as Angelo's. Both men
decide to give their sensual race the rein, Pentheus taking the masochist's route, wearing women's clothes and suffering the brutal-
izations of the very women he vowed to punish, and Angelo turning
sadist and punishing the "feminine" forces that excite the urge to
lose "masculine" control. According to Deleuze, "sadism is in
every sense an active negation of the mother and an exaltation of
the father who is beyond all laws."[12] Thus, Angelo rejects Mariana,
a figure of the mother (even her name has maternal resonance) and
ascends to the position of father of the land, or at least ruthless
enforcer of the Law of the Father, effecting a severity that, as
later events confirm, counters a contrary pull toward the feminine.
Angelo's punishment of Claudio thus achieves additional significance: Mariana's double, Juliet, the woman to whom Claudio suc-
cumbs, is visibly pregnant and hence explicitly maternal. For
Angelo, Juliet is a groaning "fornicatress" whose pregnancy is
proof of female corruption (2.223). The disguised Duke seems to
ratify this reading of Juliet's pregnancy, characterizing her fetus as
the "sin she carries" and contending that her crime—refusing to
repel the passion she ignites—is greater than Claudio's (2.3.26–28),
thus reading the female body as both sign and source of sin.[13]

Isabella so bedevils Angelo because she presents herself, albeit
involuntarily, as a potential Juliet, an alluring female body that

recalls him to his own. By stridently rebuffing his lecherous overtures, however, she makes him alone bear the burden of the sinful lust she arouses, impregnates him with "the strong and swelling evil of my conception" (2.4.7). In effect, she makes him the source of sin, turns him into Juliet, effectively effeminizing him.

By afflicting Angelo with desire, Isabella forces Angelo to retrieve the discarded creaturely self personified by Claudio. Indeed, when Angelo exclaims, "O let her brother live! / Thieves for their robbery have authority when / Judges steal themselves" (2.2.174–76), he makes the very concession Isabella labors so strenuously to extract: He and Claudio, the condemned fornicator, are kin. While such fellow-feeling has the effect of moving him momentarily to mercy, ultimately it breeds a vindictive desire to punish Isabella for having effected it. Beset by degrading lust, he stands in relation to Isabella as Claudio previously stood to him—a wretched sinner, a damnable lecher contemplating a lofty and unassailable figure.

Far more provocatively than Claudio, Isabella represents a bodily "feminine" self that Angelo must reject and punish. She therefore takes Claudio's place as the object of Angelo's retributive violence. No sooner has he safely enchained and imprisoned Claudio than Isabella, figuratively speaking, enchains and imprisons Angelo. So he must, in turn, enchain and imprison her. She has made him feel her power; now she must feel his.

Isabella seems scarcely aware of the power she wields, at least initially. "My power," she protests to Lucio when he bids her "assay" it on her brother's behalf, "alas, I doubt," (1.4.75–77). Claudio, in fact, has already defined that power, telling Lucio

> in her youth
> There is a prone and speechless dialect,
> Such as move men; beside, she hath prosperous art
> When she will play with reason and discourse,
> And well she can persuade.
>
> (1.2.182–86)

The "speechless dialect" that "moves" (arouses) men is Isabella's sexual charisma—her body language. The word "prone," connoting both recumbence and receptivity, suggests that Isabella's body speaks the language of sexual availability—or is at least made to speak it.[14] Lucio twice urges Isabella to assume a prone—or at least kneeling—position, first at the nunnery when extolling the efficacy of female "weeping and kneeling" (1.4.81) and secondly in Angelo's chambers when arresting her premature exit and admon-

ishing her to "kneel down and hang upon [Angelo's] gown" (2.2.44).
"You are too cold," he reprimands her, implicitly requesting that
she infuse her supplications with warmth and sensuality, that she
be passionate as well as subservient. Lucio essentially asks her to
"be a woman," anticipating Angelo's more menacing demand that
she put on the "destin'd livery." Thus, when Isabella begins to
work her will on Angelo and to weaken his resolve, Lucio exclaims,
"O, to him, to him, wench! he will relent. He's coming; I perceive't" (2.2.124–25). Lucio calls Isabella, whom he formerly
praised as "a thing enskied and sainted," "wench" and portrays
the success of her appeal in language suggestive of sexual arousal.
Angelo's proposition to Isabella, and Claudio's plea for her to com-
ply, simply literalize the outcome of the metaphorical seduction
she carries out.

Isabella's speechless dialect is, however, a male language, the
only mode of signification that her body commands in a phallocentric economy. Thus, during her second meeting with Angelo, as
she laments the weakness of women, Angelo "arrests her words"
and declares,

> Be that you are,
> That is, a woman; if you be more, you're none;
> If you be one (as you are well express'd
> By all external warrants), show it now,
> By putting on the destin'd livery.
>
> (2.4.134–38)

"Arrest your words" means not only "take you at your word" but
"stop your words." Angelo wishes to deny Isabella the agency of
speech, to make her words mean what he wants them to, construing a lament for female weakness as an admission of sexual desire
and therefore as a cue for propositioning her. He aims to confine
her speech—her signifying power—to the speechless dialect of her
body. The destin'd livery he urges her to wear is the mantle of
sexual subjugation that replaces the nun's habit, which, to his great
vexation, renounces the sexual availability that her speechless dialect signifies. To eschew this mantle of subjugation is to be "more
than a woman" and therefore "none" (or "nun"). In Isabella's response—"I have no tongue but one; gentle my lord, / Let me en-
treat you speak the former language" (2.4.139–140)—one hears an
echo of Hermione's protest to Leontes, "you speak a language I
understand not." In Isabella's case, the complaint might more precisely be, "you make me speak a language I understand not." In a

Lacanian context, the scene confirms the impossibility of female speech within a phallocentric system of signification.[15]

Angelo's determination to impose an image of "Woman" on Isabella takes on sadistic and pornographic dimensions. Indeed, he seems intent on enacting what Susan Griffin considers the quintessential pornographic fantasy: despoiling an idolized virgin.[16] In accordance with this fantasy, Angelo seeks to demystify his own mystification of Isabella as exalted, unattainable goddess, to expose her as pure flesh, to affirm her essential sordidness.[17] By attempting to defile the goddess remade in the image of whore, Angelo seeks to regain his "masculine" identity, to mortify the fleshly "feminine" self by mortifying Isabella.

Perhaps the most telling phrase of his first soliloquy, then, is "What is't I dream on?" (2.2.178). Angelo struggles not so much against sexual feeling in general as against the specific "dream," or fantasy, of debauching Isabella, a struggle that lies at the heart of his second soliloquy. Angelo assumes a position similar to Claudius's: He finds his prayers to heaven empty and unavailing. While he has not, like Claudius, done the dirty deed, he has apparently savored his sexual fantasy sufficiently to experience a racking guilt. Angelo's attempt to confess and repent his lurid dream seems only to intensify its imaginative rehearsal and further tempt its enactment, bringing to mind Barthes's observation that Sade's method for nurturing sexual fantasy closely resembles the spiritual exercise of Ignatius Loyola: Retreat, darkness, imagination, and repetition. This process "dictates" a pornographic text that demands enactment.[18]

Angelo's pornographic text betrays a tortured fluctuation between sadism and masochism. Masochism, according to Deleuze, reverses the dynamics of sadism, enacting the negation of the father and the exaltation of the mother, a submergence in the "feminine" and dismissal of the "masculine."[19] The masochist fetishizes his female tormentor—an image of the forbidden, desired mother—symbolically surrendering the phallus to her and investing her with the power of law, achieving sexual pleasure by purging through pain the guilt that precludes it.[20] As Deleuze puts it, the masochist de-sexualizes his relation with his tormentor in order to achieve re-sexualization.[21]

On the one hand, Angelo flirts with masochistic feminization. "This virtuous maid / Subdues me quite" he declares (2.2.184–85). Isabella subdues Angelo—that is, subjugates and emasculates him. Desire for her has made him "fond" (2.2.186), he admits—foolish and infatuated and thus potentially feminized like the "fond father"

of a Duke whose "rod" is "more mock'd than fear'd" (1.3.23,26–
27). She leads him to a longing for "levity," for an unmasculine loss
of control: He would gladly let go of his "gravity," he confesses,
in exchange for "an idle plume / Which the air beats for vain"
(2.4.9–12). One may read in this line a masochist's savoring of
powerlessness, an unmanly coveting of vanity that invites
"beating."

Moreover, inasmuch as the self-torturing Angelo elevates Isabella to the status of goddess—who competes with God for his
prayers—and verbally flays himself for his forbidden desire, he
implicitly assumes a masochistic posture.

> When I would pray and think, I think and pray
> To several subjects. Heaven hath my empty words,
> Whilst my invention, hearing not my tongue,
> Anchors on Isabel; heaven in my mouth,
> As if I did but chew his name,
> And in my heart the strong and swelling evil
> Of my conception.
>
> (2.4.1–7)

The self-lacerating language suggests that Angelo might, in performance, actually flagellate himself during this speech, physicalizing
the masochistic pose by excoriating himself at the feet of his (absent) goddess/mistress, enacting an enslavement derived from a
guilt-inducing sexual vexation that can only be purged through
pain.[22]

In imagining himself pregnant with his "conception"—the sexual
fantasy that Isabella has implanted—Angelo evokes a parody of
the virgin birth in which his God, Isabella, descends from on high
and impregnates him, leaving him with the unwanted child of lust,
the sin he carries.[23] In Janet Adelman's resonant phrase, Angelo is
"pregnant with his own sexuality," and Isabella is the inseminat-
ing agent.[24]

Angelo cannot, however, as the masochist must, desexualize the
object of his desire, so his would-be masochistic self-mortification
becomes autoerotic self-stimulation. His obsessive fixation on the
sexual fantasy of ravishing his goddess clearly arouses him—in
concrete physical terms the "swelling" to which he refers can only
be phallic. Since Isabella seems to have come to occupy the place
of God, she has come, in Lacanian terms, to occupy the place of
the Other, of ultimate truth or rather ultimate fantasy, the supposed
end to which Angelo's vexatious, insatiable desire drives him.[25]
This Lacanian notion of drive—ultimately beyond satisfaction as

Angelo's case seems to prove—tallies with Susan Sontag's treatment of pornography as an outlet for "high-temperature visionary obsessions," as the vehicle of a sexual passion "beyond love" and "beyond sanity" that aims at the "limits of consciousness."[26]

Yet Angelo elects not to confine himself to mystical autoeroticism, adhering instead to the Sadean imperative of enacting his fantasy, which, in the face of what he comes to believe is Isabella's deliberate provocation of a lust she refuses to gratify, shifts from masochistic to sadistic. "Lay by all nicety and prolixious blushes / That banish what they sue for" (2.4.162–63), he demands, now believing her chastity to be a seductive affectation. Angelo begins to associate Isabella with the strumpet whose "double vigor" of "art and nature" (2.2.183) suggests a cunning enhancement of sexual appeal. Previously he measured Isabella's attractiveness in terms of her difference from the whore. Now he collapses the difference.

Earlier in the scene, Angelo essentially appoints Isabella a whore's fate in asking her to trade places with the "fornicatress," Juliet, pregnant with sin: "give up your body to such sweet uncleanness / As she that he hath stain'd" (2.4.54–55). Angelo, pregnant with his own sexuality, essentially asks Isabella to duplicate and thereby terminate his pregnancy. He aims to transfer the sin he carries to Isabella, make her pregnant—if only metaphorically—with a "staining" sexuality. He may, in dirtying her ("pitching his evil"), cleanse himself.

Angelo's strained, oblique courtship culminates in a proposition that becomes, once repelled, a vicious threat, a demand that Isabella satisfy his lust or else accept responsibility for her brother's gruesome death:

> Redeem thy brother
> By yielding up thy body to my will,
> Or else he must not only die the death,
> But thy unkindness shall his death draw out
> To ling'ring sufferance.

(163–67)

Here Isabella's status as mortified stand-in for Claudio becomes explicit. If the violently aroused Angelo, giving his sensual race the rein, cannot brutalize Isabella, he will brutalize her brother by torturing him to death. Angelo openly avows that his violent passion for Isabella fuels his sadistic flaying of Claudio: "Answer me tomorrow," he tells her, "Or by the affection that now guides me most, / I'll prove a tyrant to him" (167–69).[27] Angelo's lust, which he perversely calls love, transmutes into a sadistic urge to subjugate and inflict suffering. Isabella must "yield" to him, submit to his "sharp appetite." The violence of his language turns his vicious demand into the verbal equivalent of a rape. Here too the director may choose to physicalize the violence of the lines, staging the moment as an attempted rape, which Isabella manages to thwart.[28] If Angelo, in his second soliloquy, fondles a fantasy that eventuates in his assault on Isabella, one might well invoke Robin Morgan's celebrated aphorism, "pornography is the theory and rape the practice." For Angelo, pornographic fixation begets sadistic enactment, the punishment of the threatening female who afflicts him with effeminizing desire.[29]

Critics have often noted that Isabella's first speech in the play expresses a request for "more restraint," a wish that the notoriously strict order of St. Clare were even stricter. What has been less noted is the peculiarity of the question that precedes the wish: "and have you nuns no farther privileges?" (1.4.1). It seems decidedly odd that a young woman coveting "farther stricture" should begin by asking after further privileges. Either she masochistically equates stricture with privilege or chafes under stricture but is shamed by Francisca's testy reply—"are these not large enough?"—into shamming a desire for more.[30] In either case, she seems ill-suited to the cloister, either balking at sexual renunciation or embracing it with a vigor that invites suspicions of sexual guilt, as though the severity of the restraint she covets matches the fervor of the passion she wishes to restrain. The actress Juliet Stevenson, who played a warm and sensual Isabella for Adrian Noble in 1983, seems to have favored the latter interpretation:

> I think she recognizes her own sexuality and the need to apply strict control over it. I don't think she's frightened or surprised by it; she wants to dominate it. Hence her choice of the St. Clares. The severity of the order is, I think, commensurate with the scale of those latent passions in her, which she feels must be harnessed, controlled.[31]

Isabella's chastity need not be reduced to a pathology, of course. But even if the urge to dominate her sexual impulses may be imputed to youthful self-excitement or monastic imperative, the extremity of that urge, coupled with the sexual corruptiveness of the patriarchal world she flees, tempt the conclusion that she must curb sexual drives that might otherwise propel her into the perilous

territory of male sexuality.[32] In a telling exchange, Isabella agrees
with Angelo that women are "frail":

> Ay, as the glasses where they view themselves,
> Which are as easy broke as they make forms.
> Women? Help heaven! men their creation mar
> In profiting by them. Nay, call us ten times frail,
> For we are soft as our complexions are,
> And credulous to false prints.
>
> (2.4.124–30)

Isabella presents female sexual experience as a process of loss,
as the breaking of chastity and the making of "false" forms—the
begetting of bastards.[33] In Isabella's mind, it would seem, a
woman's sexual experience is one of despoliation, impregnation,
and abandonment, such as Juliet and Kate Keepdown actually suffer. Isabella's construct presupposes not only male rapacity—men
"break the glass" and "mar their creation" by using women—but
female wantonness. Men corrupt women because women are corruptible, receptive as well as vulnerable to sexual use. Isabella first
refers to such women as "they" and then as "we." By implication
she portrays herself as sexually susceptible, as though confirming
that she would rather restrain her sexual impulses than pursue
them into a ruinous encounter with a rapacious male. Rather than
wear the harness of sexual vassalage, she seeks to harness her own
sexuality. In this regard, she resembles Angelo and the Duke: She
wishes to achieve "masculine" self-mastery, to disown the "feminine" self, to mortify the flesh. Her choice of the cloister, then,
seems simultaneously an act of self-actualization, self-suppression,
and self-defense.

If Isabella is a passionate young woman whose only outlet for
passion in this patriarchal society is the impassioned championing
of monastical chastity, then the task of winning Claudio's pardon,
which soon becomes the task of "moving" Angelo, provides a new
outlet, one that, far from submerging her in institutionalized masochism, provides for the temporary experience of power: Isabella
dominates and sexually arouses the most dominant, seemingly
most desexualized man in the land. The director and actress must
of course establish the extent to which Isabella is conscious of her
effect on Angelo. Certainly it seem plausible that she discerns
Angelo's faltering resolve and enjoys the experience of wielding
power and weakening his will. From the standpoint of performance,
it is not only possible but desirable that Isabella actually harbor
an unconscious attraction to Angelo, fueling her implorations with

sublimated desire. Certainly Stevenson understood and played the
scene as a sublimated sexual encounter, asserting that Isabella and
Angelo "copulate across the verse."[34] The text does not overtly
substantiate Isabella's attraction to Angelo but, from the standpoint of performance, it is the strongest, most emotionally generative choice, the choice that sets up maximum conflict for Isabella.
In fact, this attraction hardly seems implausible if one concedes
to Isabella sexual impulses in conflict with her sexual renunciation
and considers Angelo as a kind of alluring forbidden object.

In addition, Isabella hints at a subterranean sexual drive during
her second interview with Angelo. "I am come to know your pleasure," she announces upon arriving (2.4.31), a perhaps guileless
greeting that nonetheless registers a double sexual meaning, as
though Isabella were acknowledging—consciously or not—the
sexual undercurrents of their encounters. Isabella's most sexually
charged pronouncement comes, however, when she finally begins
to grasp the nature of Angelo's proposal:

> were I under the terms of death,
> Th' impression of keen whips I'd wear as rubies,
> And strip myself to death as to a bed
> That longing have been sick for, ere I'd yield
> My body up to shame.
>
> (2.4.100–4)

Once more we seem to be nearing the realm of pornographic sadomasochism: Isabella, in piercingly sensual language, imagines herself being whipped.[35] She will not accept a whore's fate but will
accept a whore's punishment, spurning the bodily violation of vindictive rape for that of punitive beating. This fantasy bespeaks a
guilt-ridden compulsion to punish her own sinning flesh, to enact
the penitential imperatives of a monastical conscience. Isabella
may be sufficiently aware of her provocation of Angelo, sufficiently
appreciative of the power she thereby commands, sufficiently dis-
tressed by a sting of reciprocal attraction, to feel that her own
stimulated, errant flesh stands in need of corrective flaying. From
one angle, Isabella employs the discourse of martyrology, drawing
on legends and images of female saints cruelly tortured or killed.
She reiterates, with martyrish intensity, her readiness to die on
Claudio's behalf. On the other hand, the violently erotic imagery
of her resolution links martyrology and pornography, associating
Isabella and her tortured female saints with the tortured—or in any
case sadistically objectified—women in pornography.[36] As Griffin

asserts, "the metaphysics of Christianity and the metaphysics of pornography are the same. . . . All the elements of sadomasochistic ritual are present in the crucifixion of Christ."[37] On one level, at least, *imitatio Christi* means to savor fleshly mortification. Perhaps, for Isabella as well as for Maria Magdalena of Pazzi and Elizabeth of Genton, self-mortification is the vehicle of a spiritual ecstasy imaged as sexual union with Christ the bridegroom. Certainly the erotic imagery of her "rubies" speech commingles flagellation with the sexual act. For Isabella as well as for Angelo, the mystic's ecstatic self-flagellation becomes linked with masochistic autoeroticism.

Isabella's vision registers as an autoerotic fantasy because the fantasized flagellator is simply an empowered aspect of the self, a personified superego, a cultural "masculine" self that inflicts punishment on the feminized body. Thus, Isabella savors in fantasy what her brother suffers in reality. Unlike Angelo, she does not mortify the flesh by persecuting a feminized ego-substitute but by submitting to the persecutions of a masculine superego-substitute. She takes the part not of flagellator but of flagellant. Indeed, she seems to accept the destin'd livery of "lack" that ensures her place in the sexual system, surrendering an active sexuality and embracing masochistic eroticism.

While Isabella's beating fantasy seems to confirm her predilection for mortifying or at least restraining the flesh, it does not, strictly speaking, qualify her as a masochist. She seems to covet a desexualized relation with a forbidden father figure, but not, like the masochist, as a means to resexualization, but as an end in itself. Initially Isabella seems to wish to identify Claudio with her father.[38] Before telling him of Angelo's loathsome proposition, she protests that Claudio's acceptance of it "would bark honor from the trunk you bear, / And leave you naked" (3.1.71–72). If Claudio were to agree to his sister's despoliation, he would forfeit identification with his father. Thus, when Claudio protests his willingness to "encounter darkness as a bride / And hug it in mine arms" (83–84), Isabella exclaims, "There spake my brother; there my father's grave / Did utter forth a voice" (85–86). Claudio's momentary resolution would have the effect of saving Isabella from sexual violation and so links him with her protective father. On the other hand, when Claudio implores Isabella to satisfy Angelo's demands, he becomes not his father's but his mother's son: "Heaven shield my mother play'd my father fair! / For such a warped slip of wilderness / Ne'er issu'd from his blood" (140–42). In so doing, as Adelman points out, Isabella implicitly protects her father from sexual contamination, as though needing to perpetuate the image of an idealized, desexualized father figure who will protect her from sexual defilement.[39] One might even say that such a figure corresponds to God the father, illuminating another facet of her attraction to the nunnery.

Claudio's refusal to facilitate Isabella's desexualization, his suggestion that she might, for his sake, suffer Angelo's brutalization of her flesh, compels her to turn into a flagellator. Indeed, she verbally brutalizes him, transforms him, as did Angelo, into a personified corrupt flesh that must be mercilessly lacerated. In one sense, Claudio once more plays the part of Angelo's chastened surrogate: Charged with incest and thus made complicit in Angelo's assault on his sister, he suffers a vituperation that surely feeds on rage against Angelo even as Hamlet's chastisement of Ophelia channels disgust with his mother. In another sense, Claudio plays the part of Isabella's chastened surrogate, a whipping boy absorbing whatever guilt she feels for igniting Angelo's lust. She identifies Claudio with her own traitorous flesh and punishes him as a feminized ego-substitute, assigning him the role she had assigned herself in the fantasy of flagellation. Claudio now stands in relation to Isabella as Isabella does to Angelo.

Angelo stands in the same relation to the Duke: as scagegoated flesh-monger, mortified "feminine" self. The play's opening scene makes clear that Angelo functions as the Duke's double.[40] He is portrayed—and portrays himself—as the stamp upon which the Duke's image is fixed (1.1.16, 48–50). "Be thou at full ourself," the Duke urges him (1.1.41, 43). Both men are reclusive ascetics ruled by sexual disavowal. Indeed, when Lucio, addressing the disguised Duke, praises him as one who, unlike the frigid Angelo, "had some feeling of the sport" which "instructed him to mercy," the Duke protests, "I have never heard the absent Duke much detected for women; he was not inclined that way" (3.2.119–22). The Duke implicitly prefers to be linked with Angelo, whom Lucio disparages as freakish ("not made by man and woman"), preternaturally cold ("his urine is congealed ice"), and impotent (he is a motion ungenerative") (3.2.104–5, 110–12).

In addition, the Duke enters into intimate attachments with the women to whom Angelo is intimately attached: Isabella and Mariana. His desexualized disguise gives him access to their sexual lives. For Isabella, the Duke takes over the role of salvific father-brother that Claudio declined. He addresses her as "young sister" (3.1.151) and she twice calls him "good father" (238, 269). Indeed,

Adelman calls the Friar/Duke the "embodiment of the fantasied asexual father who will protect Isabella from her own sexuality."[41] At the same time, his friar's disguise affords him two covert intimate meetings with Isabella in a "dark corner" of Vienna's prison—and we hardly require Pompey's direct linking of prison and brothel (4.3.1–4) to discern in these meetings an image of sexual tryst. The titillating effects of being alone (for the first time in his life, one imagines) with a young woman in secluded crannies of the prison could be made quite clear in performance, especially at the close of their second interview, when a leering Lucio could discover them in some mildly compromising position—touching, hand-holding, embracing—that might discommode the Duke and set up Lucio's later insinuating line, "But yesternight, my lord, she and that friar, / I saw them at the prison. A saucy friar, / A very scurvy fellow" (5.1.134–36).[42]

Moreover, the text offers hints of the Duke's attraction to Isabella. When first intercepting her, he speaks of "the satisfaction I would require" and later, in the same speech, uses the word in its explicitly sexual sense, urging Isabella to give Angelo "promise of satisfaction" (3.1.154–56, 264). In addition, the Duke secretly (and voyeuristically) witnesses Isabella's excoriation of Claudio and appears to find the sensual fervor of her speechless dialect as provocative in rage as Angelo found it in supplication. Left alone with her, he extols the same chaste allure that exercised Angelo:

> The hand that hath made you fair hath made you good. The goodness that is cheap in beauty makes beauty brief in goodness; but grace, being the soul of your complexion, shall keep the body of it ever fair.
> (3.1.180–84)

From the Duke's perspective, Isabella exercises a sexuality free of corruption, uniting the chastity and beauty that Hamlet accuses Ophelia of having sundered. The Duke might say "get thee from a nunnery," especially since his later proposal of marriage requires such a displacement.[43]

On the surface, the Duke's proposal seems a far cry from Angelo's brutal proposition. Yet his wooing of a would-be nun could also be construed as an attempt to possess a self-possessed woman, to subdue a female force that subdues him. In one sense, the Duke's attempt to wed Isabella is analogous to taming a shrew: like the shrew, she demonstrates a willfulness and self-sufficiency, a daunting capacity for fearless raillery, a provocative "openness" that invites patriarchal enclosure.[44] Until his proposal, the Duke seems determined to make Isabella feel as helpless as possible. He resolves to keep her ignorant of Claudio's survival in order, he says, "to make her heavenly comforts of despair / When it is least expected" (4.3.110–11). In other words, as befits the play's sado-masochistic dynamics, he will hurt her in order to please her, play God in order to secure her devotion, manipulate her into an indebt-edness favorable to his proposal. "Give your cause to heaven," he instructs, overruling her urge toward masculine revenge ("O, I will to [Angelo] and pluck out his eyes" [4.3.119]) and recommending a retreat into iconic femininity (urging "wisdom," "patience," and "forbearance" [118, 124]). That he really means "give your cause to me" seems clear from his ensuing admonition that she seek "grace of the Duke" (4.3.119–36). The Duke seemingly deifies him-self in order to justify the coercion of Isabella's will.

In the final scene, the Duke increases Isabella's helplessness, orchestrating the public besmirching of her honor. He manipulates her into unchaste public utterances that he scornfully censures, accusing her of madness and wantonness and thereby converting her defamations of Angelo's sexual perfidy into admissions of her own. He places her under arrest, and if, in performance, he also places her in chains, the stage picture recalls the mortified Claudio, the original image of the body shamed.[45] As Angelo had threatened, her attempt to indict him redounds to her shame and makes her "smell of calumny." Having reduced her to absolute powerlessness, the Duke proposes marriage, seemingly consummating a careful plot to bind Isabella to him, to place her in the chains of a possibly unwanted wedlock.

With Mariana the Duke similarly achieves intimacy and mastery. Mariana testifies to their closeness by describing the Duke as "a man of comfort whose advice / Hath often still'd my brawling dis-content" (4.1.8–9). The Duke, it seems, has repeatedly enjoyed intimate meetings with Mariana, the likely subject of which is her obsessive, unrequited passion for Angelo, which adds intrigue to his claim to have confessed her (5.1.527). His desexualized pose as father-confessor gives him access to Mariana's private life, sanc-tioning the disclosure of potentially titillating secrets. Barthes writes of Sade's fondness for inserting rituals of confession into his sadomasochistic orgies in order not only to "parody the sacra-ment of penitence" but to "illustrate the sadistic situation of the subject submitting to her executioner."[46] Thus Mariana, whose thralldom to Angelo already suggests a desperate masochism, sub-mits to the Duke, whose manipulations of her border on the sadis-tic. As with Isabella, he oversees the sullying of her honor by mocking the intimate testimony he himself elicits. Even after he drops his disguise, the Duke subjects her to further torments, marrying her off to Angelo and then commanding his immediate execution (5.1.377, 414–16).

The Duke essentially punishes Angelo for pursuing heedlessly the same ends that he achieves carefully, converting Angelo to the personification of a wayward flesh that must be disciplined— a discipline that has distinctly oedipal reverberations. The Duke, whose "rod" is "more mock'd than fear'd," hands Angelo the phallus of cultural authority, gives him "all the organs / Of our own pow'r" (1.1.20–21), seeming to emasculate himself. In orchestrating the bed-trick, however, the Duke effectively emasculates Angelo, commodifies and feminizes his body, makes him an object of female sexual use. The Duke punishes Angelo as Angelo punished Claudio, similarly staging a piece of sadomasochistic street theater, publicly emasculating him for falling prey to the female sexuality whose clutches the Duke escapes. In assuming the role of a chastened sinning flesh, Angelo finally trades places not only with Claudio but with Isabella and Mariana, whose humiliation the Duke also stages. The Duke forces Angelo to enter the space of shame, the space of "the feminine."[47] Unworthy to bear the sword of heaven or the rod of governance, Angelo must submit to the "mightier member" of the Duke, who confirms his utter powerlessness by wedding him against his will to a devouring (or at least overtly desiring) woman whom he has already rejected. Angelo, who sought to dominate one woman, must now submit to another.

Lucio similarly suffers consignment to an unwanted marriage as punishment for fleshly transgression—specifically for recalling the Duke to his own flesh. Lucio, who "sticks like a burr" to the offended Duke, perhaps shares Angelo's fate because, to an extent, he shares his function, representing a sinning flesh from which the Duke wishes to distance himself. Indeed, more than any other character, Lucio forces the Duke to confront his fleshly self—albeit in the image of Lucio's slanderous caricature. The Duke undertakes to mortify Lucio's unruly flesh not by whipping him but by wedding him to a whore, yoking him to a degraded female sexuality that shames and emasculates him (5.1.508–18).

The Duke mortifies the flesh not only by mortifying Angelo and Lucio but by mastering Isabella. The Duke essentially asks Isabella to embody the "feminine" self that, projected onto his male double— the weak and degenerate Angelo—he disowns and depreciates. The Duke can embrace the "feminine" only by embracing a woman he would coerce into embodying it. The Duke consequently endeavors to disguise the coercions as miraculous deliverances. To the extent that he "resurrects" her brother and hopes to convert her gratitude into devotion, he offers himself as the God who, metaphorically speaking, was her original choice of husband, and, to the extent that he rescues her from sexual shame, not simply by exposing Angelo's perfidy and proving her innocence but by offering to marry her, he seems still to play the protective father figure who safeguards her chastity.[48]

Yet the Duke's manipulations may leave Isabella with feelings inhospitable to his pose as father-savior. Indeed, in one sense, the Duke tricks Isabella in much the same way that he tricks Angelo. Isabella thinks that she has enjoyed a kind of intimacy with one man, the desexualized holy friar, and discovers that, in fact, she has been intimate with another, the duplicitous and newly sexualized Duke. The Duke has known Isabella while she knew not that she ever knew him.

The Duke implicitly asks Isabella to function as the object of conquest and figure of closure for his oedipal narrative, which must end in his birth as both man and sovereign. The opening scenes of the play establish the Duke's need for initiation into manhood, linking his ineffectual governance to sexual disavowal. Having failed to wield the phallus with authority, the Duke claims that his "rod" is now "more mock'd than fear'd" (1.3.26–27), an image of both political and sexual impotence. He proceeds to undergo a phase of liminality, taking off his breeches and donning a friar's dress, aligning himself with women, circulating reports that he has died or entered a monastery, sending letters whose "uneven and distracted manner" and contradictory contents provoke Angelo to wonder if the Duke has lost his mind (4.4.1–5). These images of bisexuality, death, anti-worldly withdrawal, and witlessness are all aspects of liminality.[49] Thus, from one angle, the Duke authors his own ritual of rebirth, passing through a phase of temporary "death" in order to give birth to himself as a man or, in this case, as an ideal sovereign who embodies ultimate masculinity, wielding the phallus magisterially in the final scene and maneuvering a seemingly unconquerable woman into a position of conquest.

To say that narrative is the production of Oedipus is to say that each reader—male or female—is constrained and defined within the two positions of a sexual difference thus conceived: male-hero-human, on the side of the subject; and female-obstacle-boundary-space, on the other . . . narrative endlessly reconstructs [the world] as a two-character drama in which the human person creates and re-creates himself out of an abstract of purely symbolic other—the womb, the earth, the grave, the woman.[50]

Isabella is not simply an erotic agent who must be mastered—the personification of an erotic wilderness that the civilizing hero must tame—but the symbolic other out of whom the Duke wishes to create himself, the redemptive "feminine" force who enables his paternity, restores his potency, and affirms his sovereignty—in short, makes a man of him. In bedeviling Angelo and seeking to marry Isabella, the Duke simultaneously punishes one feminine double and seeks to possess another.

In the final scene, when Isabella brings suit to him, the Duke seems to have her where he wants her: On her knees, a prone, powerless, impassioned supplicant, utterly dependent upon him for deliverance. He then maneuvers her into a second posture of proneness when condemning Angelo to death, goading Mariana into a desperate plea that Isabella "take her part" and sue for his pardon. Earlier in the scene, Mariana presents herself as a kind of statue that can only be animated by Angelo's acceptance of her as wife:

> He knew me as a wife. As this is true,
> Let me in safety raise me from my knees,
> Or else for ever be confixed here,
> A marble monument!
>
> (5.1.230–33)

The pose in which she proposes to freeze herself is that of the prone supplicant, or submissive wife. In taking Mariana's part, Isabella functions as surrogate submissive, assuming the statue's pose of eternal proneness. Mariana, on her knees before Angelo, essentially pleads for permission to become a subservient wife. When Isabella assumes the same posture before the Duke, she involuntarily elicits his permission, assumes the very position he may intend for her in marriage.

Indeed, when the Duke extends his hand to Isabella at the play's end, he implicitly hopes for one final and decisive assumption of the prone position on Isabella's part. Isabella of course says nothing in response to his proposal. Her silence has generated voluminous debate and multifarious performance choices, ranging from joyful, unhesitating acceptance to hostile defiance.[51] Yet the complexity of the play seems to require a less simplistic resolution. Certainly Isabella's silence could signify resignation, as though the Duke had hounded her into mute submission. Yet it might also manifest resistance, evoking if not reenacting her original rejection of patriarchy, signified by the vow of silence she was poised to take at the nunnery. Her muteness may not signify the helplessness of an actress who has run out of lines, as Riefer suggests,[52] but the resistance of a woman who no longer wishes to speak someone else's.

Ultimately of course, Isabella's speechlessness is ambiguous and open-ended, a mystery for every director and actress—and critic—to solve. In my view, Isabella's silence best supports an attitude of ambivalence and irresolution that returns her to the position she assumed when first forced to reenter the world of men: At war twixt will and will not. Her silence strands her between autonomy and patriarchal inscription and thus generates the unresolved tension that, in Teresa de Lauretis' estimation, attends the representation of female subjectivity, according to which an individual woman is both a woman and Woman, a subject in her own right forced to assume the status of object of male desire, forced to play figure of closure in the Oedipal plot.[53] Her resistance or nonreply to the Duke's proposal, her suspension of his patriarchal narrative, suggests that the subject-object contradiction "cannot and perhaps even need not be resolved."[54] In sum, Isabella's silence signifies neither "yes" nor "no" nor even "maybe" but enigmatically manifests the impossibility of expressing an inner experience too complex, too female, to register meaningfully in a male economy of meaning. Once more, the Lacanian postulate of an impossible female language seems to come into play. Yet, in the theater, there is surely speech in Isabella's dumbness—to steal another line from *The Winter's Tale*. Her speechlessness becomes itself a mode of speech, a dialect that cannot be silenced, even if it cannot be fathomed. Isabella herself, through the actress who represents her, remains a body that cannot be easily fitted to the destin'd livery, a mystery for every spectator—and critic—to solve.

NOTES

1. In my own production of *Measure* at University of California, Berkeley (April 1992), I staged the scene in precisely this way.

2. The sadist "has a powerful and overwhelming superego and nothing else. The sadist's superego is so strong that he has become identified with it; he is his own superego and can only find an ego in the external world . . . when the superego runs wild, expelling the ego along with the mother-image, then its fundamental immorality exhibits itself as sadism. The ultimate victims of the sadist are the mother and the ego. . . . The sadist has no other ego than that of his victims"

(*Coldness and Cruelty*. Trans. Jean McNeil, *Masochism*, New York: Zone Books, 1989).

3. See, for instance, Susan Griffin, *Pornography and Silence* (New York: Harper, 1981) and Andrea Dworkin, *Pornography: Men Possessing Women* (London: The Women's Press, 1982). Pornography is an exceptionally complex subject. Even within feminist ranks attitudes toward it differ sharply. For instance, Linda Williams, who calls herself an "anti-censorship feminist" finds the attitude of Griffin and Dworkin and other "anti-pornography" feminists to be needlessly prosecutorial and untenably utopian, arguing that "a whole and natural sexuality that stands outside history and free of power" is purely mythical and that power is an ineradicable part of human sexuality. See the opening chapter of her fascinating study of pornographic films, *Hard Core: Power, Pleasure, and the Frenzy of the Visible* (Berkeley: University of California Press, 1989).

4. *Coldness and Cruelty*, 29. In an undergraduate Shakespeare class, I screened several versions of the eye-gouging scene from *King Lear*. The students unanimously agreed that the cruelest Cornwall was Peter Brook's Patrick Magee (who, fittingly, also played Sade in Brook's *Marat/Sade*) because he was so inhumanly passionless.

5. I put "feminine" and "masculine" in quotation marks in order to make clear that I am using them to designate subject positions—powerless flesh and powerful law—rather than gender.

6. "Erotic Religious Flagellation and Shakespeare's *Measure for Measure*," *English Literary Renaissance* 16 (1986): 139–165.

7. "Erotic Religious Flagellation," 144.

8. L. A. Parry, *The History of Torture in England* (Montclair, New Jersey: Patterson Smith, 1975; [reprint, London: Sampson Low Marston, 1934), 41.

9. *Discipline and Punish: The Birth of the Prison*, trans. Alan Sheridan (New York: Vintage Books, 1979).

10. *Discipline and Punish*, 49. In a fascinating essay, Gillian Murray Kendall argues that, in Shakespearean drama, "the excessive violence associated with real executions accompanies instead the killings done by subjects against the state, by those using murder to gain political power," "Overkill in Shakespeare," *Shakespeare Quarterly* 43 (Spring 1992): 34.

11. Beatrice Faust discerns a continuity between religious art and pornography: "It was only with Christianity that sex and aggression became hopelessly confused. Erotica was driven underground and sadomasochism—with predominantly homoerotic overtones—replaced it in the formally accepted visual arts. Beside the gentle image of the madonna and her child we find the *pieta*, in which Mary cradles her son's mangled body, the crucifixions, stations of the cross, and multitude of martyrdoms—often depicting langorous young men, less often showing beautiful women. The flagellation literature of the nineteenth century and the recent wave of violence in both pornography and television, may be seen as continuations of a long and sordid Western tradition. Perhaps secular sadomasochism developed to replace the declining religious art," *Women, Sex, and Pornography* (New York: Macmillan, 1980), 86.

12. *Coldness and Cruelty*, 55.

13. Janet Adelman connects the Duke's characterization of Juliet's fetus to his overwrought censure of Pompey: "in both instances the language of sexual origin and maternal dependence carries the weight of the Duke's disgust, as though the facts of conception and maternal nursery were in themselves enough to turn one

away from life," *Suffocating Mothers: Fantasies of Maternal Origin in Shakespeare's Plays, Hamlet to The Tempest* (New York: Routledge, 1992), 87–88.

14. Brown relates the "proneness" urged on Isabella to the flagellant's position and therefore to Isabella's pledge to "strip [her]self to death," "Erotic Religious Flagellation," 163–65.

15. See Jacques Lacan, *Feminine Sexuality,* trans. Jacqueline Rose (New York: W. W. Norton, 1985), 144–45.

16. "Over and over again, the pornographer's triumph, the *piece de resistance* in his fantasy, occurs when he turns the virgin into a whore," *Pornography and Silence,* 22.

17. See Griffin, *Pornography and Silence,* 29–35.

18. *Sade Fourier Loyola,* trans. Richard Miller (New York: Hill and Wang, 1976), 145.

19. *Coldness and Cruelty,* 63. Deleuze contends that sadism and masochism are distinct phenomenon that have been inappropriately linked. He thus contests Freud's characterization of masochism as a manifestation of the death instinct that when turned against the "object" (the mother), produces sadism. See *Beyond the Pleasure Principle,* trans. and ed. James Strachey (New York: Norton), 48–49.

20. *Coldness and Cruelty,* 31–32, 76, 88–89.

21. *Coldness and Cruelty,* 104.

22. In my production at the University of California at Berkeley, the scene opened with Angelo's flagellating himself, suggesting that he had been at it for quite some time.

23. See Robert N. Watson's fascinating discussion of the many ways in which the play evokes the Virgin Mary as a shadow for both Isabella and Angelo, "False Immortality in *Measure for Measure:* Comic Means, Tragic Ends," *Shakespeare Quarterly* 41 (1990): 425–26.

24. *Suffocating Mothers,* 93.

25. See Lacan, *Feminine Sexuality,* 153–54.

26. "The Pornographic Imagination," in *Perspectives on Pornography,* ed. Douglas A. Hughes (New York: St. Martin's Press, 1970), 112. Though Sontag's philosophical treatment of pornography seems to differ sharply from the ideologically driven critiques of the anti-pornography feminists, her implication that the pornographer ultimately aims at self-transcendence seems perfectly compatible with the feminists' view. The latter, however, associate this self-transcendence with a self-denial that casts women in the role of denied material self.

27. Brown makes much the same point in "Erotic Religious Flagellation," 158.

28. I so staged the scene in my production at the University of California at Berkeley. The scourge with which Angelo had beaten himself at the outset of the scene became Isabella's means of repelling his assault. Trevor Nunn also staged the moment as a near-rape in his recent RSC production.

29. Male dread of female power and of effeminizing desire springs from the association of femaleness with "lack." See Madelon Sprengnether's classic essay, "'I wooed thee with my sword': Shakespeare's Tragic Paradigms," in *Representing Shakespeare: New Psychoanalytic Essays,* ed. Murray M. Schwartz and Coppélia Kahn (Baltimore: Johns Hopkins United Press, 1980), 174–75. For highly illuminating discussions of Angelo's fear of female power and of effeminacy, see David Sundelson, *Shakespeare's Restorations of the Father* (New Brunswick, N.J.: Rutgers University Press, 1983), 91–92; Wheeler, *Shakespeare's Development and the Problem Comedies,* 115; and Adelman, *Suffocating Mothers,* 92.

30. For the first view, see Brown, "Erotic Religious Flagellation," 153; for the

second, see Marvin Rosenberg, "Shakespeare's Fantastic Trick: *Measure for Measure*," *The Sewanee Review* LXXX (1972): 54.

31. Quoted in Carol Rutter, *Clamorous Voices: Shakespeare's Women Today* (London: The Women's Press, 1988), 41.

32. This point figures very prominently in Marcia Riefer's provocative essay, "'Instruments of Some More Mightier Member': The Constriction of Female Power in *Measure for Measure*," in *Modern Critical Interpretations: William Shakespeare's Measure for Measure,* Harold Bloom, ed. (New York: Chelsea House Publishers, 1987), 131–44. See especially 136–37.

33. The image recalls Angelo's characterization of Claudio's crime: Putting "mettle" in "restrained means" to make "a false [life]" (2.4.48–49)—impregnating an unmarried woman and engendering an "unlawful" child. It also anticipates Isabella's later dread of giving "unlawful birth" (3.1.189–91).

34. quoted in Rutter, *Clamorous Voices*, 49.

35. For Harriet Hawkins, these lines seem "deliberately designed by Shakespeare to arouse Angelo as saint, sensualist, and as a sadist. And so, of course, they do," "'The Devil's Party': Virtues and Vices in *Measure for Measure*," in Bloom, *Modern Critical Interpretations*, 85.

36. Paul Tillich's wife, Hannah, describes his taste for pornographic slide shows depicting women lashed on crosses: "There was the familiar cross shooting up the wall . . . A naked girl hung on it, hands tied in front of her private parts. Another naked figure lashed the crucified one with a whip that reached further to another cross, on which a girl was exposed from behind. More and more crosses appeared, all with women tied and exposed in various positions. Some were exposed from the front, some from the side, some from behind, some crouched in fetal position, some head down, or legs apart, or legs crossed—and always whips, crosses, whips," *From Time to Time* (New York: Stein and Day, 1973), 14. The image of a publicly revered theologian's privately exercising a sexual vexation that conflates religious and pornographic imagery seems chillingly apposite to *Measure for Measure*.

37. *Pornography and Silence*, 14, 68.

38. My reading of Isabella's father-fixation is heavily indebted to Adelman's account in *Suffocating Mothers*, 96–98.

39. *Suffocating Mothers*, 97.

40. Many critics note the extent to which Angelo functions as aspect of the Duke's self. See, for instance, Sundelson, *Shakespeare's Restoration of the Father*, 90, Alexander Leggatt, "Substitution in *Measure for Measure*," *Shakespeare Quarterly* 39 (1988): 345–46, and Nancy S. Leonard, "Substitution in Shakespeare's Problem Comedies," *English Literary Renaissance* 9 (1079): 296–97.

41. *Suffocating Mothers*, 98.

42. Something of this effect was apparently achieved in Michael Bogdanov's 1985 production at Stratford, Ontario. See Anthony B. Dawson, *"Measure for Measure,* New Historicism; and Theatrical Power," *Shakespeare Quarterly* 39 (Fall 1988): 339.

43. The director and actor must of course determine the extent to which the Duke's desire ought to be evident to the audience. His proposal at the end will obviously be the more surprising—even shocking—if it is unexpected and inexplicable. On the other hand, an antecedent attraction could possibly make the proposal more troubling, especially if the attraction is mutual, if Isabella has developed a deep affection for the Friar—or even a desire sublimated and sanctified by his status as fatherly rescuer. Seen in such a light, the Duke's proposal

forces Isabella to face her feelings for him while violating the trust that enabled them.

44. See Charles R. Lyons for a fascinating account of Isabella's resemblance to a shrew, "Silent Women and Shrews: Eroticism and Convention in *Epicoene* and *Measure for Measure,*" *Comparative Drama* 22 (1990): 123–40, especially 136–38. The notion of a female "openness" that invites "enclosure" I borrow from Peter Stallybrass's influential essay, "Patriarchal Territories: The Body Enclosed," *Rewriting the Renaissance: The Discourses of Sexual Difference in Early Modern Europe,* eds. Margaret W. Ferguson, Maureen Quilligan, and Nancy J. Vickers (Chicago: University of Chicago Press, 1986), 123–42.

45. The image may also recall the mortifications of Pompey and Mistress Overdone, whose arrests were also turned into humiliating public spectacles in my production at University of California Berkeley. Isabella thus becomes linked with a fornicator, a bawd, and a brothel-keeper.

46. *Sade Fourier Loyola,* 145.

47. See Lynda E. Boose for a discussion of the homology of shame and femininity in the punishments of early modern England, "Scolding Bridges and Bridling Scolds: Taming the Woman's Unruly Member," *Shakespeare Quarterly* 42 (1991): 179–213, especially 185–94.

48. Wheeler also ascribes to the Duke a strategy of rescuing Isabella from the public sexual shaming that he himself has staged, *Shakespeare's Development,* 129–30.

49. See Victor Turner, *The Ritual Process: Structure and Anti-Structure* (Chicago: Aldine Publishing Company, 1969), 95–107.

50. Teresa de Lauretis, *Alice Doesn't: Feminism, Semiotics, Cinema* (Bloomington: Indiana University Press, 1984), 121.

51. For an illuminating discussion of the different ways directors have staged this final moment, see Philip C. McGuire, *Speechless Dialect: Shakespeare's Open Silences* (Berkeley: University of California Press, 1985), 63–93. For other helpful accounts of the play in performance, see Graham Nicholls, *Measure for Measure: Text and Performance* (London: Macmillan, 1986); Ralph Berry, *Changing Styles in Shakespeare* (London: George Allen and Unwin, 1981), 37–48; Michael Scott, *Renaissance Drama and a Modern Audience* (London: Macmillan, 1982), 61–75; Jane Williamson, "The Duke and Isabella on the Modern Stage," *The Triple Bond: Plays, Mainly Shakespearean, in Performance,* ed. Joseph Price (University Park: Pennsylvania State University Press, 1975), 149–69; and Richard Paul Knowles, "Robin Phillips Measures Up: '*Measure for Measure* at Stratford, Ontario, 1975–76)," *Essays in Theatre* 8 (1989): 35–59. For a provocative discussion of the play's resistance to feminist performance, see Kathleen McLuskie, "The patriarchal bard: feminist criticism and Shakespeare: *King Lear* and *Measure for Measure,*" *Political Shakespeare,* Jonathan Dollimore and Alan Sinfield, eds. (Ithaca, N.Y.: Cornell University Press, 1985), 88–108. For a discussion of the possibilities of feminist intervention in performance, see Rutter, *Clamorous Voices,* 27–42.

52. "'Instruments of Some More Mightier Member,'" 142.

53. *Alice Doesn't,* 186.

54. Ibid., 153.

Absolute Bodies, Absolute Laws: Staging Punishment in *Measure for Measure*

ARTHUR L. LITTLE, JR.

THERE are a few Shakespeare plays about which I have not been able to imagine myself writing. *Measure for Measure* is one of them. But after being invited to participate in a *Measure for Measure* symposium at UCLA and in Gillian Murray Kendall's seminar on Shakespearean Power and Punishment at the Shakespeare Association of America meeting—all of this happening within the span of a few days and also as one term ended and another started—I began to ask myself whether power and punishment was not indeed a way into *Measure for Measure*.[1] This question was about more than killing two academic sessions with one paper. It was, however superficially, a way of making sense of Shakespeare's play, a way of involving it in my thinking about—if not my obsession with—what I understand to be the sixteenth- and seventeenth-century's thinking about—if not its obsession with —publicly staging the political uses and abuses of the body.

Since those academic sessions and this most recent essay, *Measure for Measure* is (for me now) about the problem of getting to know the Duke's body. His body is a problem because it seems so impenetrable, so closed off and dissociated from its own interrogations—that is, from its own final assertions that the body (at least that of his subjects) is knowable and deconstructible. The bodies of the Duke's subjects are, as he seems to show through all his measured punishments, neither impenetrable nor unknowable. And here I am not only talking about the Duke's body but his power, since the one is thoroughly invested in the other. As far as this play is about the Duke's impenetrable and unknowable body and power, I cannot sympathize with the persona it dramatizes. His absolutism seems politically incorrect and dramatically uninteresting. Does Shakespeare really fancy himself here as a mouthpiece

113

for the absolutist ideas and ideals of James I, who has come to the English throne just a few months before the first production of *Measure for Measure*?[2] Not my Shakespeare. Yet, it is difficult not to hear those echoes between the Duke who lays claim to divination and James I who argues that God has made the monarch "a little God."[3] The greatest transgression to the Duke's authority is a subject's licensing himself or herself to see (and critique) the Duke's physical body. As his supposed model, James I stringently insists throughout *Basilicon Doron* that the royal subjects should be concerned only with the King's divine body. His physical body is a mere accident, and for a subject to scrutinize, take as real, the King's divine body is, in effect, to commit treason against the King, his divine persona.[4] But the issues do not end here. The Duke is, after all, only one of many voices in Shakespeare's play.

The Duke, critics often argue, averts the play's propensity towards tragedy by entering upon the scene as some kind of divine or comic savior.[5] If this is true, it must still be acknowledged that the tragedy from which he saves his subjects has its origins in the Duke himself. This is evident whether the critic constructs the origins of the play as the moment the law falls into disuse some fourteen or nineteen years before the play opens or the instant the Duke hands over his "absolute power" to Angelo. According to those who think of the Duke as a comic savior, starting with his more explicit manipulations of his subjects in the first scene of Act Three, the Duke (or Shakespeare) imposes the resolution of comic form on the tragic possibilities of Vienna. Harriet Hawkins exemplifies this view when she argues that "dramatically, as well as socially, the Duke's contrivances and evasions, and final pardons to everyone on the criminal docket, in effect revoke (or transcend) the rule of law, and to revoke (or transcend) the rule of law is to negate necessity," suggesting that the Duke or Shakespeare transforms what is potentially tragic into "a kind of divine comedy." This divine comedy, for Hawkins, is manifested in the advent of the Duke as *deus ex machina*, bringing with him salvation and beatification.[6] The Duke's punitive theatrics do work towards revoking or transcending the rule of law, but is the final scene really a kind of divine comedy? Does he manipulate the comic any less than he does the tragic?

What *is* the relationship between the Duke theatricalizing his absolute self and Shakespeare dramatizing an absolutist duke? I have found some guidance in Michel Foucault and Mikhail Bakhtin. Foucault has written about the performative and ritualistic uses of the punitive body, arguing that public punishment "belongs to a whole series of great rituals in which power is eclipsed and restored (coronation, entry of the king into a conquered city, the submission of rebellious subjects); over and above the crime that has placed the sovereign in contempt, it deploys before all eyes an invincible force.[7] And as Foucault also insists, "It is always the body that is at issue—the body and its forces, their utility and their docility, their distribution and their submission."[8] Bakhtin has studied the performative and ritualistic uses of the body, particularly the sociopolitical body. In his corporeal scheme, he represents the body as being either classical or grotesque. The classical body transcends its physical form and function. The grotesque body, on the other hand, is incapable of any such ecstasy or abstraction. It most relentlessly depicts the human body as waddling in its animalism. For Bakhtin, the classical body is the body of the state, its official icon. The grotesque body, as its opposite, figures in the state as an iconoclastic and unstable thing that threatens to deconstruct the way the state wishes officially to represent itself. (The supposed two bodies of the king, as mapped out by Ernst H. Kantorowicz, may be read as examples of Bakhtin's classical and grotesque bodies.)[9] The grotesque body is, as Bakhtin writes, "a body in the act of becoming. It is never finished, never completed; it is continually built, created, and builds and creates another body."[10] For both Foucault and Bakhtin the body remains the primary signifier of public performance and ritual. The Duke uses his power of punishment in order to assure his subjects of their non-absolute or unfinished status, that is, in the simplest terms, of the inability of their bodies to survive without him. The main argument I am making in this essay is that the Duke attempts to deconstruct his subjects' absolutist fantasies by undermining the bodies, laws, and places through which they are able to construct (from the Duke's perspective) such naive political fantasies. And finally I am arguing that the Duke's staging of his political theater cannot be separated from the politics of Shakespeare's staging of an absolutist ruler.

BODIES, ICONS, AND THE ICONOCLAST

The Duke appropriates the political myth of a divine or comic transcendence in order presumably to come into a nondeconstructible absolutism. In so doing, he attempts to shift his absolutist power away from the physical or tragic and to an even more impenetrable and invisible realm than can possible be signified by his own physical body. He does so primarily because his subjects have begun to imagine that they are more than physical bodies. The Duke mocks the aspirations of his subjects to identify their bodies with various absolutes: Isabella with chastity, Angelo with morality, Claudio with mortality. These absolutes are the very texts that the Duke's theatrics set out to undermine. The Duke's absolutist fantasies force him to challenge the absolutist fantasies of his subjects. "More than our brother is our chastity" (2.4.185),[11] says Isabella, for example, indicating that more than our body is our soul (to borrow from Foucault), or better still, our soul—our essence, or meaning—signifies more than our physical body.[12] And does the Duke really take himself seriously, for example, when he says to Claudio, who apprehensively awaits execution, "Be absolute for death" (3.1.5)? Here at the beginning of the third act where the Duke commences his improvisational toying with his subjects, he begins by satirizing an absolutist rhetoric that is pietistic and disingenuous. As Robert N. Watson has argued, the Duke's speech transforms *contemptus mundi* and *ars moriendi* commonplaces into cliches.[13] But here, over the issue of life and death, the Duke satirizes not so much the pietistic formulas of the church as he does Claudio, who momentarily (and perhaps egotistically) believes that he can find resolve in such an absolute reading of his body. The shift of the essential self from the physical body to the soul perhaps explains why the Duke pardons the earthly Barnadine: The Duke finds him irrelevant to the new agenda of punishment—"Sirrah, thou art said to have a stubborn soul, / That apprehends no further than this world" (5.1.483–84).

Even though Foucault places such a shift some one hundred fifty years later, the Duke seems everywhere to exemplify this kind of move in the manipulation of his absolutist power. Foucault argues that the shift in the meaning (and method) of punishment is intrinsically related to what the subject's body means to its ruler. As Foucault writes,

> It was an important moment. The old partners of the spectacle of punishment, the body and the blood, gave way. A new character came on the scene, masked. It was the end of a certain kind of tragedy; comedy began, with shadow play, faceless voices, impalpable entities. The apparatus of punitive justice must now bite into this bodiless reality.[14]

For Foucault, this bodiless reality is the "soul," and it has necessitated "a punishment that acts in depth on the heart, the thoughts, the will, the inclinations."[15] As the hooded and "old fantastical Duke of dark corners" (4.3.159–60), the Duke seems to enact this

Foucauldian "new character." Consequently, both he and his subjects have at the outset outgrown the old, physical uses of punishment, those "strict statutes and most biting laws" (1.3.19) that have become the useless, extracted teeth on display in a barber's shop (5.1.320–23). The Duke argues that if he is to have absolute power, it is not enough for him to have absolute power over the physical body; he must have absolute power, period. It is time too, the Duke suggests, for him to bite into—to counter or match—this new reality.

The Duke's drama intends to challenge these bodies that presume to have moved beyond the strictures of human blood and warmth. These (absolute) bodies have become Vienna's statuary, its icons. This point is especially applicable to Isabella and Angelo. When Lucio first meets Isabella, for example, he says to her that he esteems her "a thing enskied and sainted, / By your renouncement, an immortal spirit" (1.4.34–35). And in her first confrontation with Angelo, he talks about her as a thing "too cold" (2.2.43–45). More emphatic still are the play's references to Angelo whose "mettle" and "character" get linked to the metal and character of coins (1.1.16–50). Furthermore, he is described as "a man whose blood / Is very snow-broth; one who never feels / The wanton stings and motions of the sense" (1.4.57–59), and as someone "not made by man and woman after this downright way of creation" (3.2.106–8). And as the Duke himself says about Angelo, he is one who "scarce confesses / That his blood flows, or that his appetite / Is more to bread than stone" (1.3.50–53). These images of metal, stone, and coldness work to define Angelo as an inanimate thing, a statue. To the point also is the Duke's portrayal of the Angelo who witnesses Mariana's tears after Angelo breaks his betrothal to her: "And he, a marble to her tears, is washed with them, but relents not" (3.1.233–34). The Duke conjures up Ovid's Niobe who "there upon a mountaines top / . . . weepeth still in stone: from stone the drerie tears do drop."[16] Here Angelo as "marble" figures as a Niobe to the supposed Niobean state of Mariana. To be considered here, too, are Mariana and Claudio. Near the end of the play, Mariana says to the Duke as she begs for his mercy towards the condemned Angelo, "Let me in safety raise me from my knees [as a result of Angelo's pardon], / Or else forever be confixed here, / A marble monument" (5.1.231–33). And finally, were Claudio to be decapitated as Angelo demands, his head would become a statuesque thing—a mere death's head (4.2.177–81)—a point made all the more convincing by the substitution of Ragozine's head (4.3.70–77). Isabella, Angelo, Claudio, and Mariana are all part of or are all threatening to become part of Vienna's statuary—its finished bodies—and this is precisely what the Duke does not want.

Their ability to be or become statues challenges his power in Vienna. His power is manifested not by any talent he has for creating statues but by his ability to destroy or deconstruct them. He becomes himself an iconoclast, leaving only himself unbroken. These statues represent what would be the classical body in Bakhtin's corporeal scheme. Here in *Measure for Measure,* the Duke challenges those bodies that are potentially classical but are not his own. He intervenes in the process of their completion and transforms them back into grotesque and unfinished bodies.

What challenges the Duke are not the grotesque bodies but those potentially absolute bodies whose mere existence seems to compete with the Duke's own absolutism. Those who are not the "generous and gravest citizens" of Vienna (4.6.13), namely Mistress Overdone, Pompey, Elbow, and Barnadine, constitute Vienna's grotesque citizenry. In them sex, morality, law, and mortality have become parodic. Their presumed grotesqueness is particularly defined through their sectarian adherence to matters of the physical body, a trait that is so often the case in many other underworlds in sixteenth- and seventeenth-century English drama. The permanently grotesque subjects (who are never complete) ultimately serve to foil and, paradoxically, make more convincing the Duke's classicism; their bodies always already stand as testimonials to his power.

If the Duke were simply concerned about achieving power, then his attention would probably be directed towards the grotesque bodies. However, the Duke has power. His objective is to attain absolute power, and his manipulations focus most pointedly on destroying all classical bodies except his own. For despite all their supposed moral deficiencies, Vienna's grotesque citizens are not politically opposite Vienna's classical citizens: The main difference between them is that the grotesque community seems already circumscribed by a pronounced sense of self-consciousness or mockery. And the Duke attempts to deconstruct the classical community by introducing to it the self-consciousness or mockery that seems already a vital part of the grotesque world's identity. The underworld is only a more grotesque depiction of how the Duke wishes to render the classical society of Vienna.

In finally unveiling himself to Vienna's classical society, the Duke concomitantly prevents the completion of their absolute bodies and reveals them as bodies in the process of being constructed—or, perhaps, as bodies that are always deconstructible. Their bodies come to represent the grotesque in the Duke's classical theater.

His reentry at the end of the play stages a Foucauldian ritual of public punishment. During this scene, this ritual splinters into or is made to cohere around a coronation (here in the form of the Duke's unhooding), an entry proclaiming ducal power, and a submission of both slandering and potentially absolute subjects. The quintessential body his reentry stages is similar to the absolute body in Bakhtin's corporeal scheme:

> The body of the new canon is merely one body; no signs of duality have been left. It is self-sufficient and speaks in its name alone. All that happens within it concerns it alone, that is, only the individual, closed sphere. . . . All actions and events are interpreted on the level of a single, individual life. They are enclosed within the limits of the same body, limits that are the absolute beginning and end and can never meet.[17]

The absolute body, like the monarch's divine body, is not a physical body but a name—the body as a logos, an idea, and an ideal. This is the body of apotheosis, the Duke as saint, as "perfect patriarch."[18] He seems to have transcended the epistemology of the body when he is unveiled and Angelo speaks of him as "Grace, like pow'r divine," Isabella of his "unknown sovereignty" and the Duke himself of his own "hidden pow'r" (5.1.372, 390, 395). To leave the issue here, however, would be to accept and perhaps celebrate the Duke's body as absolute and to celebrate, too, his iconoclastic approach to the bodies of his subjects. It would also mean accepting the Duke's theater as Shakespeare's own, a point to which I will return in the last section of this essay.

Overruling Vienna's Laws

The Duke stages his power by challenging not only the bodies of his subjects but the laws as well. The most immediate focus of his campaign against potentially absolute laws is, ironically, given the Duke's complaints, Vienna's "strict statutes and most biting laws," the dissipation of which has led to the destruction of "all decorum" (1.3.19–31). But the enforcement of these laws is not the primary issue: More to the point is the fact that these strict or absolute laws work against the Duke's own absolute power. He wishes not to reenforce these laws, which could be easily accomplished. By finally overruling these laws, he uses them as a means to achieve his absolute power. According to the Duke's testimony, fourteen years before the time of the play he used strict mechanisms of punishment in order to terrify his subjects, not actually to punish them. After finding these mechanisms "more mocked than feared" because of his failure to use them, the Duke does not intend now to bring back the mechanisms of punishment but rather to take their place. It is not the law that will terrorize the people of Vienna but the Duke himself, and he will presumably prove more effective because he replaces the physical and local threat of the old law with the *idea* of an omnipresent and terrorizing Duke.[19]

No matter how strong or absolute the laws are, the Duke reveals them as being ineffective, mere forfeitures. Shortly before the unveiling of the Duke, the supposed moment of salvation, the Duke authorizes the mockery of the law. The strict statues of Vienna are effectively ridiculed and transformed into the grotesque figures of scarecrows and teeth.

His deconstruction of the law is most profoundly directed at the *lex talionis,* the law that demands an exact or absolute retribution. For the Duke, the *lex talionis* is important not so much for any role it has in the actual legal workings of Vienna, but because it symbolizes the attempt to render the law absolute—in both a finalizing and an equalizing sense. This law, too, must be mocked by the Duke, and as Shakespeare's play title suggests, this law emerges as the dominant trope in the Duke's theater. Announcing the sentencing of Angelo, his most intricately plotted punishment, the Duke claims that "the very mercy of the law cries out / Most audible, even from his proper tongue, / 'An Angelo for Claudio, death for death!' / Haste still pays haste, and leisure answers leisure; / Like doth quit like, and Measure still for Measure" (5.1.410–14). Here he appropriates not only Jesus's text from the Sermon on the Mount where Jesus says, "Ivdge not, that ye be not iudged, / For with what iudgement ye iudge, ye shal be iudged, and with what measure ye mette, it shal be measured to you againe," but also Moses's words on Mount Sinai, where Moses says, "But if death followe, then thou shalt paye life for life, / Eie for Eie, tothe for tothe, hand for hand, fote for fote, / Burning for burning, wonde for wonde, stripe for stripe."[20] The Duke takes the word "measure" from the New Testament and reinscribes it in the Old Testament.

Given that in Christian thought the first is interpreted as the "old" law of justice and the latter as the "new" law of mercy, the Duke advocates an absolutist reading—not as is commonly done of justice—but of mercy. In his fusion of the old and the new, the Duke uses the absolutism of the old punishment as the contextual framework for the new punishment, making the mercy of the new law no less absolute than the justice of the old law. If to move from the old to the new law means to move from the absolute letter of the law to the absolute disposition of the judge, then in the Duke's meshing of these Testaments, mercy finds itself at the mercy of the Duke's absolute power. In the end, neither the old nor the new law speaks; only the Duke's testament reigns.

Still, the Duke does more here than appropriate the words of certain biblical texts. Present here are also those familiar images of the speaking Duke and his listening subjects: The Duke's tongue has become the mercy of the law, crying out to his enraptured auditors (Escalus, whose name is derived from the Latin word "*auscultator,*" meaning "one who listens or obeys," is the most nominally symbolic of the Duke's listeners). Moses on Mount Sinai, Jesus on the Mount, the Duke at the gates of Vienna: These are moments not simply about punishment but about the staging of it—at least this is how the Duke's "most audible" rendition of the old and new law seems most effectively to foreground these archetypal, biblical moments in which the laws of punishment are formalized. Shakespeare's play has been mainly the Duke's preparation for this final theatrical event. His enacting of a Last Judgment at the city's gates attempts to preempt the performance of such rites at the gates of heaven.[21] He desires to assert in this judgment scene a more earthly and immediate version of what the biblical Last Judgment tries to impress upon its subjects—what Roman law calls *merum imperium,* that is, the ruler's absolute power over the life and death of his subjects, or what James I in a 1609 speech before Parliament would espouse as his divine rights:

Kings are iustly called Gods, for that they exercise a manner or resemblance of Diuine power vpon earth: For if you wil consider the Attributes to God, you shall see how they agree in the person of a King. God hath power to create, or destroy, make, vnmake at his pleasure, to giue life, or send death, to iudge all, and to be iudged nor accomptable to none: To raise low things, and to make high things low at his pleasure, and to God are both soule and body due. And the like power haue Kings: they make and vnmake their subjects: they haue power of raising, and casting down: of life, and of death: Iudges ouer all their subiects and in all causes, and yet accomptable to none but God onely. They haue power to exalt low things, and abase hight things, and make of their subiects like men at the Chesse.[22]

As the sole arbitrator, he takes the place of all absolute civil and religious laws.[23] If the Duke has metamorphosed into the absolute law, he has become the entity Foucault understands to oversee and regulate public punishment. Most of the Duke's maneuvers throughout the play have been occasioned by the eclipse of his laws; this final scene of judgment and punishment is his moment of legal restoration.

DISPLACING PLACE IN VIENNA

The play moves from the privacy of the ducal court to the public streets and the gates of Vienna. This ducal but public domain displaces the other potentially absolute places: Isabella's nunnery, Claudio's prison, Mariana's moated grange, Angelo's ducal court, and the enclosed garden, the *hortus conclusus,* where Angelo unwittingly consummates his betrothal to Mariana.[24] Like the absolute bodies and laws, these absolute (that is, self-sufficient) places threaten the Duke's confirmation of his absolute territorial power in Vienna. The Duke metaphorically brings these absolute places of Vienna into the public streets, including most especially the ducal court, which is then itself made subservient to the Duke. He distances himself from his own court and then goes on to protect his subjects from it. He becomes the savior *par excellence.* In terms of hegemony, there is only one absolute place in Vienna, and that is the Duke's own self.

The Duke's return to Vienna sharply contrasts with his departure from it. After quickly giving Angelo his ducal powers, the Duke says, "I'll privily away; I love the people, / But do not like to stage me to their eyes" (1.1.68). A few lines later, he is gone. His return is, of course, much more public and ceremonious. When Angelo learns of the Duke's manner of return, he asks, "And why meet him at the gates, and redeliver our authority there?" (4.4.5–6). And a few lines later he asks, "And why should we proclaim it in an hour before his ent'ring, that if any crave redress of injustice, they should exhibit their petitions in the street?" (4.4.8–11). Why proclaim? Why the gates of the city? Why the streets? Having compromised all other absolute places, the Duke moves his subjects to the marketplace, where he exposes their grotesque (or marketplace) nature and presumably affirms his own classicism.

The marketplace is the essential place in Bakhtin's imagings of the grotesque, particularly the marketplace spectacles, its theater scaffoldings.[25] For Bakhtin, the marketplace stands in contradistinction to the official or absolute world; it is also the place of "familiar speech"—curses, profanities, and oaths—and the *cris de Paris,* the cries of street vendors. Bakhtin describes the marketplace as "the center of all that is unofficial; it enjoyed a certain extraterritoriality in a world of official order and official ideology, it always remained 'with the people.'"[26] The marketplace is the ideal location for the Duke's classical theater, since it represents the place where the state keeps its grotesque bodies. Nonetheless, the Duke's classical marketplace should not be confused with the real marketplace of Vienna, the permanent underworld inhabited by Mistress Overdone and Pompey, for example. That world seems always already to exist and has no salient theatrical or political function in the state's demonstration of its absolute power. (Even Angelo seems to discern no great symbolic import in this underworld. He gives it over to Escalus, who, confused by the rhetorical limitations of Elbow, calls Pompey's trial to an end without really resolving anything [2.1.41–256].) The classical marketplace gets nearest the real marketplace when Mariana is accused of being a prostitute and the Duke a rascal. The Duke's strategic use of the marketplace is twofold: For one, the marketplace exposes the absolutisms of his subjects as being of no consequence when their absolutisms are put before the Duke himself. Secondly, and no less importantly, by transforming the marketplace into something more official, something more in line with his own absolutist ideology, the Duke is able to assert his complete and absolute authority over the territories of Vienna.

The marketplace may be characterized most succinctly as a place where there is much rampant speech. More so than any other scene in Shakespeare, this final scene is replete with references to speaking. Very often the Duke's subjects do not simply talk about speech but they talk about others speaking justly, boldly, madly, abusively, villainously, and so on. Throughout, there are numerous explicit mentions of prattling, confessing, swearing, vowing, accusing, charging, complaining, slandering, and silencing. The Duke himself indulges in the marketplace's excess of speech: During this final scene, the Duke continuously introduces the word "slander" into his speech and it is he (as friar) whom Escalus accuses of being a "slander to th'state" (324). The Duke appropriates and subverts the cries and noises of the marketplace when he pronounces his sentence against Angelo, arguing that "the very mercy of the law cries out / Most audible, even from his proper tongue" (410–11). Rather than eradicate the marketplace, the Duke wishes

to transform it into his own space. And he does so most construc-
tively by laying claim to the marketplace as his own theater.

STAGING THE POWER OF THEATER

The final scene, where the Duke is unveiled and presumably
stops acting for his onstage audience, is where he becomes most
susceptible to the interrogations of the offstage audience. This moment is not only theatrical (as have been the Duke's machinations
throughout) but metatheatrical, directed ultimately not at the
Duke's theatrical play with his subjects but at the Duke as a maker
of theater. The Duke is not mainly a "comic authority figure . . .
who increasingly uses the art of theatre to order a disordered society."[27] Rather, the Duke stages what Foucault reads in nonliterary
context as the theater of punishment. This theater—acted out on
a scaffold—exists not first and foremost to create order but primarily as a way for the state to display its absolute power.[28] His power
is not over any abstractions but over the body itself.

And more politically useful than the state's right to punish bodies, argues Foucault, is its absolute power to stage the bodies it
punishes. When the Duke decides to don the disguise and not
simply play the tyrant (1.3.34–45), he in effect chooses the power
to stage scenes over the right simply to punish crimes. Once it is
understood that, as Foucault says, the scene of public punishment
is not only a judicial but a political ritual,[29] the Duke's mockery
becomes more easily discernible. The final scene is most prominently a scene of trajectories from justice to power, from punishment to theater, and from judgment to politics. In the end, the
Duke emerges as the only classical or authorized body in Vienna.
He alone presumes to be its serious and nongrotesque citizen. If
the Duke is to have a coup de theatre, the offstage audience realizes
that it must be here, where the Duke reveals to his subjects his
manipulations of them. This scene is his moment of political and
theatrical triumph. It draws into the theatrical spotlights the
Duke's unveiling, his meting out of punishments, and his final displacement of the major players into marriage couples, that is, into
the conventions of comedy.

Ultimately, this scene (and particularly the unhooding) betrays
the Duke's attempt to have power over the theater itself. Once
revealed and understood to be something divine, unknown, and
hidden, his power would become real. The ontology of his power
is inseparable from his apotheosis, and his unveiling is not finally

about what his subjects are made to see but what they come to suspect and fear they do not or cannot see. His power is absolute once he becomes a power greater than his physical self. The Duke's unveiling is important not because it reveals some kind of cosmological or universal reality.[30] As Jean E. Howard has argued, "In the end no one is convinced that the Duke's visions merely reveal a preexisting social reality."[31] On the contrary, the moment of his unveiling creates and gives meaning to this Viennese social reality. The Duke's unhooding reveals the reciprocity between Vienna's social reality and the Duke's theater.

What does it mean to take the Duke's theater seriously, to take it for real? Not to take it seriously is what critics do who want to believe that there really can be a transcendence that allows the Duke and the play to achieve the status of a kind of divine comedy, or that the Duke really is a savior, "someone who can substitute true criminals for false ones, make distinctions among apparently equivalent crimes, and so reveal the operation of justice."[32] Not to take the Duke's theater seriously is to buy into the euphoria of the Duke's illusive rituals that not only permit but encourage the nondifference between punishment and marriage: A punishment for a marriage in the case of Claudio and Juliet, a marriage for a punishment in the case of Lucio and Mistress Keepdown, and a real inability to distinguish between marriage and punishment in the case of Angelo and Mariana.

I believe, however, that *Measure for Measure* is to be taken seriously. When the Duke unveils, it may certainly be argued that his object is to inspire awe and ensure a comic closure.[33] To take the Duke's theater seriously, however, it is necessary to distinguish between the onstage and offstage audience. The moment when the Duke inspires awe in his subjects and brings comic resolve to his theater is also the moment when the offstage audience most clearly acknowledges two theaters: the Duke's and Shakespeare's. The Duke stages his own absolute body as a way of countering and mocking the serious absolutisms of his subjects. The play invites its audience to mock and pull back from the Duke's construction of himself as its one and only serious subject. The play challenges its offstage audience not to heed the absolutism demanded by a measure for a measure but to fancy at least that some kind of critical difference exists between a punishment and a marriage.

The play's real mockery seems to be directed at the Duke. Even while the play admits to the effective power of an absolute ruler, it strongly suggests too that such absolutism is predicated upon self-delusion. Perhaps here the play comes closest to talking back to James by both celebrating and distancing itself from his power. Such a dyadic response to James could also attest to the power of drama to pay homage to the body of its patron without becoming fully incorporated into that body, even if that body advocates itself as the inheritor of a divine right and an absolute power.[34] James may fantasize himself as the absolute body of the state when he proclaims to Parliament in 1603, "I am the Husband, and all the whole Isle is my lawfull Wife; I am the Head, and it is my Body,"[35] but Shakespeare's play suggests that there is (as long as it lasts) a power more absolute than the ruler, and that is the power to stage him.

NOTES

1. I wish to thank those participating in either session, since the conversations in both sessions proved quite helpful in my ongoing work with the play and with the issue of power and punishment. I would most especially like to thank Emily Bartels and Gillian Murray Kendall, who made detailed suggestions about an earlier draft. I also owe a debt of gratitude to my research assistant, J. C. Stirm. The shortcomings of this essay, however, are mine and not theirs.

2. This question is central to the *Measure for Measure* (1603/4) vs. *Basilicon Doron* (1599/1603) debate, in which critics argue whether *Measure for Measure* takes seriously James I's precepts to his son about the divination and absolute authority and power of the monarch. Critical opinion ranges from those who discern some kind of ideological affinity between these works to those who find an ideological opposition between them to those who find the explicit association non-existent. See respectively, Roy W. Battenhouse, "*Measure for Measure* and King James," *Clio* 7 (1978): 193–226; Richard Levin, "The King James Version of *Measure for Measure*," *Clio* 3 (1974): 129–63; and Terrell L. Tebbetts, "Talking Back to the King: *Measure for Measure* and *The Basilicon Doron*," *College Literature* 12 (1985): 122–34. The relationship between Shakespeare's and James's text seems undeniable. How the critic decides the relationship depends largely on how the critic perceives the connection in *Measure for Measure* between the Duke's theater and Shakespeare's.

3. See James I's *Basilicon Doron*, 3–52, in vol. 1 of *The Political Works of James I*, with an introduction by Charles Howard McIlwain, Harvard Political Classics, 2 vols. (Cambridge, Mass.: Harvard University Press, 1918), 12. *Basilicon Doron*, like *Measure for Measure*, is especially concerned throughout with the monarchal (or ducal) use of punishment. Also see Jonathan Goldberg, "James I and the Theater of Conscience," *English Literary History* 46 (1979): 379–98. Goldberg focuses mainly on *Basilicon Doron* and examines James's manipulation of the "familiar metaphor of the player king."

4. See especially James I's introductory letter to the reader of *Basilicon Doron* in vol. 1 of *The Political Works of James I*, 4–11.

5. For some germinal studies of the Duke's divinity, see G. Wilson Knight on the Duke's divine ethics in "*Measure for Measure* and the Gospels," *The Wheel of Fire* (London: Methuen, 1930; reprint, 1970), 73–96; and Roy W. Battenhouse, "*Measure for Measure* and Christian Doctrine," *PMLA* 61 (1946): 1029–59, in

which Battenhouse speaks of Shakespeare's play as a "divine romance." Also of a germinal but more secular nature is Robert Hunter's reading. His operative construct is the "good ruler" as opposed to the divine persona. Nonetheless, Hunter argues that a good and absolute ruler is "like power divine." *Shakespeare and the Comedy of Forgiveness* (New York and London: Columbia University Press, 1965). For more recent studies discussing the problematics or failure of the Duke's comedy, see Richard P. Wheeler, "Vincentio and the Sins of Others: The Expense of Spirit in *Measure for Measure*," in *Shakespeare's Development and the Problem Comedies* (Berkeley, Los Angeles, and London: University of California Press, 1981) 92–153 (also 5–19); and Jean E. Howard, *"Measure for Measure* and the Restraints of Convention," *Essays in Literture* 10 (1983): 149–58.

6. See Harriet Hawkins's critical study, *Measure for Measure* in Twayne's New Critical Introductions to Shakespeare (Boston: Twayne Publishers, 1987), 85–87.

7. Michel Foucault, *Discipline & Punish: The Birth of the Prison,* trans. Alan Sheridan (New York: Vintage Books, 1979), 48.

8. Foucault, 25.

9. According to Ernst H. Kantorowicz, medieval political mythology understood the king to have two bodies, one political or divine and the other physical or natural. While the former body is impenetrable and immutable, the latter is subject to age, disease, and chance. *The King's Two Bodies: A Study in Mediaeval Theology* (Princeton: Princeton University Press, 1957), 3–23, 294–313. I am drawing a simple comparison here between Kantorowicz's and Bakhtin's corporeal scheme, since Bakhtin's classical body signifies more an ideational or idealized body and his grotesque body represents a more physical and functional one. A more in-depth comparison of these corporeal schemes would most likely further elucidate the theories of both.

10. Mikhail Bakhtin, *Rabelais and His World,* trans. Helene Iswolsky (Bloomington: Indiana University Press, 1984), 317. For a more elaborate definition of Bakhtin's corporeal scheme, see especially 24–36, 315–25. Also see Peter Stallybrass and Allon White, *The Politics & Poetics of Transgression* (Ithaca, New York: Cornell University Press, 1986), 6–26, where they give a concise but substantial reading of the classical and grotesque body in Bakhtin's *Rabelais.*

11. All *Measure for Measure* quotations are from The Signet Classic Shakespeare, ed. S. Nagarajan (New York: New American Library, 1964).

12. Marc Shell in *The End of Kinship: "Measure for Measure," Incest, and the Ideal of Universal Siblinghood* (Stanford: Stanford University Press, 1988) strongly suggests that Isabella's choice is between body and spirit. But for Shell, the choice is between a physical chastity and a spiritual one, and because Isabella chooses not to engage in sexual intercourse with Angelo she is faulted for interpreting chastity to be a physical entity, (102–3). Also see J. W. Lever's introduction to the Arden edition (1965), 78. Her choice is not between types of chastity. It is between her brother's body (for which she would exchange her body—hence, Shell's "incest") and her spirit (which represents a kind of disembodied or transcendent self). Because she chooses chastity does not mean that she understands chastity to be a physical thing. On the contrary, it is her choice of the chaste spirit over the incestuous body that, at least retrospectively, motivates the Duke to use his friar self to counter or match Isabella's spirit or soul and ironically to convert her from the spiritual and back to the corporeal.

13. Robert N. Watson, "False Immortality in *Measure for Measure:* Comic Means. Tragic Ends," *Shakespeare Quarterly* 41 (1990): 411–32. See especially

421–22. Watson argues that Claudio accepts these pietistic formulas "only formally, only superficially." This seems to be the Duke's point. As the Duke begins his more theatrical plot maneuvers, he desires to put forth all such adherences to absolutisms (outside himself) as being formal and superficial.

14. Foucault, 16–17.

15. Foucault, 16–17.

16. Ovid, *Metamorphoses* (trans. Arthur Golding, 1567); Carbondale, Illinois: Southern Illinois University Press, 1961), bk. 6, lines 394–5. All Ovid references are to this edition.

17. Bakhtin, 321–22.

18. Tebbetts states that (for patriarchy) "apotheosis is the only just reward for the perfect patriarch:" 124.

19. For a more elaborate reading of the kind of physical and ideational contrast I am making here, see Elaine Scarry, who argues that the aim of torture is to move the victim from a strict experiencing of physical pain to the experiencing of pain because of the very *idea* that he or she could be tortured, *The Body in Pain: The Making and Unmaking of the World* (New York and Oxford: Oxford University Press, 1985), 51–59.

20. *The Geneva Bible* (1560), Matt. 7:1–2; Exod. 21:23–25.

21. Watson argues that the Duke's Judgment at the gates of the city as opposed to the gates of heaven "is a culminating instance of the way *Measure for Measure* parodies pious archetypes in asserting the priority of earthly order and human survival:" 430–31. I agree with the reading that the Duke does parody pious archetypes, giving final priority to earthly matters. While the Duke does parody heaven's Last Judgment, this is only a method to an end. The Duke's objective here is to displace and then take over and embody the absolute power of heaven's Last Judgment. I am also reminded here of James's "little God" comment in *Basilicon Doron* (see my endnote no. 3).

22. Foucault, 48; James I, vol. 1, *The Political Works of James I,* 307–8.

23. See Tebbetts, 130–31, although Tebbetts is speaking only of civil laws.

24. The bringing of acts from private places and into the public is very significant aspect of this final scene. See, for example, 5.1.9–16. Consider James's address to the reader of *Basilicon Doron,* where he threatens that all deeds, however secretly committed, will be "publikely preached on the tops of houses," 4. Cf. Luke 12:3 (along with Mark 4:22 and Matthew 10:27). There is also George Whetstone's *Promos and Cassandra* (1578) (most probably Shakespeare's main source) in which there is also a scaffold scene. See Battenhouse, *"Measure for Measure* and King James,"* where he argues that there is no "scaffold scene" in Shakespeare's play, 199. Also see the history of the Duke and messer Remirro de Orco in the seventh chapter of Niccolo Machiavelli's *The Prince.* This history is similar to the story of the Duke and Angelo in Shakespeare's play, as some critics have already noted. In Machiavelli's history, the Duke holds a public court and punishes Remirro by having his body cut in half and put on display in the public square at Cesena.

25. Bakhtin, 155.

26. Bakhtin, 153–54.

27. Jean E. Howard, "Renaissance Antitheatricality and the Politics of Gender and Rank in *Much Ado About Nothing,"* in *Shakespeare Reproduced: The Text in History & Ideology,* ed. Jean E. Howard and Marion F. O'Connor (New York and London: Meuthuen, 1987), 182. Also see Leonnard Tennenhouse, *Power on*

Display: The Politics of Shakespeare's Genres (New York and London: Methuen, 1986), 154–55.

28. Foucault, 48.

29. Foucault argues that a crime personally violates the body of the sovereign, since the "force of the law" and the "force of the prince" are one. For this reason, the *raison d'etre* of the public execution is not to bring back justice but to reactivate power (47–49).

30. This is in part a response to Tennenhouse, who does not question whether any real critical difference exists between Shakespeare's play and the Duke's all-encompassing patriarchalism, 159.

31. Howard, "Renaissance Antitheatricality," 182.

32. Tennenhouse, 158.

33. See for example, Tennenhouse, 158.

34. Brian Gibbons argues that James's subjects had a growing need to understand more empirically the way divine right gets translated into absolute power. See *Jacobean City Comedy: A Study of Satiric Plays by Jonson, Marston and Middleton* (London: Rupert Hart-Davis, 1968), 50–60.

35. Goldberg, 396. Also see Kantorowicz on the *corpus verum* (the physical body of an individual) and the *corpus fictum* ("The corporate collective"). James speaks here of his *corpus fictum*. There are a hierarchy of the *corpus fictum*, ranging from the head of the household to the head of the universe (209–10). What it means to represent the corporate collective in the *corpus verum* is one of the issues raised by Shakespeare's play.

The State of Life and the Power of Death:
Measure for Measure

ROBERT N. WATSON

A MORAL COMEDY

MEASURE for Measure comes closer than any other Shakespeare play to having a schematic, articulable moral. Its primary topic is sexuality, and its primary argument is that neither individuals nor societies can thrive unless license and repression keep each other in balance. Naturally critics are reluctant to admit that sexual morality is what the play is about, because that is what it *seems* to be about.[1] But in this case it may pay to surrender our ingenuity in the face of the obvious. The polar outposts of this play are brothels and convents, prudery and lechery are what chiefly characterizes its characters, and its two crucial actions are bouts of sexual intercourse—one a premarital impregnation, the other a form of attempted rape. From beginning to end, the dominant motive is the need to convert lustful fornication into marital fecundity. Vienna's Sigmund Freud defines as perversion any sexual activity not primarily directed toward heterosexual genital intercourse;[2] Shakespeare's Vienna defines as treason any such intercourse not directed toward legitimate procreation. For the individual, marriage becomes—as in the patristic commonplaces—a way of reconciling unruly sexual desire with necessary sexual restraint; for the state, it becomes a way of maintaining the substance and order of the social fabric. Though *Measure for Measure* is notorious for its strayings from comic sentiment, it thus builds toward the typical comic conclusion far more forcefully and logically than most comedies: by the end, marriage becomes an overdetermined resolution.

The premise of the play is that the Duke of Vienna—by preferring fornication, which creates life, however unlawfully, to execution, which destroys life, however lawfully—has allowed sexual license to corrupt his city. This is an understandable error in a humane ruler, all the more understandable in a theater that had been closed by epidemic plague the previous year (1603), in a city that had lost close to a quarter of its population to the plague over the preceding decade. Despite some bad harvests in the 1590s and some complaints about the tendency of young people to procreate before they were ready to support a family,[3] population explosion was hardly to be feared; on the contrary, a common measure of a state's health was the growth of its population. So there would have been some sociological force to Lucio's warning that Angelo's more severe policy might "unpeople the province,"[4] an inverted reminder of the Biblical injunction so often emphasized by Renaissance preachers: "Be fruitful and multiply." Even Puritanical figures such as Phillip Stubbes—who laments that "untill every one hath two or three Bastardes a peece, they esteeme him no man," and furiously condemns anyone who argues that "Otherwyse the World wold become barren"—stress the obligation to multiply *within* marriage.[5]

The Duke's problem is that, though his former course may have been understandable, it has not been understood. Lucio remarks that before the Duke "would have hanged a man for getting a hundred bastards, he would have paid for the nursing a thousand. He had some feeling of the sport; he knew the service; and that instructed him to mercy" (3.2.113–17). This is intolerable for the Duke, for both the motives and the numbers it claims to reveal. One pious Jacobean tract argued that "it is more Prince-like to save then to destroy, and more difficult to revive one dead man, then to kill a thousand living,"[6] but Lucio's analysis presents the problem as a disease spreading outward from the Duke's unruly body to his entire body politic, rather than as an enlightened choice for mercy and healthy growth. It also suggests the exponential growth of the problem, in a world where even one bastard child is one too many: The villains of Jacobean tragedy are often illegitimate children who necessarily attack the social order that excludes them. So the Duke stages for his city, as Shakespeare does for his, an averted tragedy that characterizes all aberrations from married procreation as collaborations with death.

Angelo applies a simplistic system of accounting to this political commodity, the legitimate son; the Duke's calculations are more complex and seemingly humane, but perhaps ultimately more cynical as well. According to Angelo, the making of a counterfeit coin, the forging of that aspect of the state's wealth, is a theft equivalent to the stealing of a real coin (2.2.42–49).[7] The comparison is typical of Angelo in being too cold and abstract to be wholly convincing, but given the trends, Lucio's speech reveals (however slanderously and hyperbolically), the exchange rate in Vienna has shifted disastrously, devaluing legitimacy against desire. The Duke is thus obliged to intervene with a temporary didactic choice of order over passion, a morally instructive bit of tragicomic theater. The laxity of the Duke's own reign leads directly to the excessive restraint promised by Angelo. When Lucio asks the manacled Claudio, "Whence comes this restraint," Claudio replies, "From too much liberty, my Lucio. Liberty, / As surfeit, is the father of much fast; / So every scope by the immoderate use / Turns to restraint" (1.2.116–20). His individual experience is significantly parallel to that of the state, not just the result of it.

Sex and death were conventionally associated in the Renaissance, of course, but (as in its emphasis on venereal disease) *Measure for Measure* uses that association in a particularly tendentious way. Lucio's final words—"Marrying a punk, my lord, is pressing to death, / Whipping and hanging" (5.1.520–21)—echo a theme pervading the play. The covert and unholy alliance between these supposed mighty opposites—fornication and repression, conception and execution—surfaces again when the Duke assigns Pompey the bawd to work for Abhorson the executioner. Both men object to the partnership, but Pompey soon concedes, "I have been an unlawful bawd time out of mind, but yet I will be content to be a lawful hangman. I would be glad to receive some instruction from my fellow-partner" (4.2.14–17). The Provost insists that they "weigh equally" in any ethical scale, and Pompey eventually discovers that "many of [his] old customers" from the brothel require his new services at the jail (4.3.1–4). The pun lurking in Abhorson's elided name neatly encapsulates the pattern: The executioner is evidently an abhorred whoreson. Promiscuity again appears to generate its own punishment; the executioner has been created by the fornicator.

If excessive liberty leads to excessive restraint, as the appointment of Angelo demonstrates, then excessive restraint leads to excessive liberty, as the corruption of Angelo demonstrates. Behind the closing down of whorehouses in Vienna lurks the relatively recent memory of closing down monasteries in England. The case of Isabella reinforces the same ideas more subtly: that discipline can lead to perversion, that severe rectitude provokes repressed sensuality into a guerilla war against outward propriety. Angelo insists that Isabella's virgin modesty is what paradoxically inspires his lust; again, extraordinary self-restraint—hers as well as his own—becomes the provocation to an extraordinary self-indulgence. The erotics of Isabella's renunciation could hardly be more lurid:

> were I under the terms of death,
> Th'impression of keen whips I'd wear as rubies,
> And strip myself to death as to a bed
> That longing have been sick for, ere I'd yield
> My body up to shame.
>
> (2.4.100–4)

The erotic undertones of religious flagellation throughout *Measure for Measure,* the ways mortification of the flesh becomes gratification instead, have been well documented.[8] Furthermore, she extends her death wish (as does Angelo) to all the fallen creatures around her. On hearing the tale of Mariana's star-crossed love for Angelo, Isabella exclaims, "What a merit were it in death to take this poor maid from the world! What corruption in this life, that it will let this man live!" (3.1.231–33). Her advice to the lovelorn is invariably execution, Robespierre ghostwriting for Ann Landers. The moral rectitude of Angelo and Isabella becomes nearly indistinguishable from their masochistic sexual appetites.

So *Measure for Measure* is a tragicomedy not only because a convincing threat of barrenness or death appears before sexual desire resolves itself into marriage, but also because the play exposes the potentially deadly attributes of sexuality itself. Both fornication and its extreme repression are wastrel expenditures of the bodies natural and politic. If a society suspects that the monastic life breeds perversion rather than immortality, then the only remaining answer to death—the answer of Protestant society—is fruitful marriage.

A Tragedy of State

Within this relatively commonplace moral admonition about physical, social, and psychological decadence, Shakespeare develops a potentially heretical, even blasphemous, meditation about the fate of the human individual. *Measure for Measure* evokes a tragic resistance to comic solutions, not only by emphasizing the destructive potential of sexuality, but also by widening our perspective on its creative potential. Valuing procreation as a demographic contribution rather than as individual assertion and gratification may not sound especially sinister. But the anti-Malthusian conclusion that all is well as long as the population of Vienna keeps growing does not really answer the fears roused by the various threats of execution, and particularly by Claudio's confused but eloquent terror of death. The man whose first fear is that his body is doomed "To lie in cold obstruction, and to rot," then that his spirit may "be imprison'd in the viewless winds / And blown with restless violence round about / The pendent world," hardly encourages the happy surrender of the worldly self to dispersal:

> The weariest and most loathed worldly life
> That age, ache, penury and imprisonment
> Can lay on nature, is a paradise
> To what we fear of death.

(3.1.117–31)

So it is not surprising that Claudio finds no consolation in the disguised Duke's argument that, from the standpoint of atomistic philosophy, he really has no self to lose (3.1.19–21); nor is he reconciled to his fate by the idea that he has fathered a child to take his place.

On the contrary, he is confronted with a literal version of the commonplace that haunts parents such as Prospero, and perhaps sons such as Hamlet as well: What condemns him to death is the visible evidence of his biological replacement. When the disguised Duke speaks to Juliet about this fetus, he calls it "the sin you carry"; and for Claudio this is precisely the sin whose wages are death.[9] The lineal succession that is satisfactory for the purposes of the state may not eradicate our terrifying vision of the individual will and consciousness obliterated by nature and mortality.

Tragicomedy commonly abets the comfortable illusion that procreative love is the opposite of death. What makes *Measure for Measure* so disturbing is its subversion of that binarism. While the plot of the play appears dismissive toward the asceticism of Angelo and Isabella, a thematic countermovement endorses their intuition that sexual intercourse is a surrender to mortality, not a cure for it. The comic triumph in *Measure for Measure* belongs not to love or to the hero, but instead to a version of what Michel Foucault calls "bio-power": specifically, the need of the state, under the guise of personalized benevolence, simply to keep the procreative machine running. Indeed, *Measure for Measure* refutes Foucault's claim that this concern was an invention of the eighteenth century, since the ending of this Jacobean play could be trenchantly described in exactly the terms Foucault uses to describe this supposedly post-Enlightenment mode of government: "It is no longer a matter of bringing death into play in the field of sovereignty, but of distributing the living in the domain of value and utility."[10]

In *Measure for Measure,* domestic bliss is exposed as a euphemism for the domestication of the human animal; it is not only bawds (as Elbow supposes) who "buy and sell men and women like beasts" until "all the world drink brown and white bastard" (3.2.2–3). That is the leading industry of the state, and all other industries depend on the successful management of that breeding-farm. Elbow's complaint immediately follows the Duke's scheme to trick Angelo into impregnating Mariana with a legitimate fetus. Again, human bodies are the fungible coins—and the indifferent food—of the state. Fifty lines later, we learn that the "dear morsel" Mistress Overdone—worn out in the "service" of nine husbands— "hath eaten up all the beef, and is herself in the tub" (3.2.54–57).

The comic dance of marriage is, measure for measure, also a Dance of Death, and the disguised ruler in the dark cowl may carry a sickle as well as a pardon. The state has reached an accommodation with the jealous god Death, and as we play out our biological roles, each of us becomes a propitiary sacrifice. No wonder statecraft is so oddly associated with pregnancy in Vienna (for examples, 1.1.11, 4.4.18). Against the ongoing devastations of the Grim Reaper, *Measure for Measure* pits a Duke who might be called the Grim Breeder, hardly more appealing in his ways of creating people than the Reaper is in destroying them. Vienna is left without eternals, with only maternals and paternals to take their place.

The Reformation encouraged people to find some version of immortality in their legitimate progeny, yet was obliged to acknowledge that this was not really immortality at all. In the near term, the idea that resurrection occurs "dayly" through "generation" was heretical.[12] Furthermore, the process "whereby the *Parents* were said . . . to *live again* in their *Posterity*" was absurdly inadequate to replace the promise of full bodily resurrection of each individual at the Last Judgment.[12] As the Duke retrieves his citizens both from convents and from brothels to enlist them in the work of orderly social replication, we may feel how badly the social compromise fails to satisfy either our spiritual or our narcissistic cravings.

While thus questioning the adequacy of procreation as a response to human mortality, *Measure for Measure* also subjects honor and piety to similarly cynical psychological and political inspection. These virtues, and the hopes commonly attached to them, stand exposed (from Freudian and Machiavellian perspectives) as merely illusory forms of personal redemption. This devastating interrogation of all the "heroic" modes in which individuals attempt to perpetuate their individuality brings me to my main topic: false immortality. *Measure for Measure* resists its genre by undermining the three modes in which comedy usually promises immortality—fame, salvation, and procreation—and by replacing them with an emphasis on the destruction of the individual, an emphasis that is typical of tragedy. Whether or not we accept the pseudobiographical impression that Shakespeare here vandalizes his own comic form in deference to the great tragedies he had recently begun to write, we can hardly deny the inadequacies of the comic resolution of *Measure for Measure,* the darkness it fails to dispel. It is tragicomic not only because death is strongly present prior to the resolution, but more crucially because mortality remains imperfectly refuted at the center of that resolution.

Neither progeny nor Christianity, neither self-indulgence nor self-denial, provides an adequate response. The ailments of the Duke's city take the classic alternative forms—libertine and ascetic—of a psyche confronting the terror of mortality.[13] As Freud warned that psychoanalysis could only convert neurotic dysfunction into normal human unhappiness,[14] so the Duke aspires only to limit social dysfunction so that death can resume its normal functions. There is finally domesticity again in the slaughterhouse, and good and evil make undifferentiated contributions to a system whose only absolute law is supply and demand.

"One can see *Measure for Measure* as a play that opens with the law being invoked to punish fornication by death and that closes with the law being utilized to punish fornication by marriage."[15] This witty observation cuts deep: It opens for inspection the common discomfort with the "comic resolution" of *Measure for Measure*: two marriages tainted by unwilling and undesirable bridegrooms, the other two compromised by their peculiar brides, one arguably reluctant and still in a nun's habit, the other newly out of jail and barely back on her feet after childbirth. Given the fact that even the most promising marriages in Shakespeare's plays often teeter on the brink of tragic collapse, we can hardly foresee great good coming of all these awkward alliances, except perhaps in tidying up the bookkeeping of the Viennese bureaucracy. And yet it is not so cynical or unreasonable for a government to treat marriage as merely another, preferable instrument for controlling desire—which is one plausible definition of punishment. From the perspective of the state, choice and love are subordinate values. The state cannot finally concern itself with the motivation behind marriage any more than it can condemn citizens for unacted evil desires: "Thoughts are no subjects," Isabella tells the Duke, "Intents, but merely thoughts" (5.1.451–52).

So, amid the threats of death to characters in this play, which fit it to most definitions of tragicomedy, lurks a threat to expose supposedly transcendent values as mere instruments of state, to expose the hope for individual survival as a hollow fantasy subserving the survival instincts of the body politic. As in the heraldic structure of aristocratic Jacobean funerals, which insisted on including indifferent technical heirs to the exclusion of genuine mourners, the demand for an assurance of social continuity far outweighed the demands of personal emotion.[16]

The cure for mortality offered in *Measure for Measure* thus works far better sociologically than psychologically. The resurrection of Claudio and the pardons for Angelo and Barnardine are political tricks that only defer the question of mortality. Claudio was told that Angelo's ill-won pardon would gain him merely "six or seven feverous winters"; will the Duke's nobler pardon gain him so much more? The one gesture toward a truly eternal solution—Isabella's religious vocation—apparently yields to the demands of dynastic survival, and the play does not audibly mourn for it. The essence of the Duke's final triumph (and Shakespeare's comic solution) is marriage—not as individual fulfillment, but as a practical, worldly, even legalistic solution to the problem of maintaining the size and structure of the Viennese population, and to the no more romantic problem of controlling illegitimacy and venereal disease among the city's many wayward citizens. The focus on government appears to offer some respite from the question of individual death, but that anxiety nonetheless finds ways to break through to the surface.

Measure for Measure opens with the Duke fashioning Angelo into a son and heir to the throne:

> I say, bid come before us Angelo.
> What figure of us, think you, he will bear?
> For you must know, we have with special soul
> Elected him our absence to supply;
> Lent him our terror, drest him with our love,
> And given his deputation all the organs
> Of our own power.

(1.1.15–21)

The Duke intends thus to make Angelo "at full ourself." Angelo responds to the suggestion that he is to bear a figure of his predecessor when, later in the scene, he expresses his anxiety about having "so great a figure . . . stamp'd upon" him (1.1.48–49); in the next act he will use the same coining metaphor to refer to procreation (2.4.45). The Duke's implicit fantasy of parthenogenesis is common in the struggle of Shakespeare's tragically misguided men (such as Coriolanus and Leontes) against their own mortality.[17] Only when the Duke sees, mirrored back by Angelo, the life-defeating implications of this death-denying narcissism can he accept his own place in the procreative economy of the state.

To be mere coins in some usurious biological economy can hardly satisfy the desire for transcendent personal significance, whether the usurer is perceived as an earthly monarch or a heavenly one. The Duke's introductory remarks make the practices of heaven in this regard seem suspiciously congruent with those of nature:

> Heaven doth with us as we with torches do,
> Not light them for themselves; for if our virtues
> Did not go forth of us, 'twere all alike
> As if we had them not. Spirits are not finely touch'd
> But to fine issues; nor nature never lends
> The smallest scruple of her excellence
> But, like a thrifty goddess, she determines
> Herself the glory of a creditor,
> Both thanks and use.
>
> (1.1.32–40)

"Thanks, but no thanks," might be the reply of the heroic actor cast as a mere torchbearer. Ben Jonson's epitaph "On My First Son" demonstrates that this loan-shark aspect of God could elicit bitterness, despite all the standard gestures of submission to divine will. When Gertrude remarries so hastily, Hamlet remarks no less bitterly on the way "thrift" has been valued over grief for his dead father. Death tenaciously shadows the procreative process, and the efficiency of the biological economy is an insult to the human spirit, especially when a Ben Jonson is asked to accept the loss of a Ben Jonson, or a Hamlet the loss of a Hamlet.[18]

By staging his own miraculous return, in the manner of the disguised-ruler plot so popular on the early Jacobean stage, the Duke fulfills another fantasy familiar from Elizabethan drama: namely, the return of a father from death (or at least from a great distance or great poverty) to remedy the wrongs of the prodigal heir who has forgotten him and his ways. King Hamlet and King Lear are grim variations on this theme. The immediate provocation of such stories may have been anxieties about royal succession in England, but their persistent appeal probably resides in their implicit denial of death. In the case of *Measure for Measure*, the Duke's purpose in this arrangement is twofold, and will be served only to the extent that Angelo stumbles in the footsteps of his patron. First, the Duke must show his citizens the dangers of provoking excessive restraint. Second, he must prove that even an apparently pure embodiment of his moral law makes a very poor substitute for his own wit and kindness, for the individual humanity that shines redeemingly through his disguise. The Duke thus entangles himself in a contradiction much like the one that agonized Jacobean society as a whole: trying to prove to his citizens that replacing oneself procreatively is more important than indulging selfish desires, yet aspiring to do so in a way that will prove himself irreplaceable.[19] Furthermore, the Duke's effort to end illegitimacy in Vienna involves making Angelo, in one sense, the Duke's own bastard son. Angelo's failure as a dynastic heir, precisely by the way it bolsters the Duke's claim to lasting political glory, ruins the Duke's figurative version of procreative survival.

The ending of the play questions whether the Duke's paternalistic stratagem with Angelo, the growth of Vienna's population, or even his fame-winning masterstrokes in the theatricalized arts of state can adequately substitute for a fruitful marriage. In steering his subjects toward matrimony, the Duke discovers not only a worthy spouse but also the fact of his own mortality that obliges him, too, to marry. If there is any validity to the argument that *Measure for Measure* was written partly in tribute to the accession of King James, it would make sense for the play to contain some endorsement of a monarch who could offer a lineal successor (such as Prince Henry) rather than merely an appointive one, some transformation of the literary legacy that had worshipped a Virgin Queen.[20] Power was intimately bound up with paternity for James,[21] and his legacy to his son Henry was the *Basilikon Doron,* a text on the proper management of a kingdom. From its very first lines, the Duke's obsessively paternalistic play presents itself as this sort of mixed representation of authority; but power, fatherhood, and authorship all fall short of assuring personal immortality.

The Duke pursues another well-worn path toward immortality in his quest for fame, including the putative immortalities of honor and of art. He spreads news of his death (4.2.200) and slips back into town (like Tom Sawyer) to study the reactions, but Lucio's

gossip spoils the anticipated canonization. Of course, the Duke
claims to be indifferent to fame, even to dislike it:

> I'll privily away. I love the people,
> But do not like to stage me to their eyes:
> Though it do well, I do not relish well
> Their loud applause and Aves vehement.
>
> (1.1.67–70)

He doth protest too much, methinks; his nagging resentment of
Lucio's casual slanders suggests that he cares very much about
his audience and his reviews.[22] Vainly determined to convince
Lucio that the Duke is a paragon, he soliloquizes bitterly about
the injuries that await even the most carefully built public reputation, and promptly begins fishing shamelessly for compliments
from Escalus (3.2.137–45, 179–82, 254–75, 224–31). Though it
might be something King James would be pleased to hear,[23] the
Duke's assertion that "slandering a prince" deserves "pressing to
death, / Whipping, and hanging" (5.1.520–21) seems revealingly
severe.

When he reappears as himself at the start of the fifth act, the
Duke seems to mock his own quest for a glorious place in future
Mirrors for Magistrates. He extols Angelo's reign, which he intends soon to expose as mortally corrupt, as deserving "with characters of brass, / A forted residence 'gainst the tooth of time / And
razure of oblivion" (5.1.12–14). The Duke's irony presses uncom-
fortably on Shakespeare's earlier explorations of the quest for immortality, in *Love's Labor's Lost* and the sonnets. The facts of
fallen flesh and blood have already overthrown this immortalizing
project, before time and nature could even begin to erode gilded
monuments.

Escalus's authoritative announcement to his disguised and un-
recognized sovereign that "The Duke's in us" (5.1.293) would have
summoned the doctrine of the monarch's two bodies in the minds
of the audience. In a play so concerned with the paradoxical quest
for personal immortality, this doctrinal echo (like Hamlet's "the
body is with the King" at 4.2.27–30) invites our attention but finally
offers no reassurance. After Angelo's corruption of the law renders
him instant "carrion" (2.2.167), the royal self no longer resembles
that metal stamp of divine justice; it becomes indistinguishable
from the sinful flesh. Angelo describes Isabella as "deflower'd . . .
by an eminent body that enforc'd / The law against it!" (4.4.19–21).

This phallic body politic becomes a source of corruption and death, rather than symbolic immortality, to its citizens.

The Duke's immortal longings also lead him to experiment with piety, with the abjuration of the things of this world in hope of a place in the next. One very popular Jacobean tract asserted that "It is *Piety* that *enbalmes* a *Prince his* good name,"[24] and *Measure for Measure* offers various hints that the Duke desires that sort of embalming, ranging from his claim to have always "lov'd the life remov'd" (1.3.8), to his request for reassurance of his reputation for preferring contemplation over pleasure (3.2.224–31) and the peculiar evidence that he has long served as a holy confessor to Mariana. But he uses his monkish traits finally as a ploy to effect the civil education and earthly salvation of Claudio, and to lure Isabella away from her own pious choice—away from her betrothal to Christ and into his own earthly marital embrace. Furthermore, the essentially hollow tone and ulterior motivation of his monkish lessons to Claudio serve to undermine the entire belief-system— both on stage and off—that views death as a blessing. Within the play-world these religious postures all prove to be ploys of state, designed to foster stability, in the form of dynamic equilibrium.

A PARODY OF PIETY

The Duke's speech to Claudio at the start of the third act is essentially a compilation of *contemptus mundi* and *ars moriendi* commonplaces, marked as cliches by their role in a theatrical performance (Duke as monk) that aims at civic reform through pietistic deception, rather than at any pious conversion that would mitigate the state's punitive power. The Duke's overall project clearly demonstrates that he is not actually scornful of this world and this life, and here he sedulously avoids any mention of the afterlife that might lead Claudio to value it above his imminent fatherhood.[25] It is also clear that Claudio accepts these formulaic assurances only formally, only superficially. Such pragmatic, even hypocritical, uses of the consolation ritual—making Last Things the means to a worldly end—evokes the views reportedly held by the boldest of Renaissance blasphemers: Centuries before Karl Marx criticized religion as the opiate of an oppressed populace, these radicals suggested that priest and preacher were merely dummies for the Machiavellian ventriloquists who held material power.[26]

In comforting Isabella for the supposed death of her brother, the unveiled Duke reverts to some of his monkish commonplaces, in a form that again suggests their hollowness:

> That life is better life, past fearing death,
> Than that which lives to fear. Make it your comfort,
> So happy is your brother.
>
> (5.1.395–97)

Editors struggle vainly to find more in this statement than double-talk. If Claudio has overcome his fear of dying, it is only by no longer having any life to lose; he has become (supposedly) a corpse, not a laughing philosopher. The Duke's remark can be taken as a simple endorsement of the afterlife, but (absurdly) the sole virtue it identifies in that afterlife is that it lacks the fear of death; immortality consists only of nonmortality.

Arguably the Duke is mimicking good Christian practice by encouraging penance through mortification in Claudio, his sister, and his fiancée; and one reward of pious daily dying is the seeming daily demonstration of Resurrection. But the theater of God's judgments begins to look like an ordinary stage fiction. Claudio's supposed demise is made acceptable to the tragicomic form because we learn that the death, no less than the consolation, is merely a piece of playacting.

The standard complaint against the marriages of *Measure for Measure*—that the comic resolution seems a forced and insufficient response to the tragic elements and atmosphere of the story—applies to the threatened deaths as well. Death is not refuted any more wholeheartedly than marriage is affirmed. Furthermore, death is assigned rather arbitrarily (in Claudio's condemnation and Ragozine's illness) and avoided the same way (in the pardons of Barnardine and Angelo); we are given no compelling justification for the choice of corpses, any more than for the choice of spouses, beyond the mechanisms of biology and statecraft.[27]

Terrible deaths have been averted, but in a way that provokes a modern suspicion that ordinary deaths are the most terrible of all. At the end, the Duke's fame is under attack from Lucio's slanders, those nagging interruptions from the lower stratum of body and body politic that mar Shakespeare's artistic resolution as well as the Duke's conclusive statecraft. If the raising of Claudio from the dead is a consoling spectacle, it also threatens to shift our perspective on the more fundamentally consoling story of Christ raising Lazarus: *Measure for Measure* transforms that Gospel truth into a markedly theatrical fantasy, perhaps even a fraud. If the Duke's glorious return from supposed death echoes the story of Christ's own Resurrection, it seems at times a travesty designed to endorse the most cynical reading of the Resurrection: as a trick engineered by a fake holy man for his own aggrandizement.

The play alludes to the commonplace that the entire world is a prison from which death is the only true escape,[28] yet several characters are eventually released from Death Row into worldly pleasures. The pardons constitute a happy ending, but one that (precisely because it *is* happy) subverts a crucial metaphor frequently employed in the Renaissance, within and beyond this play, to reconcile human beings to mortality. Furthermore, the two pleas we hear for bail from prison are hardly reassuring models of redemptive prayer: Claudio's becomes a solicitation of his sister to fornication—a striking perversion of the prayer to the Virgin for salvation that resonates throughout the play—and Pompey's is met only by diabolical jeering (3.2.40). We cannot know whether such veiled but persistent blasphemies were the reason—the monastic aspects of the story would naturally have drawn attention—but it is interesting to note that, when an English Jesuit censored Shakespeare's works for the Inquisition in the 1640s, *Measure for Measure* was the only play he removed entirely. Occasional words and passages were blotted out in other plays, but *Measure for Measure* was amputated like a cancer, the stubs of the pages cut back almost to the binding.[29]

The skeptical potential of the play threatens the vital organs of the Christian body politic, compromising functions and mythologies essential from Shakespeare's time to our own. Procreation is exposed as essentially a mechanism of biology manipulated as a ploy of the state, which (aided by the church) strives to harness, rationalize, even sentimentalize, the relentless directionless march of nature. With Isabella apparently about to surrender her virginity, Mariana (by the convention of such stories) probably newly impregnated, Juliet newly delivered, and Lucio's whore the mother of his young child, *Measure for Measure* presents a kind of time-lapse photograph, showing the self-perpetuating natural system to be far more in control than the vagaries of individual human will. Angelo presses Isabella to show that she is a woman "By putting on the destin'd livery" (2.4.137); this equation of her identity as a woman with sexual submission earns Angelo the jeers of even the most mildly feminist audience, yet the very play that thus makes him the villain suggests that the procreative sheets—and the swaddling clothes, and the burial shroud—are indeed the destined livery of each human being, for all our protestations of free will. A feminist critic understandably complains about the lack in *Measure and Measure* "of women's personal autonomy—her right to control her body,"[30] but men hardly seem to fare better in that category, whether in bed or in prison. It is not only social hierarchy, as some political critics assume, that the state must mystify to sustain itself: The bodily cycle of birth and death seems to demand and receive a similar disguise.

Isabella is determined to abjure physical pleasure, public life, and procreation, yet she is repeatedly pulled back from the pursuit of salvation to the businesses of body, family, and state. When she tells Angelo that she would "rather give my body than my soul" to save her brother, Angelo is curtly amenable: "I talk not of your soul" (2.4.74, 56–57). Throughout the play, Isabella is steadily drawn into the marketplace of the physical, into a mentality that thinks more about desire than about religion; more about the threat of death than about the hope of immortality; more about bodily confinement (a jail or a grave) than about a spiritual injury (disgrace or damnation) that would be a "restraint / Though all the world's vastidity you had."

For Isabella, there is no way out of the human prison, no way to avoid the compromises and corruptions of her place in the human family. From the very start, her dedication as a spiritual Bride of Christ is subverted and even parodied by her conversion into a procreative bride for the body politic. Isabella's name proclaims her devoted to God, but Vienna, through an ingenious translation of that devotion, enforces its claim on her womb.[31] For her first fifteen lines, Shakespeare's Isabella is allowed to profess asceticism; then Lucio rings the bell at the convent and says, "Hail virgin, if you be" (1.4.1–16). This might be an unremarkable greeting under the circumstances, except that it awakens some truly remarkable echoes. Lucio's salutation translates the beginning of the basic prayer to the Virgin Mary, and then questions whether Isabella is actually suited to the role.[32] Furthermore, that hailing of the Virgin (in a Roman Catholic society such as the play depicts) immediately followed the ringing of a bell, a bell that (even under Elizabethan Protestantism) was known as the Angelus bell.

Lucio arrives to lure Isabella out of the convent, and arrives as both an agent of Angelo (who wants to turn her into a sexual object) and of the Duke (who then wants to turn her into a procreative agent). Furthermore, "*Ave virgo*" marks the opening of the Annunciation, as reported by Luke (whose name surely recalls Lucio)—precisely the event the Angelus prayer celebrates, the summoning of the Virgin to the task of redeeming human immortality by bearing the son of the Lord. Theologians of course stressed that the Annunciation was by no means an angelic rape but instead the occasion of the Virgin's free consent to the patriarchal Lord of whom the angel was merely a deputy (and Angelo is called Vincentio's "deputy" a dozen times in the play). The process of Isabella's seduction reduces the decorum of the Annunciation to a "good cop, bad cop" tactic employed by the interrogating figures of Angelo and the Duke. Indeed, it looks oddly similar to a bawdy story in the *Decameron,* in which a friar disguises himself as the Angel Gabriel in order to seduce a reluctant woman;[33] and Marlowe's supposed assertion that "the Angell Gabriell was baud to the holy ghost, because he brought the salutation to Mary" further demonstrates that this satiric idea was available in Shakespeare's cultural milieu.

The setting Angelo chooses for his tryst with Isabella is heavily marked as a version of the *hortus conclusus* that is the iconographic home of the Virgin Mary (4.1.28–36). Isabella is positioned as a holy virgin only to be displaced into an object of sexual and reproductive desire, her symbols degradingly recontextualized.

The impressment of Isabella into the reproductive economy is marked from the beginning as a queasy burlesque of her religious mission. In the initial conversation, Lucio tells Isabella, "I hold you as a thing enskied and sainted / By your renouncement, an immortal spirit"; she answers, "You do blaspheme the good, in mocking me" (1.4.34–38). It is not clear whether Lucio is indeed mocking Isabella as he here calls her back to the earthly business of the body; but it does seem clear that Shakespeare is making a mockery of the pious notion that virginity is a plausible or even socially permissible way to pursue immortality. Isabella turns the immediate task of bearing Angelo's burden over to Mariana—another refraction of the Mary, with a moated grange for her *hortus conclusus* and an Angelo for the agent of her paradoxical chastity— but soon enough the bells will ring for Isabella as well. Presumably she surrenders her quest for immortalizing chastity by taking the Duke's hand in the final silence of the play, much as Coriolanus surrenders his own heroic immortality strategy by silently taking his mother's hand in the generational panorama.

When the revenant Duke suggests that Isabella accuses Angelo "in th' infirmity of sense," she replies,

> O Prince, I conjure thee, as thou believ'st
> There is another comfort than this world,

That thou neglect me not with that opinion
That I am touch'd with madness.

(5.1.51–54)

This conjuration makes it all the more interesting that her sanity—
and thereby, implicitly, all faith in that otherworldly comfort—is
repeatedly called into question as the scene continues, not only by
Angelo but by the Duke as well: Her complaint against Angelo is
"somewhat madly spoken" (5.1.92), and her plea to spare his
worldly life runs "against all sense" (5.1.431). Given the memorable
evocations of sexual repression, the audience may already have
been prepared to suspect a connection between Isabella's faith and
her possible psychological infirmities, and her oath of affirmation
here directs that suspicion against belief in the afterlife. It reminds
us that this belief can be interrogated precisely because it is so
necessary a comfort, just as romantic sentiment and the institution
of marriage can be analyzed as by-products of biological and political imperatives. If there were not conjugal desire, it would be necessary to invent it. Indeed, the Duke seems desperate to simulate
both marital love and divine justice, precisely because his city
seems to have lost track of the original models.

As soon as one begins to look behind these necessities, to doubt
these comforts—as *Measure for Measure* subtly but persistently
invites us to do—the immortality strategies of Isabella and the
others may indeed appear insane. But remaining stubbornly irrational about one's biological doom may be the only alternative to
becoming insane from confronting it. A culture of religious faith
(such as the Renaissance) commonly diagnoses atheism as a form
of insanity;[34] an atheistic culture will tend to follow Freud in interpreting faith as a neurotic symptom. The perspective of modern
science threatens to expose culture and religion as ludicrous cover
stories designed to keep our excessively contemplative species
from rebelling against either the earthly or the heavenly lords who
tell us to be fruitful and fill out the census. *Measure for Measure*
hovers uneasily between an old faithful world and a new skeptical
one, leaving Isabella to make a bewildering shift from a religious
to a procreative model of immortality. From another perspective,
like so many of Shakespeare's audience, she must find a way from
the old Roman theology to a new Reformed theology that argues,
more than our chastity is our progeny.

Angelo is in many ways Isabella's dark shadow, and like her, he
studiously rejects the allure of procreation (1.4.57–61) in favor of
an immortality strategy based on fame, honor, and purity.[35] In his

sensual restraint, his reluctance to consummate the marriage to Mariana, even in his suicidal impulses in the final scene, Angelo refuses to become merely another link in the long chain of corrupt and corruptible human flesh, which transmitted Original Sin (and therefore mortality) through the concupiscence of the generative act.[36] He seeks to be otherworldly here on earth; the coining metaphors may reflect the mercenary tendencies that led him away from Mariana, but they also suggest that he is ready to be stamped into the other kind of "angel," a suggestion that again conflates his official stature with holy transcendence. Yet—like Coriolanus in search of a similar transcendence[37]—Angelo cannot finally retrieve the coining metaphor from its conventional reference to procreation; the Duke converts him back into a marker of the fleshly aspect of the state's usuriously breeding wealth.

As soon as Angelo recognizes that his quest for immortal purity has foundered (if indeed it survived the wreck of Mariana's treasure), he compares his moral failure to the rotting of dead flesh in the sun (2.2.167). This is the same macabre view of mortality, the emphasis on the merely decaying body, that haunts Claudio and haunted Western Europe through the late Middle Ages. At the start of the play, Escalus describes Angelo as worthy of the "ample grace" for which he has been "elected" (1.1.18–24); the vocabulary makes public reputation (what Cassio calls "the immortal part of myself" in *Othello,* 2.3.263) an alternative model of eternal salvation. But when the truth about his fleshly failings becomes public as well as private knowledge, Angelo tells the Duke that "your Grace, like power Divine / Hath look'd upon my trespasses . . . and sequent death / Is all the grace I beg" (5.1.367–72). Equating earthly judges with divine ones, he expects a sentence of death— mortality as annihilation—and reaffirms the association by imagining that oblivion is the best to be hoped for from this visitation of grace. He sounds rather like Donne in the Holy Sonnet "If Poysonous Mineralls": "That thou remember them, some claime as debt, / I thinke it mercy, if thou wilt forget." As Angelo's brittle pride leads him to despair, so his fragile narcissism leads toward self-obliteration.

Angelo is fooled by the substitution of Mariana's maidenhead for Isabella's, and again by the substitution of Ragozine's head for Claudio's. The Duke is doubtless right that "death's a great disguiser" (4.2.174) and that the head of Barnardine might be thereby mistaken for Claudio's. But that reassurance to the Provost must be a disturbance to the audience: however indirectly, it invokes the *transi* figure of Medieval tomb-sculpture, the stark reminder that in decay all human bodies reveal their horrible sameness. This is the dirty secret that *Measure for Measure* half-reveals in half-concealing it: just as these two women's bodies (even at the moment they are supposedly expressing their most intimate qualities) may be virtually indistinguishable, so are all the rest of us when we fall into the clutches of the omnivorous Angel of Death. Shakespeare links the Ovidian comic commonplace that all women look alike in the dark with the darker preacherly commonplace that all bodies are food for worms. More subtly disturbing is the renewed recognition that, from the perspective of nature or the state, in the functions of biology or politics, indifference makes perfect sense. Any body will do.

While humiliating the transcendent strategies of honor and piety that characterize Angelo and Isabella, the play seems, perversely, to reward and endorse the utter negligence of immortality that characterizes Barnardine. He is a kind of reverse synecdoche, a whole man symbolizing an autonomic nervous system. As Claudio hovers at "dead midnight" on the brink of the death that will make him "immortal," Barnardine is described as sleeping too soundly to be put to death (4.2.61–66) and as "A man that apprehends death no more dreadfully but as a drunken sleep; careless, reckless, and fearless of what's past, present, or to come: insensible of mortality, and desperately mortal" (4.2.140–43).

Barnardine is a representative man in an unattractive disguise; despite superficial differences, he could stand in for almost anyone, as the Duke insists (4.2.169–74). Barnardine aptly represents all of us who wander through this mortal world with an unaccountable complacency, "as a drunken sleep . . . insensible of mortality, and desperately mortal." As long as we have "the liberty of the prison," we remain bizarrely impervious to the death sentence hanging over our heads, even on the occasions when a priest appears to remind us (4.2.142–45; compare Claudio's "restraint / Though all the world's vastidity you had" under Angelo's sentence at 3.1.69).[38]

Barnardine will finally be pardoned because the state can much better tolerate an unregenerate soul than an unregenerating body, but again the Duke feels obliged to obscure the distinction with his rhetoric:

> Sirrah, thou art said to have a stubborn soul
> That apprehends no further than this world,
> And squar'st thy life according. Thou'rt condemn'd;
> But, for those earthly faults, I quit them all,

And pray thee take this mercy to provide
For better times to come.

(5.1.478–83)

Barnardine is spared on earth because there is so little hope for him beyond. Perhaps the same worldly assumption underlies, and therefore undermines, the "resurrection" of Claudio and the pardon of Angelo that follow so quickly. Again, as with Gloucester on Dover Beach, providence seems to be an illusion manipulated by earthly leaders in vague imitation of a myth of grace, to conceal the possibility that human civilization is really only a confused crowd huddled together against an overwhelming and uncaring ocean—that is, an indifferent God indistinguishable from the flux of nature. Matthew Arnold's famous poem attempts to set romantic love on the same beach to take the place of the absent God; but Shakespeare had centuries earlier seen through that ploy, watching the waves make toward the pebbled shore, and our minutes hasten to their end (Sonnet 60).

The Duke's timely performance of a Last Judgment at the gates of his city, rather than the gates of heaven, is a culminating instance of the way *Measure for Measure* parodies pious archetypes in asserting the priority of earthly order. The critics who assert that (for example) "The Duke's ethical attitude is exactly correspondent with Jesus'"[39] fall victim to the same manipulation of pious reflexes by which the Duke controls his citizens. They overlook the fact that the Duke prepares his redemptive intervention by its opposite: this Lord turns judgment over to a bad son who insists on the punitive letter of the law rather than the established principle of mercy. The Duke strategically regresses Vienna from the New Testament to the Old so that he can claim credit, as head of state, for reinventing Christian forgiveness. It may be true, as one Jacobean tract asserts, that "a Prince, that is slow to punish [and] sory, when hee is constrained to be severe . . . doth most resemble the Prince of Princes."[40] Resemblances, however, are not identities—that is the problem with procreative immortality—and this version of redemption serves to defend, not faith or moral purity, but the public procreative order of Vienna. For all its gestures toward divine comedy, *Measure for Measure* generates a tragic and parodic attack on our fundamental hopes for individual survival: tragic in challenging the sufficiency of procreation as an answer to mortality, parodic in mocking the conventional fantasies of an existence above and beyond the bodies that make us slaves to the state and to our biological mortality. If providence and eternal life are nothing more than consoling metaphors, then the human body is a machine-like organism seeking automatically to reproduce itself, and so is the body politic.[41]

Perhaps *Measure for Measure* is a product of the plague year 1603 not only in its emphasis on the replenishment of the population, but also in its Puritanical portrayal of a city abandoned by its benevolent but exasperated Lord to an agency of deadly retribution. Like some reactionary analyses of the AIDS epidemic, the sermons and literature of 1603 predominantly characterize the plague as God's scourge visited on an increasingly immoral nation. At times, the Vienna of *Measure for Measure* must seem to its citizens much as the world seems to those who feel—as Reformation theology led many to feel—that God has mysteriously absconded and left his children in an inscrutable universe, and in the cold hands of Death:

> The Duke is very strangely gone from hence:
> Bore many gentlemen—myself being one—
> In hand, and hope of action: but we do learn
> By those that know the very nerves of state,
> His giving out were of an infinite distance
> From his true-meant design. Upon his place,
> And with full line of his authority,
> Governs Lord Angelo; a man whose blood
> Is very snow-broth; one who never feels
> The wanton stings and motions of the sense;
>
> *   *   *
>
> All hope is gone,
> Unless you have the grace by your fair prayer
> To soften Angelo.
>
> (1.4.50–70)

The resemblance to Prospero's "And my ending is despair / Unless I be reliev'd by prayer" indicates how strongly this speech partakes of more eschatological pleas for forgiveness, for relief from the condemnation common to fallen flesh. Lucio is hardly a Job or a Christ, but in this speech he might as well be asking why He has forsaken us, why He has surrendered us to the dark fallen angel?

Isabella's warning to Angelo about the Last Judgment (2.2.73–79) sounds plausibly like a warning about the promised death of Death after its temporary merciless reign of terror over humankind. Angelo tells Isabella that though Claudio must die under his sentence, "Yet may he live a while; and, it may be, / As long as you or I" (2.4.35–36). At the end of the play, Claudio is out of his manacles, but he is still in the food chain. Nor is this Existential perspective on human freedom anachronistic in reference to earlier seventeenth-century England. A parable proposed as a consolation for bereaved parents carries the same implications: "A Cart full of Prisoners are brought to execution; what skills it which is first, or third, or sixt, or tenth, or sixteenth? All must dye. What gets hee that is delayed till the afternoone, above him that was executed in the morning?"[42]

Let me therefore propose one more imperfect but evocative allegory lurking in a play that has perhaps already been allegorized too often and too ingeniously:[43] The Duke, not simply as *imitatio dei*,[44] but as *imitatio dei absconditi,* Angelo as the Angel of Death, Claudio as Everyman, and Isabella as Faith. In this system, Barnardine may represent the body, the stupid force of heartbeat, survival instinct, physical appetite that is unwilling to die in the condemned Everyman, and is (here) finally spared. Lucio, finally, embodies doubt, baffling every path to immortality in mocking Isabella's pious virginity, the Duke's reputation, and the entire procreative process. The state can order that nagging cynical voice to be pressed to death, whipped, hanged, and married to shame, but it cannot be silenced. Even in the triumphant final scene, it persists, ruining any hopes—the Duke's, Shakespeare's, ours—that the tragic facts of life can be dispelled (not just disguised) by the warm glow and consoling figurations of comedy. If life goes on, then so does death. "This news is old enough, yet it is every day's news" (3.2.223–24).

NOTES

1. For example, Paul Hammond's "The Argument of *Measure for Measure,"* *English Literary Renaissance,* 16 (1986): 496–519, resists its own title by asserting that there is finally no moral argument discernible in the play.

2. Freud, "Three Essays on the Theory of Sexuality," *Complete Psychological Works,* Standard ed., trans. James Strachey (London: Hogarth Press), VII, 149–50.

3. See for example Phillip Stubbes, *The Anatomie of Abuses* (London, 1583), sig. H4^r.

4. 3.2.168; all references to *Measure for Measure* are based on the Arden edition, ed. J. W. Lever (London: Methuen, 1965).

5. Stubbes, sigs. G8^v-H8^r. Like Duke Vincentio, Stubbes concludes, "let all men that have put away their honest wyves be forced to take them again, and abandon all whores, or els to taste of the law." Jacques Rossiaud, *Medieval Prostitution,* trans. Lydia G. Cochrane (New York: Basil Blackwell, 1988), 86–103,

suggests that some medieval Europeans felt obliged to procreate in order "to save both city and Christendom before they were overwhelmed" by the devastations of war and plague, and that this obligation led to an increasing tolerance of brothels and a decreasing valuation of pious celibacy. These attitudes—reflected in Guillaume Saignet's fifteenth-century allegory that showed Nature under attack "by two frightful harpies, Pestilence and War, accompanied by a maiden of virtuous appearance but shameful behavior, Chastity"—offer an enlightening context for *Measure for Measure*. Duke Vincentio appears to share Saignet's belief that "Marriage is a good thing, for it permits the multiplication of men at the same time as it avoids fornication."

6. Thomas Tuke, *A Discourse of Death, Bodily, Ghostly, And Eternall* (London, 1613), 13.

7. Compare an observation in a Jacobean sermon by Thomas Adams: "There is law against coiners; and it is made treason justly, to stamp the king's figure in forbidden metals. But what is metal to a man, the image of God?"; *The Sermons of Thomas Adams, The Shakespeare of Puritan Theologians,* ed. John Brown (Cambridge, 1909). Brown's subtitle proves only to mean that Adams was eloquent, but I have found so many close echoes of Shakespearean rhetoric throughout the sermons that I strongly suspect Adams was an avid playgoer, despite his Puritan theology.

8. Carolyn E. Brown, "Erotic Religious Flagellation and Shakespeare's *Measure for Measure*," *English Literary Renaissance,* 16 (1986): 139–65.

9. Janet Adelman, *Suffocating Mothers* (New York: Routledge, 1992), 87, reads this ominous locution as marking the play's mistrust of sexuality and maternal origins. Here as elsewhere, I would amend her argument by reading this mistrust as part of a general mistrust of mortal bodies, linked in this instance by the doctrine that original sin is transmitted as the moment of conception. Sir Thomas Browne's warning about the inadequacies of earthly love seems painfully germane: "Thus I perceive a man may be buried alive, and behold his grave in his owne issue" (160).

10. Michel Foucault, *The History of Sexuality,* trans. Robert Hurley (New York: Pantheon, 1978), I, 144. Foucault maintains that

> In the eighteenth century, sex became a "police" matter—in the full and strict sense given the term at the time: not the repression of disorder, but an ordered maximization of collective and individual forces . . . One of the great innovations in the techniques of power in the eighteenth century was the emergence of "population" as an economic and political problem: population as wealth, population as manpower or labor capacity. . . . At the heart of this economic and political problem of population was sex: it was necessary to analyze the birthrate, the age of marriage, the legitimate and illegitimate births, the precocity and frequency of sexual relations, the ways of making them fertile or sterile, the effects of unmarried life or of the prohibitions . . . this was the first time that a society has affirmed, in a constant way, that its future and its fortune were tied . . . to the manner in which each individual made use of his sex. (I, 25–26).

Surely this description fits the governmental work that propels *Measure for Measure*. Perhaps Shakespeare is once again being prescient—or perhaps Foucault is once again exaggerating the disjunctions in recent human history. On "bio-power" as an eighteenth-century invention, see I, 138–45; on its strained relation to the death-penalty—again anticipated by *Measure for Measure*—see I, 138.

11. Nicholas Guy, *Pieties Pillar* (London, 1626), attributes this idea to "Helvetian Hereticks."

12. Thomas Pierce, *Death Consider'd as a Door to a Life of Glory* (London,

1690), 13, scoffs at this consolation as "all the Resurrection those Hereticks would allow."

13. Gnosticism provides some intriguing parallels to this darker, blasphemous side of *Measure for Measure*. The Gnostics commonly protested that the individual spirit was trapped in a degradingly physical universe controlled by a demiurge claiming to be the sole and benevolent deity, and their strategies for defying his mortal limitations followed the ascetic and libertine extremes. See Hans Jonas, *The Gnostic Religion*.

14. Freud, "On Hysteria," II, 305.

15. Philip C. McGuire, *Speechless Dialect: Shakespeare's Open Silences* (Los Angeles: University of California Press, 1985), 71. Victoria Hayne, in her forthcoming U.C.L.A. dissertation, will argue against this perspective by demonstrating that the reluctant grooms are merely forced to honor the marital commitments they have already made by word or deed.

16. Glare Gittings, *Death, Burial and the Individual in Early Modern England* (London: Croom Helm, 1984), 175.

17. Robert N. Watson, *Shakespeare and the Hazards of Ambition* (Cambridge: Harvard University Press, 1984), passim. Becker, 118, associates a man's desire "to bypass the woman and the species role of his own body" with a determination "to procreate himself spiritually through a linkage with gifted young men, to create them in his own image," rather than "to be used as an instrument of procreation in the interests of the race."

18. The argument that Angelo's "virtues" (a word with seminal implications) must go forth in "issues" (1.1.27–43) echoes the commonplace arguments for procreation in Shakespeare's sonnets and in fact throughout Renaissance literature, exhortations not to waste nature's finest models by failing to reproduce them in a new generation. In the same passage, the Duke talks about Angelo's life story as if it were a stable and legible text to be read, and such writing (again with pun on "character") becomes another metaphor for procreation at 1.2.144. This wordplay further interweaves the procreative and artistic aspects of the Duke's immortality-strategy—the same pair of projects linked so persistently in Jonson's epitaph and in Shakespeare's sonnets. Yet as those sonnets demonstrate, Shakespeare remains painfully aware that these modes of immortality are merely figurative and highly vulnerable; see Gillian M. Kendall, "Shakespeare's Romances and the Quest for Secular Immortality," Diss. Harvard University, 1986, which insightfully explores Shakespeare's highly equivocal endorsement of these answers to death.

19. Gittings, 175, describes the role-based funeral practices of the period, yet notes that "This view of society, in which no one was indispensable and everyone could simply be replaced by another person of similar rank, was greatly at odds with the growing feeling of individualism, with its emphasis on personal uniqueness."

20. On the other hand, it might have been awkward for Shakespeare to suggest that James' rather indirect accession resembled Angelo's.

21. Jonathan Goldberg argues that the paternal metaphor permeates James' assertions of authority; see "The Politics of Patriarchy," in *Rewriting the Renaissance: The Discourses of Sexual Difference in Early Modern Europe*, ed. Margaret Ferguson, Maureen Quilligan, and Nancy Vickers (Chicago: University of Chicago Press, 1986), 3–32.

22. The excellent BBC-TV "Shakespeare Plays" production emphasizes this

trait when the Duke triumphantly stages himself to the people's eyes in the final scene.

23. Gless, 161–62, compares the Duke's complaints about slander with those of King James; others, notably Josephine Bennett, *"Measure for Measure" as Royal Entertainment* (New York: Columbia University Press, 1966), pursue the connection more extensively. However, Richard Levin, *New Readings vs. Old Plays* (Chicago, University of Chicago Press, 1979), 167–93, forcefully refutes this instance of "occasionalist" interpretation. Critics are now likely to depict the play as allegorically attacking James' leadership, not endorsing it. My contention, comparably, is that the play can be read as allegorical blasphemy no less forcefully or coherently than as a positive Christian allegory. Perhaps the tragicomic mixture allows *Measure for Measure* to straddle questions of tyranny and theodicy more easily. In any case, these arguments and ambiguities are more likely to verify the notion of Shakespeare's elusiveness than to provide any defensible paraphrases of the play as political or theological assertion.

24. Lewes Bayly, *The Practise of Pietie* (London, 1613), Epistle Dedicatory, sig. A2ʳ.

25. Brown, "Erotic Religious Flagellation," 151, summarizing an observation several critics have made, comments that the consolations the disguised Duke offers are "conspicuously devoid of the promise of a Christian afterlife." Lever, 87, characterizes the Duke's argument as "essentially materialist." Julia Reinhard Lupton, "Afterlives of the Saints," *Exemplaria* (Fall, 1990): 379, notes perceptively "the play's systematic exclusion of references to heaven and resurrection."

26. This Marxist/Machiavellian perspective on religion is most obvious in the writings of the radical Reformers, though it insinuated humanist training, and traces of it may be found in canonical figures such as Marlowe, Lyly, Montaigne, and Hobbes, as well as in Mary Gunter.

27. Indeed, the use of Ragozine invites us to ask a question that our culture, abetted by its newscasts, fiercely resists: Is death by disease any less arbitrary or important than death by accident or execution?

28. On the body as the soul's prison, see for example Zacharie Boyd, *The Last Battle of the Soul in Death* (1629; Reprint, Glasgow, 1831), 396, 413; and William Harrison, *Deaths Advantage* (London, 1602), 33, on death as escaping "from a prison, a place of libertie." On hell as the next prison, see *Death Repeal'd By a Thankfull Memoriall* (Oxford, 1638), 127, 145.

29. Roland M. Frye, *Shakespeare and Christian Doctrine* (Princeton: Princeton University Press, 1963), 291–92, records this censorship.

30. Irene Dash, *Wooing, Wedding, and Power: Women in Shakespeare's Plays* (New York: Columbia University Pres, 1981), 251. Adelman, 94, interprets Angelo's line as an effort to force Isabella back into "the taint of sexuality" that she "had hoped to escape by putting on the livery of a nun"; my suggestion is that Isabella's flight from the limitations of a female identity based in sexuality is only part of a more general flight from the limitations of a human identity based in reproductive biology.

31. Her name also matches that of a harried virgin whose mournful struggle against a series of wooers in *Orlando Furioso,* culminating in a mistaken beheading, "parodies the chastity sacred to the female saint's life"; see Lupton, 377.

32. The discussion of the Virgin Mary in Donne's *Sermons,* VI, 180, suggests how threatening Lucio's question might be: "It is not enough for a virgin to bee a virgin in her owne knowledge . . . She must appeare . . . as they that see her,

may not question, nor dispute, whether she be a maid or no." Gless, 103, notes the echo by which Lucio's "salutation mocks Catholic devotion to the Blessed Virgin," but overlooks the further resonances of the Annunciation, which make it much harder to isolate the blasphemy safely as simple antimonasticism in the mouth of a profane scoundrel. Virtually the entire Annunciation text, which the Book of Common Prayer takes directly from Luke, offers suggestive parallels to Isabella's experience, from the initial novitiate's unease at Lucio's apparently mocking greeting, and embarrassment at the sexual implications of his message, to the submission to shadowy powers that will make her the prospective mother of her Lord's son:

> And the Angel went in unto her, & said, Haile . . . And when she saw *him,* she was troubled at his saying, & thoght what maner of saltacion that shulde be. [Her child] shalbe greate, & shalbe called the Sonne of the moste High. . . . Then said Marie unto the Angel, How shal this be, seing I know no man? And the Angel answered, and said unto her, The holie Gost shal come upon thee, & the power of the moste High shal overshadowe thee.
> (Luke 1:28–35, Geneva Bible)

An eerie futurist echo of Shakespeare's twist on the Annunciation story occurs in Margaret Atwood's novel *The Handmaid's Tale* (New York: Random House, 1985), in which the few women still fertile are dressed in red nuns' habits and forced to bear the children of the patriarchs in order to perpetuate the society.

33. Lupton, 398, n. 9, adduces this precedent, and also mentions the resemblance between Lucio's name and Luke's. Her very intriguing study of the hagiographic traditions reveals that Isabella's pursuit of a saintly martyrdom is "consistently perverted by the sexual dynamics of a contemporary Vienna," and that "Angelo's langauge reduced *agape* to *eros* by rewriting Christian charity as the granting of sexual favors and by deflating the holy sexuality of ancient martyrdom to the boiling corruption of modern Vienna" (80). This argument seems clearly synergistic with my own, though I am more concerned with the fall from transcendence into biology than with the specific fall from saintliness into sin.

34. See, for example, Martin Fotherby, *Atheomastix,* 14, 150–51, construing even the most stable forms of atheism as madness. For a modern perspective on this tendency, see G. E. Aylmer, "Unbelief in Seventeenth-Century England," in *Puritans and Revolutionaries,* ed. Donald Pennington and Keith Thomas (Oxford: Clarendon Press, 1978), 33–34.

35. The willingness to die for these things—all linked in Renaissance notions of immortality—in war, duel, or suicide is no less rational a response to mortal transience than our modern determination to delay death briefly by health-care; but if the denial of death is indeed fundamental to the psychic viability of a society, we will necessarily again diagnose as a kind of insanity any conflicting version. Philippe Aries, *The Hour of Our Death,* trans. Helen Weaver (New York: Random House, 1981), 215, discusses "the difficulty in separating the idea of supernatural survival from the idea of fame acquired during earthly life. . . . After the sixteenth century, rational and scientific thought, like Protestant and Catholic religious reform, tried to dissociate the two forms of survival," but "did not immediately succeed." Between the Counter-Reformation defense of "the ancient communication across the barrier of death," and the way, "in Puritanism, worldly success remained attached to the idea of predestination," the neat distinction between worldly deeds and otherworldly destiny would have been under attack from all sides.

36. See 3.2.100–108. This resistance—predictable in a narcissistic age, according to Becker's theory—had parallels across Renaissance culture. See Browne, "Letter to a Friend," 402, praising Robert Loveday for his determination to leave "no Earnest behind him for Corruption or Aftergrave, having small content in that common satisfaction to survive or live in another, but amply satisfied that his Disease should dye with himself. . . ." Donald R. Howard, "Renaissance World-Alienation," in *The Darker Vision of the Renaissance,* ed. Robert S. Kinsman (Berkeley: University of California Press, 1974), 59–60, discusses the Cathar belief (echoing Gnosticism) that "the worst of crimes was procreation, because it imprisoned another good soul in another evil body."

37. Watson argues that Coriolanus's effort to extricate himself from the mortal flesh he shares with his fellow Romans obliges him to define his "coining" as a mechanical rather than a procreative process; see 145–61, 169–70, 178, 183, 188.

38. The fact that, until Angelo's reign, Vienna lacked "undoubtful proof" confirming Barnardine's death-sentence (4.2.136–37) may reflect the fact that, until Angelo fell, it lacked confirmation that all men are merely mortal flesh.

39. G. Wilson Knight, *The Wheel of Fire,* 5th Edition (Cleveland: World Press, 1964), 82. Huston Diehl, "To Put us in Remembrance," in *Homo, Memento Finis, Early Drama, Art and Music Monograph Series 6,* ed. David Bevington (Kalamazoo, MI: Medieval Institute, 1985), 192–95, compares the Duke's return to the Last Judgment. Pamela Sheingorge and David Bevington, "Alle This Was Token Domysday," in the same volume, offers the same comparison (122).

40. Tuke, 13.

41. This understanding does to individual human bodies what Averroes did to individual human minds, marking them as brief deformations of a unitary substance to which they will all eventually return. It matches a belief attributed to the radical wing of the Reformation that "the Divin essence in those persons shall be reduced into God again, but the persons shall be annihilated, for the soul is mortall and the body shall never rise frim the dead, but was annihilated; the world shall endure by way of generation from time to time without end"; Thomas Edwards, *Gangraena,* 2nd ed. (London, 1646), I, 219; quoted by Norman T. Burns, *Christian Mortalism from Tyndale to Milton* (Cambridge: Harvard University Press, 1972), 79.

42. I. C., *A Handkercher for Parents Wet Eyes* (London, 1630), 21. John Donne, *Devotions,* ed. Anthony Raspa (New York: Oxford University Press, 1988), 82, attempts to convert this Existential metaphor back into conventional terms of justice, and does so in a manner highly reminiscent of *Measure for Measure,* by discussing a fateful "*Bell* in a *Monastery*":

> If these *Bells* that warn to a *Funerall* now, were appropriated to none, may not I, by the houre of the *funerall,* supply? How many men that stand at an *execution,* if they would aske, for what dies that Man, should heare their owne faults condemned, and see themselves executed, by *Atturney*?

43. Lever, 47, cites the various Christian allegories that have been applied. Gless, 4–5, also comments on the oversupply of "personification allegory" concerning *Measure for Measure*; then, 53–60, offers a different way of allegorizing the play. On 247–50, Gless discusses the possibility of identifying the Duke with the Christian God. See also Knight, 74; Battenhouse, 1029–59; and Robert G. Hunter, *Shakespeare and the Comedy of Forgiveness* (New York: Columbia University Press, 1965), pp. 204–26.

44. Louise Schleiner, "Providential Improvisation in *Measure for Measure,*" *PMLA,* 97 (1982), 227–36, characterizes the Duke's actions as an *imitatio dei.*

Part III
The Limits to Power

Flout 'em and Scout 'em and Scout 'em and Flout 'em: Prospero's Power and Punishments in *The Tempest*

Kathryn Barbour

At Hatfield House there is a portrait of Queen Elizabeth I known as the Rainbow portrait. An idealized version of the Queen (she was nearly seventy when it was painted), the portrait has features that declare the body of the Queen to be an important site for the intersection of sexuality, chastity, wealth, and political power.[1] Political power is suggested by the rainbow—the traditional symbol of peace—as well as the motto: "No sine sole iris [No rainbow without the sun]." Frances Yates, in her "Allegorical Portraits of Queen Elizabeth I at Hatfield House," observes: "Every detail in this picture is significant".[2] The richness of the garments suggests the wealth of Elizabeth and her realm, as do the pearls that ornament her headpiece, wrists, and neck. The pearls also draw attention to both Elizabeth's chastity and her sexuality: While the pearls serve as traditional symbols of chastity, a long single strand encircles her neck, drapes her bosom, and points to her sexual parts, which are simultaneously covered by the cloak she wears over her shoulder. The amber-colored cloak is covered with eyes and ears. Referring to the *Iconologia* of Cesare Ripa, Yates argues that the "the eyes, ears, and mouths which are depicted all over the queen's cloak symbolize her Fame which is flying rapidly through the world, spoken of by many mouths, seen and heard by many eyes and ears".[3] Roy Strong agrees that the cloak "is probably intended for Fame", but he notes that "Strictly speaking there should also be mouths".[4] Yet the cloak in this portrait may also be read as a visible reminder that like the sun (with which Elizabeth is also associated in the portrait) a monarch's eyes and ears are everywhere: "She saw and she heard everything that happened in her kingdom."[5] As Michel Foucault argues, "The perfect disciplinary apparatus would make it possible for a single gaze to see everything constantly"[6], but as this is impossible, an adept monarch relies on a network of organized surveillance to maintain control over his or her subjects.

It is clear from an examination of this and other portraits of Elizabeth that a fundamental tension exists in the idea/ideal of the monarch. The monarch must be at once regarded as invulnerable and vulnerable, both ideal and real, universal and particular. It is this tension between the metaphorical and the physical aspects of bodies—the body of the monarch as well as the bodies of his or her subjects—that underlies Prospero's experiments in power and punishment in *The Tempest*. While not a monarch in Milan, since he controls only a dukedom, Prospero's conquest of the island gives him the opportunity to assume that role. In his interactions with his "subjects" and those upon whom he seeks revenge, everything possible is done to deny the physical and therefore fragile and mortal nature of the body of the monarch. Everything possible is done to remind the "body politic" of the actual, temporal existence of the bodies of the subjects. The closer in blood and station to the position of the monarch, the less likely is the imposition of physical punishment. The harshest and most physical punishments are imposed on those furthest in class and status from the monarch—vagrants, drunkards, and the dispossessed.

The reciprocal gaze, the gaze of the people upon the monarch as the monarch oversees the body politic, is an important aspect of the monarch's domination. As Leonard Tennenhouse reminds us:

> The Renaissance monarch understood himself or herself as deriving power from being the object of the public gaze. If not always in full view of his court, she or he was nonetheless visible in the institutions of state, in the church, at the courts of law, on the coin of the realm, or upon its scaffold.[7]

Rulers who fail to recognize the importance of their visible presence in person and in image run the risk of fading from the public eye.

Another significant aspect of monarchical power in the Renaissance was explained by Niccolò Machiavelli in his advice to those princes who would act towards their friends and subjects as if they lived in an ideal state:

> How we live is so far removed from how we ought to live, that he who abandons what is done for what ought to be done, will rather learn to

The Rainbow Portrait of Queen Elizabeth I, by permission of Hatfield House, Jeremy Whitaker, photographer.

bring about his own ruin than his preservation. A man who wishes to
make a profession of goodness in everything must necessarily come to
grief among so many who are not good. Therefore it is necessary for
a prince, who wishes to maintain himself, to learn how not to be good,
and to use this knowledge and not use it, according to the necessity of
the case.[8]

The Tempest is one of several plays that deal with the interplay
between the visibility of a ruler, his desire to be (or perhaps to be
perceived to be) a benevolent ruler, his ability to retain power, and
the means by which that power can be achieved and maintained.

Certainly, *The Tempest* is a play that is fundamentally concerned
with power. Much recent criticism has focused on the discourses
of colonialism and issues of expansion and exploitation.[9] Francis
Barker and Peter Hulme point out that Prospero's "denial of dispossession with retrospective justification for it, is the characteristic trope by which European colonial regimes articulated their
authority over land to which they could have no conceivable legitimate claim".[10] Paul Brown suggests that "colonialist discourse
voices a demand both for order and disorder, producing a disrup-
tive other in order to assert the superiority of the colonizer."[11] The
unending struggle for power that leads to victory over the other is
at once necessary and impossible: "The threat must be present to
validate colonialist discourse."[12] Closure becomes impossible.[13] Yet
discussions of the play that concentrate on issues of colonialism
often ignore other questions of power in the play, particularly those
that focus on gender. The white female body, for example, functions as a site for power struggles in the play. And both the bodies
of Claribel and Miranda are colonies or plantations to be exploited
by the men in the play: "I had peopled else / This isle with Calibans" (1.2.350–51).[14]

Other critics have concentrated on political power and the discourses of treason. According to Curt Breight, "the discourse of
treason is *central* to a thirty-year period of English culture beginning in the early 1580s"[15] and Prospero's project in *The Tempest*
is that of control over and revenge upon traitors.[16] Of course, Prospero plays a double game with his notion of treason. When he
practices his spells and manipulations on the courtiers, particularly
on the King of Naples and his son Ferdinand, his actions against
them can be seen as treasonous. Furthermore, his actions as monarch on the island realm are also suspect—his domination having
been gained by the dispossession and subjection of the previous
sovereign.

Still, it is also possible to read *The Tempest* as a play about the limits of power. Prospero's need for control and revenge results from his earlier failures. He had fallen from power in Milan because he succumbed to two basic impulses: a naive desire to trust his subjects, his brother, and others around him; and his desire for solitude. He was either ignorant of the importance of the monarch's gaze or he chose to disregard it:

> I thus neglecting worldly ends, all dedicated
> To closeness and the bettering of my mind
> With that which, but by being so retired,
> O'er-priz'd all popular rate, in my false brother
> Awak'd an evil nature . . .
>   . . . me (poor man) my library
> Was dukedom large enough: of temporal royalties
> He thinks me now incapable . . .
>
>   (1.2.89–111)

As Duke of Milan, Prospero committed two of the greatest monarchical blunders: He absented himself from the public gaze, and failed to observe or attend to the plotting of those around him. This combination of invisibility and blindness undermined his authority, while the outward signs and practices of authority bolstered the ambitions of his brother:

> Being once perfected how to grant suits,
> How to deny them, who t'advance, and who
> To trash for over-topping, new-created
> The creatures that were mine, I say, or changed 'em,
> Or else new-formed 'em; having both the key,
> Of officer and office, set all hearts i' th' state
> To what tune pleased his ear. . . .
>
>   (1.2.79–85)

Antonio, "executing th' outward face of royalty" (1.2.104), felt it prudent to remove Prospero and Miranda altogether from the public eye. The two are hustled away "one midnight . . . i' th' dead of darkness" (1.2.128–30), when they can successfully be hidden from the prying eyes of the people, where they can neither see nor be seen, hear nor be heard. Antonio wants nothing to distract from the gaze he has redirected to himself.

In *The Tempest,* the island functions as a kind of laboratory for Prospero, a place where he can experiment with a variety of tactics for the control of his subjects. On his arrival, there were only two inhabitants on the island: Ariel, imprisoned in the cloven pine, and Caliban. By Prospero's lights, Sycorax having died, both are masterless—and Prospero deals with these 'vagrants' as some attempted to deal with the vagabonds of the mid-sixteenth century: He seeks to amend them through work and education. Even in a kingdom with only two subjects, however, Prospero's methods are significantly unsuccessful, as the houses of correction in Elizabethan towns upon which those techniques may have been modeled were unsuccessful.[17] Even Ariel's service is maintained only by constant threats and promises. Prospero finds it necessary to shift his techniques from an unfocused and allegedly humane display of power to more clearly defined punishments. When Ariel demands his liberty, Prospero reminds him both of the servant's debt and the master's power:

> . . . Thou best know'st
> What torment I did find thee in: thy groans
> Did make wolves howl and penetrate the breasts
> Of ever-angry bears. It was a torment
> To lay upon the damned, which Sycorax
> Could not again undo. It was mine art,
> When I arrived and heard thee, that made gape
> The pine, and let thee out . . .
> If thou more murmur'st, I will rend an oak
> And peg thee in his knotty entrails till
> Thou hast howl'd away twelve winters.
>
> (1.2.285–96)

Ariel is reminded of Prospero's past and present power, which can bind as easily as free, punish as easily as reward. And while Prospero does promise to discharge Ariel after two days, it is the reminder of pain that causes the spirit to ask his master's pardon.

With Caliban, Prospero's largesse had gone further, and so had his expectation of indebtedness. Having taken Caliban into his cell, and having taught him to speak, Prospero clearly expects gratitude and compliance in return. The depth of Prospero's outrage at Caliban's lack of "gratitude" is evidenced by the harshness of his tactics for controlling Caliban's behavior:

> For this, be sure, to-night thou shalt have cramps,
> Side stitches that shall pen thy breath up; urchins
> Shall, for that vast of night that they may work,

All exercise on thee; thou shalt be pinched
As thick as honeycomb, each pinch more stinging
Than bees that made 'em.

(1.2.325–30)

Prospero's control over Caliban is achieved by physical punishment—pinches,[18] bites and cramps, forced imprisonment (reminiscent of Sycorax's imprisonment of Ariel), as well as psychological
torment: Prospero's spirits pitch Caliban in the mire, lead him out
of his way in the dark, mow and chatter at him in the shape of
apes, and "sometimes [he is] all wound with Adders, who with
cloven tongues / do hiss [him] into madness" (2.2.11–13). They are
constantly reminding him of his subjection: "For every trifle are
they set upon me" (2.2.8).

In dealing with Ariel and Caliban, Prospero practices the arts of
surveillance and discipline on those who act as servants to him—
though Ariel is, perhaps, more of a gentleman-of-the-chamber, a
favorite who should be honored by service, while Caliban functions
as a menial. With the arrival of the King of Naples's ship, however,
Prospero has a clear opportunity to examine the results of inflicting
certain types of discipline and punishment on very different classes
of individuals—some of whom match or exceed him in rank. Prospero's punishments are clearly designed to correspond to the class
of the target of the punishment.[19]

Prospero, for example, threatens Ferdinand, who has identified
himself as King of Naples, with imprisonment:

I'll manacle thy neck and feet together;
Sea water shalt thou drink; thy food shall be
The fresh-brook mussels, withered roots, and husks
Wherein the acorn cradled. Follow!

(1.2.461–65)

In the case of Ferdinand, Prospero merely *threatens* physical
abuse, choosing instead to inflict a fine-tuned psychological manipulation. While his actions against Ferdinand are preemptive, for
Ferdinand has done Prospero no harm,[20] Prospero has learned that
discipline is most effective when administered before punishment
becomes necessary. The tasks he assigns to Ferdinand are, significantly, unsuitable to his class, designed to be humiliating. He is
treated as a servant, and characterizes his labor as "baseness" and
"dishonour." Ferdinand, while identifying himself with the monarchical *role*, is made sharply aware of his physical body, a body
identical in its physicality to those of his social inferiors. This may

function as an object lesson for the prince—perhaps he won't make Prospero's mistakes.

For the other aristocratic castaways, too, Prospero uses tactics that bypass bodily discomfort for mental suffering and humiliation, avoiding the physical marking that characterizes the punishments of those of inferior class. Alonso's primary pain is that of loss, especially the loss of his son—and with that loss the chance for continuation of the male line in Naples. The Renaissance preoccupation with the establishment of dynasties makes this a bitter loss indeed. Alonso also suffers from the guilt of the awareness that it was his collaboration in the usurpation of Prospero's power that was the cause of the shipwreck, and therefore his son's death. Like Antonio and Sebastian, Alonso is tormented by the Harpy, and all together are imprisoned by Prospero's charms. Antonio and Sebastian suffer, too, the humiliation of exposure as unsuccessful fratricides. All three are exposed as impotent—they are powerless against the Harpy, against the sleep charms, against the "inward pinches" of remorse. For men accustomed to command, this must be the greatest humiliation—to be exposed as unable to control even their own minds and bodies. If the mark of princely power is the ability to control the bodies of *others,* this must be an especially severe punishment. Like Ferdinand, they are made distinctly aware of their own secondary status. (The lesson taught, that of the short-lived nature of control, is one that Prospero himself fails to learn, even while he attempts to teach it to others.) Still, it would be dangerous for Prospero to inflict physical damage on the bodies of the aristocratic characters. Twice the audience is told that the royal party has escaped the wreck without a scratch: "Not a hair perish'd; / on their sustaining garments not a blemish, but fresher than before" (1.2.217–19). Damage to the physical bodies of those closest in blood to the monarch reminds the body politic of the fragility of the monarch's own physical body. Deposed once by treason, Prospero avoids displays and punishments that recall the physical vulnerability of the monarch—and of those like him.

Stephano and Trinculo, like Caliban, are subject to more direct and physical torment. Ariel reports their punishment for their treasonous intentions:

> . . . So I charmed their ears,
> That calf-like they my lowing followed through
> Toothed briers, sharp furzes, pricking goss, and thorns,
> Which ent'red their frail shins. At last I left them

I' th' filthy-mantled pool beyond your cell,
There dancing up to th' chins, that the foul lake
O'erstunk their feet.

(4.1.178–84)

Their crimes, so similar to those of Antonio and Sebastian, receive
punishment that is much more physical and severe. Like Caliban's
punishments, the punishments of the low characters in the play—
being chained, branded, driven by whips, even enslaved—recall
the punishments enacted against vagrants in the 1500s: "Branding
and ear-boring were statutory punishments from the late four-
teenth century . . . Further forms of corporal punition included
hair-polling, the pillory, the ducking stool, ear cropping, and hanging".[21] There is an extremely clear relationship in the play between
the social class of the offender and the type of punishment inflicted
upon him. All of the physical punishment is suffered by the servants of the wealthy or the masterless men: Trinculo, Stephano,
Caliban, Ariel. The highborn characters are never touched, are
unmarked, but inflicted instead with mental punishments and
charmed confinement. As once Antonio and his coconspirators
balked at outright murder—"They durst not . . . set a mark so
bloody on the business"—so Prospero recoils from the use of physical punishment on the aristocratic body: "Not a hair perish'd; /
On their sustaining garments not a blemish, / But fresher than
before" (1.2.217–19).

The mildest treatment of all of Prospero's subjects is reserved
for Miranda. While her behavior is certainly controlled by her
father, that control has been achieved by a lifetime of manipulation,
and all that is necessary for coercion now is a sharp word or a
sleep spell (Miranda's enchanted sleep may suggest Prospero's interest in suppressing her sexuality). And even Miranda proves to
be a recalcitrant subject. This is at least suggested by his insistence
that she "Obey, and be attentive" (1.1.38), and confirmed in her
conversations with Ferdinand: "But I prattle something too wildly,
and my father's precepts I therein do forget" (2.3.56–58).

Significantly, the most important site of struggle for power is the
body of Miranda. Miranda's body can be read, like the body of
Elizabeth, as a locus of wealth, power, sexuality, and lineage—and
one that is only marginally under her father's control. Because she
is his only heir, Miranda's body is the only hope for the continuation of Prospero's line. It becomes, therefore, critically important
for him to control access to her body—and it is to this end that
he employs his experiments with power. Caliban's punishments

began when he attempted to invade this location of Prospero's potential power. For Prospero's grandchildren to be "little Calibans" could not be tolerated—and his vigilance prevented it. He is equally watchful over Ferdinand. When he first resists Prospero's control, the young man is charmed and then sexually disarmed: "For I can here disarm thee with this stick, / And make thy weapon drop" (1.2.473–74). Next, Prospero regresses Ferdinand to a presexual stage: "Thy nerves are in their infancy again / And have no vigour in them" (1.2.485–86). Later, Prospero follows Miranda when she meets Ferdinand. He monitors their conversation, and finding Ferdinand a worthy father for Miranda's children, resolves to bestow Miranda, as a gift, upon a fellow prince. He maintains control, however, over the consummation of the union, and does so, characteristically, with a combination of threats:

> . . . But
> If thou dost break her virgin-knot before
> All sanctimonious ceremonies may
> With full and holy rite be minister'd,
> No sweet aspersion shall the heavens let fall
> To make this contract grow, but barren hate,
> Sour-eyed disdain, and discord shall bestrew
> The union of your bed so loathly
> That you shall hate it both.
>
> (4.1.14–22)

Prospero's insistence on the postponement of the consummation of their relationship is more than the typical paternal admonition. Miranda's marriage into the house of Naples, not merely her physical union with its heir, is absolutely necessary for Prospero's project. And the legitimacy of children—even children of royal parentage—was not always unquestioned in the period.

Ferdinand's response that opportunity and desire "shall never melt / Mine honor into lust" shows how effectively Prospero has transformed Ferdinand, in Foucault's terms, into a docile body.[22] Prospero has mastered Ferdinand, who will serve to father Prospero's issue, and fortify Prospero's political position in Milan, and all without lust—or at least without the outward expression of lust.

Prospero broadcasts his ability to see and hear all of the struggles for control that have taken place on the island to Ariel and the audience:

> . . . My high charms work,
> And these, mine enemies, are all knit up

In their distractions: they are now in my pow'r;
And in these fits I leave them . . .

(3.3.88–92)

While Ariel has been Prospero's eyes and ears—the chief actor in Prospero's machinery of surveillance—it is Prospero who runs the show, and while the pains and punishments he inflicts on his island subjects are in the realm of fancy, they are all reflections of the real tactics a Duke of Milan might employ: In Milan, traitors may be confined indefinitely, disloyal servants tortured, pretenders manacled, heirs murdered. The ruler has power over life and death not in dream, but in reality.[23]

The apparatus of power on the island has been magic, worked through the (coerced) figure of Ariel. Upon his return to Naples, Prospero will need to establish some kind of political network to enforce his will. While his forgiveness of Antonio's crimes without any evidence of repentance on Antonio's part might suggest a bit of backsliding to a more naive position, it can also be seen as politically expedient—any punishment that recognized Antonio's lack of repentance would acknowledge the limits of Prospero's power and refocus the gaze on Antonio's subversive nature. The gaze must be diverted away from Antonio.

Of course, Prospero's experimentation with power and punishment has only been partially successful. Indeed, he has demonstrated his ability to gather ocular and aural evidence and to use that evidence to discipline his subjects. He has strengthened his dukedom by manipulating an alliance with neighboring Naples. He has come dangerously close to—perhaps even committed—treasonous behavior himself. Conceivably the offer of the body of Miranda to the son of his brother's accomplice compensates for this transgression. (Why *has* Claribel been granted to Tunis?) He will return to Milan accepting the reality that he must be the object of the public gaze, capable of imposing a range of punishments on a diverse class of subjects. Still, even in the controlled setting of the island, the results have been mixed. Sebastian shows no signs of repentance. Antonio's silence can hardly be read as anything but subversive. Caliban remains, at least according to Prospero, incapable of change: "A devil, a born devil, on whose nature / Nurture can never stick; on whom my pains, / Humanely taken, all, all lost, quite lost; / And as with age his body uglier grows, / So his mind cankers" (4.1.188–92). There is no indication in the remarks of Stephano or Trinculo that either has been improved by the lashings by briers and furzes, or the cramps and the pinches they have endured and as William Carroll notes, "the failure of punitive marking—ear-boring, inscribed letters, lashings—as a means of social control was substantial, if not total. As such, this failure replicates the subversion of semiotic intention demonstrated in state attempts to manage other punitive spectacles, especially that of public execution".[24] Even Miranda's compliance is not complete. No sooner had she recognized an object of her desire than she disobeyed her father's commands—and recognized it: "O my father, / I have broke your hest to say so" (3.i.36–37). Prospero's insistence that he had planned it all along can hardly be sufficient recompense for her transgression.

The tightrope walked by the monarch remains precariously stretched between the physical and the metaphorical. Perhaps it is only prudent that for Prospero "every third thought shall be my grave" (5.1.312). It must have been true for Elizabeth and her successor James; the lesson of the frailty of the human body of the monarch must have been thoroughly learned with the deaths of their own mothers—one in an attempt to secure the male line, the other to secure the political security of the monarch in power. In the Rainbow portrait, with its lavish rendition of the power of the monarch, Elizabeth stands against a background of almost total darkness.

NOTES

1. Andrew and Catherine Belsey argue that the portraits of the sixteenth-century monarchs were "elements in a struggle at the level of representation for control of the state." "Icons of Divinity: Portraits of Elizabeth I," in *Renaissance Bodies,* ed. Lucy Gent and Nigel Llewellyn (London: Reaktion Books, 1990), 11–35.

2. Frances Yates, "Allegorical Portraits of Queen Elizabeth I at Hatfield House," Appendix to *Astrea: The Imperial Theme in the Sixteenth Century,* (London: Routledge, 1975), 216.

3. Yates, 217.

4. Roy C. Strong, *Portraits of Queen Elizabeth I* (Oxford: Oxford University Press, 1963), 86. I believe that there are mouths on the cloak in the portrait—the eyes and ears are embroidered on the fabric of the cloak, while the mouths are concealed in its folds.

5. Lord David Cecil, *Hatfield House* (London: St.George's Press, 1973), 3.

6. Michel Foucault, *Discipline and Punish: The Birth of the Prison,* trans. Alan Sheridan (New York: Vintage, 1979), 173.

7. Leonard Tennenhouse, *Power on Display: The Politics of Shakespeare's Genres* (New York: Methuen, 1986), 155.

8. Niccolò Machiavelli, *The Prince,* trans. Luigi Ricci (New York: New American Library, 1952), 84.

9. Early discussions of the influence of pamphlets and Montaigne's essay on

cannibals are considered in Frank Kermode's Introduction to his edition of *The Tempest* (London: Methuen, 1964).

10. Francis Barker and Peter Hulme, "Nymphs and reapers heavily vanish: the discursive con-texts of *The Tempest*," in *Alternative Shakespeares*, ed. John Drakakis (London: Methuen, 1985), 200. Baker and Hulme question the assumption that the "true beginning" of *the Tempest* is Prospero's usurpation, noting that "although different beginnings are offered by different voices in the play, Prospero has the effective power to impose his construction of events on the others," (199). It is this power to silence that characterizes colonial discourse.

11. Paul Brown, "'This thing of darkness I acknowledge mine': *The Tempest* and the discourse of colonialism," in *Political Shakespeare: New Essays in Cultural Materialism*, ed. John Dollimore and Alan Sinfield (Manchester: Manchester University Press, 1985), 58.

12. Brown, 68.

13. Brown also points to Prospero's ironic identification with Caliban at the close of the play. In the epilogue, Prospero, like Caliban and Ariel, must plead for release.

14. This and subsequent quotations from *The Tempest* are taken from *The Riverside Shakespeare*, ed. G. Blakemore Evans (Boston: Houghton Mifflin, 1974).

15. Curt Breight, "'Treason doth never prosper': *The Tempest* and the Discourse of Treason," *Shakespeare Quarterly* 41 (1990): 4.

16. Although his reading of the play is not a political one, Stephen Orgel also discusses succession and usurpation in "Prospero's Wife," in *Representing the English Renaissance*, ed. Stephen Greenblatt (Berkeley: University of California Press, 1988), 244.

17. On the failure of bridewells, see A. L. Beier, *Masterless Men: The Vagrancy Problem in England 1560–1640* (London: Methuen, 1985), 164–70.

18. Curt Breight argues convincingly that "pinching," refers to the contemporary practice of torturing suspected traitors, especially on the rack, and at the end of the play, signifies the continental practice of execution by removal of the flesh of traitors with hot pincers (25–26).

19. A. L. Beier makes a useful distinction between punishment as redress and punishment as retribution. " . . . where the evil-doer is too poor to pay a fine . . . redress is no longer an appropriate form of penalty. Instead some sort of retribution, involving 'loss or suffering', is usually inflicted, and early-modern England saw a significant increase in such punishments" (158).

20. According to Curt Breight, however, Ferdinand would not necessarily have been seen as guiltless by an Elizabethan audience: "The notorious Bond of Association devised in 1584 mostly to bind members of the Elizabethan upper classes to take revenge not only on the murderer(s) but also on any political beneficiary of the queen's assassination had the effect of enlarging the circle of guilt. In this context Ferdinand would not be perceived as an innocent (eventual) beneficiary of Prospero's deposition but as a guilty conspirator susceptible to Prospero's revenge" (11).

21. Beier, 159–60.

22. "A body is docile that may be subjected, used, transformed and improved." Foucault, 136.

23. Breight argues that the punishment of the lower-class conspirators is a "grim object lesson for Prospero's upper-class enemies" (20).

24. William C. Carroll, "The Punishment of Poverty in Tudor-Stewart England" (Paper delivered at the Annual Meeting of the Shakespeare Association of America, 22 March 1991), 7.

Overkill in Shakespeare

GILLIAN MURRAY KENDALL

RENAISSANCE executions, particularly those of regicides or parricides, were often affairs of excess. The sentence for treason, for example, passed on both Raleigh and the Duke of Norfolk, was "to be hanged, cutte doune alive, your membres to be cutte of and cast into the fyer, your bowels brent before you, your head smytten of, and your body quartered and devyded at the Kynges wyll."[1] Some of the tortures and mutilations associated with execution were symbolic: A hand figuratively (or literally) raised against the king might be cut off or burnt, as if rebellion against the state were an action committed by parts of the body, rather than a product of the mind. State executions may thus be seen as a logical extension of the metaphor of the body politic, which, according to James I, dictated that "it may very well fall out that the head will be forced to garre cut off some rotten members . . . to keep the rest of the body in integritie."[2] The individual bodies that make up the metaphoric body politic must suffer, must be excised, if that is what is necessary to keep the state healthy: If thine eye offend thee, pluck it out. In Shakespeare's plays, the image of the body politic—that metaphorical entity made up of all the individual bodies of the commonwealth and headed by the monarch—informs numerous instances of excessive violence. And so the metaphor begins to suggest that the body politic is attempting to enact complete punishment on the body natural for acts against the state. The justice of the metaphor seemed to please. In this way, the frail body natural becomes the locus of state authority, an emblem on which the state inscribes its power. In contrast, the body politic seems to assume human attributes of physical vulnerability—it can be "wounded"; it can "bleed." This frailty is perhaps inevitable given that the metaphorical head of the state serves as a synecdoche for the monarch's mortal body. Titus seems to recognize this sometimes awkward slippage between metaphorical and physical

173

bodies when, in a grotesque metaphor, he says of Rome that "a better head her glorious body fits / Than his that shakes for age and feebleness" (1.2.187–88). Such seeming vulnerability to the human frailty of its component parts makes of the state a victim needing protection; at the same time, it empowers that state to dispose of the destructive elements within it, like a body purging itself of disease (a common political metaphor in Shakespeare's plays).

The appropriation of the body natural into this active metaphor of the body politic, however, often means that pain will be inflicted on the body natural—even if that body earnestly supports the state. In *Titus Andronicus,* for example, the warrior Lucius explains:

> I . . .
> . . . have preserv'd [Rome's] welfare in my blood,
> And from her bosom took the enemy's point,
> Sheathing the steel in my advent'rous body.
>
> (5.3.109–11)[3]

Lucius substitutes his body for that of the body politic, transforming figurative wounds to the state into literal wounds to himself. When the state attempts to absorb characters into an extended political metaphor through *punishment,* however, problems arise: The attempt to exact talionic justice from a body natural for crimes against a body politic will inevitably give the state less than what it considers its due. The punishment cannot always match the supposed magnitude of the crime. In some cases, moreover, death may undermine state authority by rescuing the condemned from the extended agony of execution. Indeed, when the exercise of power entails demanding the complete submission of the natural body to the state[4] (or to the authority—not always legitimate—in question), the limits to state authority become apparent. Not only are there physical limits to the obeisance a body can perform, but bodies, under the stress of execution, engage in uncontrolled natural functions—physical reactions that belie any willing acquiescence to punishment suggested by scaffold confessions. The body offers resistance to inflicted suffering; it wishes to live. And so the body natural begins to show itself as independent of the power and desires of the state. The very materiality of bodily suffering, too, could undermine the metaphor of power the state wished to create: Hangmen who were clumsy in carrying out executions (thus causing more pain to the condemned) were sometimes attacked by angry spectators and forced to flee for their lives.[5] The vision of pain could turn acceptance into rebellion.

In Shakespeare's plays, the kind of excess associated with these executions is often displaced onto those who wish to gain political power by foul means. Lawful executions, on the other hand, tend to be associated with the comedies, and are always finally cancelled or circumvented by the mercy of the ruler. By removing punishment of the body from the realm of the sanctioned ruler, of course, Shakespeare could more fully explore the radical significance of the body as state-appropriated metaphor. And so in these plays, it is often when a character metes out violence to the established state that excess becomes the watchword: Extended metaphors, like that of the body politic, can prove difficult for the body natural to kill.

Macbeth's murder of Duncan is far more violent, for example, than Duncan's execution of Cawdor, for Macbeth must kill not only Duncan the man, but Duncan the King (and head of state). Duncan's body is easily dispatched, but Macbeth must still quell the prolonged and convulsive agonies of a body politic whose head has been forcibly removed. This slippage in the discourse of bodies problematizes all political murders. Brutus and the conspirators, for example, stab great Caesar repeatedly, as if they had little confidence their violent act could kill him. Titus, who has an empress and her sons to murder and enormous crimes to avenge, performs what seems a parody of execution: He first explains to two of his victims what he is going to do, and then he does it; he cuts their throats, grinds their bones to dust, adds their blood to it, and bakes their heads in a pasty, which he feeds to their mother. His final act of revenge, then, is one of incorporation; the bodies of his enemies are utterly annihilated.[6] Such complete destruction, however, ultimately limits Titus' ability to enact vengeance.

The kind of enthusiasm for violence Titus exhibits can prove problematic. No matter how much a character may wish to take revenge on an enemy, or in the case of the state no matter how much punishment may be needed in order to exact payment for crimes, characters will not die more than once. Overkill then begins to suggest the limits of power—and not only of power that is usurped, but, by analogy, power that *is,* in the context of the play, legitimate. By examining the imagery of political overkill in plays of different genres—*Macbeth* and *The Winter's Tale,* in this instance—one can see suggestions that excessive violence performed by the body politic can lead to a recognition of the boundaries and limits to state power. In very different ways, these plays show that when treated solely as a political metaphor (as when, for example, the body becomes a symbol of rebellion), the body natural may begin to take its own kind of revenge upon the state. Before beginning my discussion, however, I would first like to explore the generically comic power struggle between state and individual in *Measure for Measure,* a power struggle that reveals basic contradictions that, in *Macbeth* and *The Winter's Tale,* result in acts of political overkill.

I

Measure for Measure closely examines the etiquette of execution, the relationship of that etiquette to the power of the state, and the kind of rebellion against authority made possible by the libidinous flesh of Vienna's subjects. In this play, as part of the movement towards comedy, the Duke must come to terms both with fleshly desire and the sometimes peculiar politics of execution: He must bow to the fact that it is not always easy either to dispatch criminals or to maintain authority over the body. The roles played out in the ceremony of execution are strict, but the Duke's subjects are considerably less willing to participate in the correct forms than a number of their historical Renaissance counterparts. The protocols of execution, in order to elevate the might of the state, demand a kind of consent on the part of the condemned—a consent, historically, rarely denied.[7] Raleigh, for example, not only cooperated with the executioner, but, with his head on the block, gave the signal for his own execution by raising his hands.[8] Criminals, moreover, must be conscious of and acknowledge the punishment being meted out to them. Those who, in the Renaissance, escaped the power of the state by committing suicide had their dead bodies dragged to the scaffold and punished in a final effort to demonstrate state control over the body natural.[9] But in *Measure for Measure,* the Duke, in Barnardine, must contend with an obstreperous and uncooperative subject—one who escapes state authority not through suicide, but through a stubborn refusal to consent to his own execution.

The hangman calls Barnardine, but finds him asleep, and a sleeping man, unconscious of his fate, cannot be made part of the ceremonies of execution. Pompey, the new assistant hangman, tells Barnardine: "You must rise and be hang'd, Master Barnardine!" Getting little response, he says: "You must be so good, sir, to rise, and be put to death." Abhorson becomes insistent. "Tell him he

must awake, and that quickly too." Pompey urges Barnardine further: "Pray, Master Barnardine, awake till you are executed, and
sleep afterwards." The execution, however, cannot go forward because Barnardine will not cooperate with the state. He even shows
indifference to the fact of being in prison ("give him leave to escape
hence, he would not").[10] Barnardine engages in an extreme form
of resistance to state power: He refuses to acknowledge authority
in any way—especially authority over his rebellious flesh.[11] One
might think of *Pericles'* Marina in the brothel, who not only refuses
the bawd's or the governor's authority over her body but, by deny-
ing the very vocabulary of the brothel, begins to restructure the
society around her. Of course, Barnardine is very different from
Marina, but in his sleepiness and his drunkenness in the face of
potential execution, in his unfitness for death, one can see that he
is asserting a power counter to the state's simply through the condition of his body.[12] This kind of rebellion is symptomatic of rebellion
in the play as a whole: The Duke must, in *Measure for Measure,*
contend with a whole city whose libidinous bodies undermine the
laws and power of the head of the body politic.[13] The very weaknesses of Barnardine's flesh, then, resist the state's attempts to
make that flesh an emblem of its power.

The provost emphasizes Barnardine's intransigence, saying that
"We have very oft awak'd him, as if to carry him to execution, and
show'd him a seeming warrant for it; it hath not moved him at all."
In the near executions of the Lord Brey, Lord Cobham, and Sir
Gervase Markham, James I apparently felt the need to engage in
a similar kind of fiction to show his power over his subjects' bodies.[14] In this play, however, while the warrant is a symbol of the
authority of the state, and a symbol that should deeply move any
prisoner(Trouble-All, in Jonson's *Barthomomew Fair,* has been
driven mad because of a warrant), Barnardine remains unmoved. In
his indifference to both warrant and execution, he proves himself a
threat to the body politic; he must be made to submit to the will of
the state before he can be dispatched. Barnardine is also acting most
unlike the usual condemned Renaissance criminal. He can be
killed, of course, and he says they can "beat out [his] brains with
billets", but violent death is not the same thing as execution. The
ceremony of execution requires the cooperation of the prisoner,
and Barnardine says he "will not consent to die this day." Finally,
the provost suggests, "What if we do omit, / This reprobate till he
were well inclined." The state capitulates to the will of the prisoner—as far as we know, Barnardine is never well-inclined. In the
end, the Duke pardons him, perhaps because Barnardine cannot

be persuaded "willingly to die" anymore than the subjects of Vienna can be purged of all sexual urges. In fact, a large part of the play involves the Duke, who has been slack about law enforcement, attempting to persuade his subjects to consent to their deaths and to forgo their sexual natures. He forces Claudio to confront the fact of mortality. His Provost transforms Pompey from a bawd into a hangman. He allows Angelo's warped sexuality to emerge so that he can crush it. The Duke tries to elicit the utter submission of his subjects' bodies to the will of the state, something Angelo, simply by passing sentence and sending a warrant for execution, cannot do. Once the consent is there, the executions need not go through—*Measure for Measure* is, after all, a comedy.

II

For the kind of textbook execution never actually realized in *Measure for Measure,* one must look to *Macbeth,* where the Thane of Cawdor meets his end in a way that both dignifies himself and legitimizes the authority that calls for his death. Duncan arranges this execution easily. He states simply:

> No more that Thane of Cawdor shall deceive
> Our bosom interest. Go pronounce his present death,
> And with his former title greet Macbeth.
>
> (1.2.63–65)

Duncan neatly severs Cawdor from his title and has him dispatched—or so it seems. Certainly, unlike Macbeth, Duncan perceives the difference between the physical body—which he easily suppresses—and titles and roles—which, in this play, tend to have a separate life of their own. He shows he can manipulate both. This execution, moreover, announced and performed publicly, exhibits all the cooperation between punisher and punished that Barnardine rejects in *Measure for Measure.* Duncan asks:

> *Dun.* Is execution done on Cawdor? Are not
> Those in commission yet return'd?
> *Mal.* My liege,
> They are not yet come back. But I have spoke
> With one that saw him die; who did report
> That very frankly he confess'd his treasons,
> Implor'd your Highness' pardon, and set forth
> A deep repentance. Nothing in his life

Became him like the leaving it. He died
As one that had been studied in his death,
To throw away the dearest thing he ow'd,
As 'twere a careless trifle.

(1.4.2–11)

Execution becomes a ritual that elevates Duncan's authority[15]—
Cawdor even seems to have "studied" for this little drama. Here
the outlaw submits utterly to the state, not only by confessing the
crime of treason, but by acquiescing in the sacrifice of his body.
He throws it down "As 'twere a careless trifle;" his confession,
repentance, and renewed subjection to the king's authority mimic
exactly the accepted norm of behavior by Renaissance traitors on
the scaffold.[16] Through ceremonies of execution, the body politic
with Duncan at its head can, seemingly, control utterly the body
private, reinscribing it into a metaphor useful for the state. The
destruction of Cawdor's body becomes a public destruction and
denouncement of treason.[17] The body politic with Macbeth at its
head, however, finally gives way to a body politic contemplating
the head of Macbeth. While in Duncan's worldview, Cawdor and
what he symbolizes (treason) are intertwined and can be simultaneously destroyed, Macbeth's political world reveals an ugly
truth—one Duncan will soon encounter—about the state's relationship to the individual: Acts of treason survive the bodies that
enact them, and political control of the individual body is largely
an illusory artifact of ceremonies associated with execution. Macbeth's final resistance to any kind of repentance or confession or
even to the fact of death itself reveals a potential kind of rebellion
that the Thane of Cawdor's execution seems to deny is possible.
Macbeth's lawless and excessive private executions, moreover, finally raise disturbing questions about the state sanctioned theater
of punishment and power.

Macbeth, like Duncan, exhibits his authority by controlling the
bodies of those around him. In so doing, however, Macbeth engages in overkill, killing families instead of individuals and inflicting
twenty wounds where one would dispatch a victim. The more physical punishment he inflicts on his victims, however, the less certain
Macbeth seems to be of their deaths—or at least of their absences.
In Macbeth's world, treason and traitor do not die simultaneous
deaths, and the body's function as political tool becomes something
all too separate from the body as something frail and mortal. Macbeth cannot seem to kill both at once. It is as if Duncan's murder
suddenly opened wide a preexisting gap in the fabric of political

suppression.[18] And as *Macbeth* continues, the finality of death (as a tool of such suppression) comes more and more into question.

Macbeth's inability as king to suppress his subjects through violence contrasts sharply with his ability as soldier: The play opens with a portrayal of "brave Macbeth", the efficient killing machine. With his sword, he "carv'd out his passage" and, facing his enemy, "unseam'd him from the nave to th' chops, / And fix'd his head upon [the] battlements." The exaggerated sword stroke hints at the violence Macbeth will later perform, but the mortality of the enemy here is never in doubt. Macdonwald dies under the stroke of the sword and leaves no ghost to haunt Macbeth. Moreover, the frailty of the human body is everywhere evident in this scene. Macbeth and Banquo, it seems, "bathe in reeking wounds,"[19] and the Sergeant who reports all this must break off in his speech to Duncan:

> But I am faint, my gashes cry for help.
> *Dun.* So well thy words become thee as thy wounds,
> They smack of honor both. Go get him surgeons.
>
> (1.2.42–44)

The Sergeant is obviously weakened by his wounds. While Duncan clearly understands the political value of both words and wounds, of language and the body ("they smack of honor both"), he also acknowledges the vulnerability of that body ("go get him surgeons"). Duncan's words gesture towards the often ambiguous place bodies occupy in a world where events move simultaneously on metaphorical and physical planes. In the pursuit of the politically symbolic, however, he does not forget the significance of wounds in terms of human pain, and perhaps this is why blood and death here remain part of the natural, as opposed to the supernatural, world. The sergeant is faint and his gashes compete with and finally silence his words in a way that Banquo's "gashes" (the murderer uses the same word to describe Banquo's wounds) do not, finally, affect Banquo, while the final "gashes" Macbeth deals out seem utterly futile. Between the first gashes inflicted and the last, something happens to the nature of death and to the way we see attempts to punish the human body in order to preserve or create a body politic.

Certainly what Macbeth does to Duncan is not the straightforward violence of the opening battle. When he murders Duncan, the play becomes bathed in the imagery of blood and of breaches in the human body—but breaches described in elaborately figurative terms. Macduff refers to Duncan as a temple, a building that has been broken into, making Macbeth's act a kind of sacrilege. Macbeth uses his own suggestive images: He speaks of the wine of life being drawn—as if he were using metaphor to distance himself from the picture of Duncan's body draining of blood. He describes Duncan's "silver skin lac'd with his golden blood" and says that the "gash'd stabs look'd like a breach in nature." With this language, Macbeth attempts to control Duncan's body as signifier, making of it a place where he can superscribe his own authority on Macduff's text of sacrilege.[20] Macbeth empowers himself by rereading the dead Duncan. He says to Malcolm and Donalbain:

> The spring, the head, the fountain of your blood
> Is stopp'd, the very source of it is stopp'd.
>
> (2.3.98–99)

Duncan is a "spring" and "head" and "fountain" not only because he is a father and therefore source of his children's blood, but because he is the "head" of the body politic—which Macbeth has sought to destroy by first attacking Duncan's frail body and then, here, by describing that body's metaphorical function as "stopp'd." Macduff's almost wry translation of Macbeth's metaphors ("Your royal father's murther'd"), however, returns us to the image of the king's corpse, and acts as a reminder that to destroy one body is not to destroy the body politic. Moreover, while Macbeth uses language that makes of the brutal facts of murder and death—of mayhem performed on the body natural—something more esoteric, the brutal facts of death are what Macbeth the soldier is best at dealing with. By eschewing the frank descriptive language associated with earlier acts of violence—when he, for example, "unseam[s]" a man "from the nave to th' chops"—Macbeth moves into a world of unfamiliar and less direct symbols. In this world, violence itself seems finally to become ineffective, as if Macbeth had, with language, distanced himself too much from his own actions.

Soon after the murder, Macbeth has clearly left the world of the soldier behind, but his furtive act of murder and the later flight of Malcolm and Donalbain also robs him of the ability (or opportunity) to act as a figure of political authority, to mete out death symbolically dressed as justice. Macbeth's body resists any single metaphor he might wish to apply to it: As he looks at his hands, he sees not the hands of a soldier or prince, but "hangman's

hands." He here takes on not only the liminal role of the executioner—but that of a self-created executioner uncleansed by ceremony or policy.[21] By killing an unconscious man spiritually
unprepared for death, Macbeth has shown disrespect for the body-
soul union of the body natural, and so has violated the mystery of
the executioner. Indeed, in a kind of talionic reversal, Macbeth's
own language draws and quarters him into fragments, into separate
parts of "hand" and "brain" and "eye", as if his acts of violence
were doubling back on him.[22]

The extent of the wounds he inflicts on Duncan and the grooms
also indicates a kind of impotence, a doubt as to his ability effectively to inflict this kind of death. The text gives such doubts room
to grow: Almost immediately after the murder, imagery of resurrection begins to surface, as if the idea of death itself were beginning to rebel against Macbeth. Macduff calls out:

> Up, up, and see
> The great doom's image! Malcolm! Banquo!
> As from your graves rise up, and walk like sprites,
> To countenance this horror!
>
> (2.3.77–80)

This, of course, prefigures Banquo's more literal resurrection, and
heralds, too, the movement from the imagery of death as an end
to that of death as something slightly less final. Duncan is dead,
but what Duncan represents is not dead—Macbeth has "scorch'd
the snake, not kill'd it." His manipulation of figurative language
cannot tie signifier and signified together tightly enough to bury
Duncan's symbolic value as head of the body politic along with his
body. The irrevocable fact of Duncan's death, as much as the un-
timely return of Banquo, threatens to preserve the vision of Scotland as a political body that cannot heal—not with Macbeth acting
as its head. Macduff says "Bleed, bleed, poor country" (4.3.31),
and Malcolm responds "It weeps, it bleeds, and each new day a
gash / Is added to her wounds" (3.3.40–41). Duncan, meanwhile,
is beyond the reach of Macbeth's sword:

> Duncan is in his grave;
> After life's fitful fever he sleeps well.
> Treason has done his worst; nor steel, nor poison,
> Malice domestic, foreign levy, nothing,
> Can touch him further.
>
> (3.2..22–26)

There is, I think, a touch of envy in this speech. Macbeth's life is a "fitful fever", a sickness to him, while Duncan is at peace. But on another level, Macbeth's words reveal the futility of the murder. For by killing Duncan, he has made him immune to murder ("steel" and "poison"). He has done his worst (and the text suggests an extreme of physical violation in the murder), only to place Duncan beyond the realm of punishment. Duncan, like Caesar, is mighty yet—his symbolic value as king, once having survived his murder, becomes invincible—even as his country seems to be dying. Macbeth cannot kill Duncan any more than Duncan has been killed; Macbeth has, essentially, destroyed his means of access to complete power by placing the King, through death, beyond his reach. Once Macbeth enters the realm of political murder/execution, he finds that death is not as simple a concept as it was for the loyal soldier in the opening of the play.

The very bodies that Macbeth robs of life seem to rebel against the authority Macbeth attempts to acquire. Unlike the Duke in *Measure for Measure,* however, Macbeth deals not with the comic rebellion of a Barnardine reluctant to give his body over to the power of the state, but with a ghost that shows the limits to Macbeth's attempts to suppress rebellion by suppressing the body natural. As a soldier, Macbeth ended rebellion by hewing down the bodies of rebels. As a king who assumes the role of illicit executioner, Macbeth has come to live in a world where what bodies represent to the state does not die with them. Moreover, Macbeth's nature as political leader—in refusing to consider the body natural on a level that acknowledges the horror of human suffering—sunders political authority from power over individual bodies, until even he seems unsure of the efficacy of violence.

When, for example, the murderer returns to Macbeth with news of Banquo's death, Macbeth questions him in a manner quite different from that of Duncan inquiring after Cawdor's execution (Duncan simply asks "Is execution done on Cawdor?" and accepts a secondhand account of the event). Macbeth seems almost unable to accept the account of Banquo's death. He asks, "Is he dispatch'd?" And later, although he has been told that Banquo's "throat is cut", he asks again, "But Banquo's safe?" The murderer replies:

> Ay, my good lord; safe in a ditch he bides,
> With twenty trenched gashes on his head,
> The least a death to nature.

> (3.4.25–27)

Banquo's throat is cut and his head gashed twenty times—an obvious case of overkill. But this, and the fact that Macbeth seems worried and to seek assurances of Banquo's death from the murderer, ultimately becomes ironic. The "grown serpent" still has not been permanently dispatched; Banquo, like Caesar, returns, and Macbeth discovers the limits of physical suppression:

> The time has been,
> That when the brains were out, the man would die,
> And there an end; but now they rise again
> With twenty mortal murthers on their crowns,
> And push us from our stools.
>
> (3.4.77–81)

Suppressions of the body natural will not end the potential for rebellion against the body politic—there is, moreover, a suggestion that in being pushed from his stool, Macbeth is pushed from his throne—and "murther" done on Banquo's crown later becomes a crown on Banquo's crown. Macbeth has violated the "humane statute" and now the dead will not stay dead, despite "twenty mortal murthers". Macbeth's blindness to the reverence due to the mortal human body limits his power: The body he has transformed into a symbol of his authority symbolically returns to question that authority. At the same time, Banquo is not alive. Macbeth cannot try swords with him.

Yet Macbeth determines to keep on wading through blood, tedious though it may have become. Even after he receives what he thinks are assurances of his own immunity to violent death—that "none of woman born / Shall harm Macbeth"—he decides to kill Macduff anyway and "make assurance double sure." Numb to murder and mayhem, Macbeth ironically seems to give death a life of its own. The dead are "rebellious dead", and in Macbeth's injunction to "rise never till the wood / Of Birnam rise" lies the image of a nation of corpses waiting to haunt their creator-king.

In the last battle, Macbeth's vision of invulnerability disintegrates as Birnan wood moves towards Dunsinane and defeat becomes inevitable. His reaction makes of him a figure of death, as he finally attempts to subjugate all life—just as he earlier dispatched *some* lives to prove himself a king:

> Why should I play the Roman fool, and die
> On mine own sword? Whiles I see lives, the gashes
> Do better upon them.
>
> (5.8.1–3)

At this point, Macbeth seems finally to be lashing out at life itself, whether in the vegetative form of the moving wood or the human form of the "lives" that surround him in battle. The ineffective "gashes" that could not dispose of Banquo he now aims at life itself. The moments preceding Macbeth's death prove the opposite of Cawdor's: he resists the weight of his own guilt; he neither confesses nor repents. His body is both metaphorical head of the diseased country he rules and, at the same time, is invested with all the energy of rebellion and resistance that the state desired to quell in traitors. In his last minutes, Macbeth might seem to be an emblem that death cannot touch, but the flickering, eliding significances of Macbeth's body do not enable him to evade his own mortality.

And when Macduff overcomes Macbeth, when we return to death in battle, the image of death seems to return to normal. Siward's death is an accepted, blunt fact. "Then he is dead?" "Ay . . . They say he parted well, and paid his score, / And so God be with him!" Macbeth's head also serves as a final reminder of a more dependable mortality. The new figures of political authority at the play's end invite us to believe that with Macbeth's death, we have returned to a politically normal world, where the dead are dead and not wandering the earth ready to haunt us, where, it seems, metaphor is not so prone to dangerous slippages, and where the disease that lurks in the body politic (in this case Macbeth) can be openly excised and destroyed—suppressed through the punishment of Macbeth's body personal.

Certainly Macbeth's indulgence in political overkill in the private sector could not accomplish this kind of suppression. For one thing, his "hangman's hands" betray him because they are not connected to what Pompey would call a "lawful hangman." For another, his use of overkill all along implies a kind of denial of humanity, of mortality—of his own or of others. The final gashes that Macbeth inflicts on life reveal an inability to accept death— which life inevitably entails. And the shield he throws before his body in the fight with Macduff is no more effective than the shield against death and displacement he tries to create through overkill. "The tyrant" is slain; "Th' usurper's cursed head" is presented as a "comfort." With Macbeth's head on a pole, the metaphor of the "head" of the body politic becomes grotesquely literalized, and the image of bodily frailty, of what political suppression means to the body natural, finally dominates the scene. Literal and titular heads unite as Macbeth's head and the head of the body politic become one in the stage prop that stands for the character "Macbeth". The rent in the political fabric caused by Duncan's death, a rent that lets us see the contradictions in the relationship between the body natural and the body politic, must be closed. And yet the final words of Macduff and Malcolm do not safely contain the energy of rebellious violence that the play has generated. Despite their protestations, Macbeth has escaped the power of the state: while the head on the pole suggests an ignominious execution, Macbeth has actually died in battle, unrepentant to the end.[23] In the tragicomic form of *The Winter's Tale,* however, we can see the kind of political overkill that creates the tragedy of *Macbeth* metamorphosed into a vision of comic violence that, to paraphrase Macbeth himself, "purg[es] the gentle weal."

III

The Winter's Tale is full of the imagery of and discussion about executions. Leontes wants to execute Hermione and Perdita. He threatens to hang Antigonus. He threatens to burn Paulina. Polixenes talks about killing Perdita and her shepherd father. Autolycus rightly fears the hangman, and, perhaps in a purgation of that fear, tortures the Clown and the Shepherd with lengthy descriptions of their executions. But Hermione doesn't go to the fire; Perdita's brains are not dashed out; she does not suffer a death "as cruel as / [she] is tender;" the Clown is not flayed and the Shepherd is not stoned. Autolycus isn't hanged. Rather, the violent imagery that permeates this play underscores—and shows the inherent limits of—Leontes' attempts to assert political power through the suppression of his wife's body. He attacks her body verbally, referring angrily to "gates," "a belly," her "cheek," her "inside lip." In this case, rebellion and treason become linked to gender, as Leontes condemns Hermione, essentially for acts committed by her genitalia and reproductive organs. Polixenes condemns Perdita for the same reasons. To elevate the authority Leontes wields, then, he tries to suppress not only the body natural, but, more particularly, the processes of fertility associated with the female body natural. In *The Winter's Tale,* it seems, bodies rebel against the state simply by virtue of performing their natural functions (a situation similar to that in *Measure for Measure*'s Vienna).

The punishment that Leontes wants to inflict on Hermione and that Polixenes wants to inflict on Perdita would appear to be talionic in nature. Not only will these women pay with their bodies for crimes against the state, but it is (apparently) with their bodies that they have transgressed.[24] Leontes interprets the way Hermione kisses Polixenes and holds his hand ("paddling palms and pinching fingers") as adulterous treason. In the same way, Perdita's "hoop[ing Florizel's] body more with embraces," that is, threatening to debase royal blood with her own, is the crime Polixenes says will require her death and disfigurement. Neither Hermione nor Perdita, of course, is guilty, although Perdita is unaware of her innocence. But the idea that trespasses of the flesh are, first, crimes against the state and, second, must be paid for with flesh persists throughout the play. The clown, in speaking to his father, says more wisely than he knows, that " . . . your flesh and blood [that is, a blood relative] has not offended the King, and so your flesh and blood is not to be punish'd by him." This almost-zeugma—which mixes figurative "flesh and blood" with a reference to the stuff itself—reveals to what extent metaphor informs and limits the repressive actions of the body politic.

Whether or not Hermione's flesh and blood is technically innocent of offense against the king, however, her pregnant body, embodying all the ambiguities of paternity, resists the authority of the state and reveals the bounds of Leontes' political power. First, when she is pregnant she is beyond the reach of the executioner: the state is powerless (to a certain degree) to act upon her body. Here the blood and pain of birth substitutes for that of execution; new life substitutes for death. Second, Leontes can do nothing to halt the process of birth or the action of her body as she "rounds apace." Only nature has authority in this realm. Paulina says:

> This child was prisoner to the womb, and is
> By law and process of great Nature thence
> Freed and enfranchis'd.
>
> (2.2.57–59)

Hermione's body and the child in it are subject to laws outside of Leontes' control—and outside of Hermione's control as well. He can lock Hermione away and, in a kind of talionic punishment, deny her the childbed privilege; he can also destroy Perdita. He cannot, however, confine his child to the womb or return her there, and, as if Perdita's existence undermined his authority over his subjects, he becomes almost hysterical with the entrance of Paulina with the infant. He promptly issues a flurry of death threats all around as if to reassert his power in the presence of the child. He tells Paulina he will have her burnt—but her reply again reveals his impotence. She says "I care not," and so, like Barnardine, robs him of authority by refusing to repent, show fear, or in any way connive and assist in the ceremonies of execution or the rituals of power. In a comic moment that also reveals the distance between Leontes' words and the actions they represent, Antigonus notes that if the king had his way in all he'd "leave [him]self / Hardly one subject." The kind of overkill that Leontes engages in verbally threatens to rob him of kingship by robbing him of a population over which to rule. He is like the Queen of Hearts in *Alice* who, because she yells "Off with their heads" so frequently, finds she has no one left with whom to play croquet.

Leontes finally resorts overtly to ceremony to reestablish his authority: He arranges a trial in order to gain authority over his wife's body—to reacquire, after the birth of Perdita, the power to put Hermione to death. When Leontes, however, by subordinating the oracle to his authority, tries to assert absolute power over his wife's body, Mamillius dies and Hermione (apparently) dies too. It is as if Leontes were being reminded that other powers, like death and nature, hold equal sway with him in Sicilia—and perhaps more sway over the human body. These two deaths end Leontes' ability to punish, pardon, or even ask forgiveness of Hermione. Paulina seems to emphasize this by revealing the Queen's death in a curious way: she catalogues potential modes of execution:

> What studied torments, tyrant, hast for me?
> What wheels? racks? fires? What flaying? boiling
> In leads or oils? What old or newer torture
> Must I receive, whose every word deserves
> To taste of thy most worst?
>
> (3.2.175–79)

Her words show the limits of his power.[25] If each of her words is deserving of his "most worst"—and the redundancy of "most worst" emphasizes the overkill of flaying *and* boiling—-she, essentially, cannot live long enough to receive punishment adequate to fit the crime. Othello reveals his frustration with this idea when he says of Cassio "I would have him nine years a-killing." Touchstone, in a comic moment, seems to parody such excessive punishment when he tells William "I will kill thee a hundred and fifty ways." In Sicilia, as in Macbeth's Scotland, the desire to express power through violence can soon threaten to escalate out of control. Bohemia, however, offers the possibility of a body politic able to coexist with the small rebellions of the body natural, as potential suppressions of the body natural become a matter of comic exaggeration.

Polixenes' initial threats to Perdita and her foster family seem dire to the onstage audience of rural folk. We, as audience, are less concerned: Polixenes is, after all, in disguise and away from his court; he is in the comic sheepshearing court where Perdita is Queen of curds and cream.[26] To the old shepherd, however, execution means his excision from the body politic. He says to Florizel:

> You have undone a man of fourscore three,
> That thought to fill his grave in quiet; yea,
> To die upon the bed my father died,
> To lie close by his honest bones; but now
> Some hangman must put on my shroud and lay me
> Where no priest shovels in dust.
>
> (4.4.453–57)

He sees execution as excluding him from family, church, society. In viewing execution in this light, the shepherd participates in the kind of rhetoric employed by the state to exalt its power by repressing the body natural. Shortly thereafter, however, overkill and execution become a matter of comedy, calling the efficacy of such repression into question. Autolycus torments the shepherd and his son by saying:

Not he alone shall suffer . . . but those that are germane to him (though remov'd fifty times) shall all come under the hangman. . . . Some say he shall be ston'd; but that death is too soft for him, say I. Draw our throne into a sheep-cote!—All deaths are too few, the sharpest too easy. (4.4.772-80)

This sounds not unlike Macbeth's attitude towards family lines, but the excess here only emphasizes the point that Paulina's speech made earlier: When "all deaths are too few" the ability of the state to exercise power becomes limited by the frailty of the body natural. Repression here becomes a dark and impossible comic fantasy about multiple executions performed on one body. Autolycus says:

He has a son, who shall be flay'd alive; then 'nointed over with honey, set on the head of a wasp's nest; then stand till he be three quarters and a dram dead; then recover'd again with aqua-vitae or some other hot infusion; then, raw as he is (and in the hottest day prognostication proclaims), shall he be set against a brick-wall, the sun looking with a southward eye upon him, where he is to behold him with flies blown to death. (4.4.783–91)

There is no room here for the body to resist the sentence passed upon it—that is, for the Clown to die before the punishment is completed. But this fantasy only reminds the audience of the reality—that Polixenes' and Leontes' authority over the bodies of their subjects has limits. Autolycus translates the rhetoric of suppression into something contradictory and comic. Moreover, the exercise of such punishment on the poor and befuddled shepherd and son would clearly tend more to show the weakness of the state than its power over "traitorly rascals".

While Autolycus transforms execution into a matter of comedy, however, in Sicilia the problem of Hermione's death remains. And Leontes, who punished flesh and blood (in a literal and figurative sense) for being under nature's jurisdiction rather than his own, comes to live in an increasingly unnatural world of winter. In this world, the violence Leontes wished to inflict leads to a nightmare vision similar to that of *Macbeth*, in which the dead will not stay dead. The play makes motions towards the kind of horror Macbeth experiences when he faces the dead and gashed Banquo, for Hermione exists not only as a Queen and a statue, but as a ghost. Although Paulina proclaims the Queen dead—in fact, she swears to it—in the next scene, Hermione has apparently broken the boundaries of her grave. Antigonus says to the infant Perdita:

> I have heard (but not believ'd) the spirits o' th' dead
> May walk again. If such thing be, thy mother
> Appear'd to me last night; for ne'er was dream
> So like a waking.

> (3.3.16–19)

This "creature", as Antigonus calls her "with shrieks . . . melted into air" after saying Antigonus would see his wife no more. This both is and is not Hermione, just as Banquo's ghost is and is not Banquo. Leontes' rhetoric of violence seems to beget even more disturbing images of resurrection at the end of the play. The idea that the lost heir will be found, says Paulina,

> Is all as monstrous to our human reason
> As my Antigonus to break his grave,
> And come again to me.

> (5.1.41–43)

The idea of Antigonus' half-eaten body breaking his grave is "monstrous"—but monstrous ideas about ghosts breaking their graves are already in Leontes' mind. Of remarriage, he says:

No more such wives, therefore no wife. One worse
And better us'd, would make her sainted spirit
Again possess her corpse, and on this stage
(Where we offenders now) appear soul-vex'd,
And begin, "Why to me—?"

Paul. Had she such power,
She had just cause.

Leon. She had, and would incense me
To murther her I married.

(5.1.56–62)

Leontes' fantasies of resurrection come from his rhetoric of violence and lead to thoughts of reanimated corpses and murder. He cannot seem to escape from his image of the body as something to punish—even if the body were that of an innocent second wife. Paulina, sounding very much like the manipulative speaker in John Donne's "The Apparition", feeds Leontes' horrific fears about Hermione's ghost:

Paul. I should so:
Were I the ghost that walk'd, I'ld bid you mark
Her eye, and tell me for what dull part in't
You chose her; then I'ld shriek, that even your ears
Should rift to hear me, and the words that follow'd
Should be "Remember mine."

Leon. Stars, stars,
And all eyes else dead coals! Fear thou no wife;
I'll have no wife, Paulina.

(5.1.62–69)

Leontes wants no wife, not even his former one if she is to make an appearance like the ghost of Hamlet's father, saying, in this case, "Remember mine" instead of "Remember me." He has learned—as Macbeth learns—that the suppression of the body personal he thought would give him rest denies him rest. The ghost of Hermione lurks in the wings, reminding Leontes of the futility of his earlier actions. In *The Winter's Tale,* however, a return from the dead is finally made a matter of wonder rather than horror.

In the final scene, Leontes finally abrogates his own authority and begins to revere the very body personal he once desired to punish for acts of treason and rebellion. Appreciation of the frail human body replaces the desire to elevate authority through its suppression. Leontes finally even accepts his own frailty, his own mortality—an acceptance that heralds the return of Sicilia to life and, by means of her resurrection, lays Hermione's ghost.

When Leontes consents to visit Paulina's house, he reverses what has been the predominant relationship between the body politic and the body natural. Paulina says:

> . . . that you have vouchsaf'd, . . .
> my poor house to visit,
> It is a surplus of your grace, which never
> My life may last to answer.
>
> (5.3.4–8)

The image of a body that cannot be punished enough to pay for its transgressions gives way to the image of a body that cannot live long enough to express adequate gratitude to the king. Moreover, while Macbeth clings to his authority and rejects his own mortality to the last, Leontes here temporarily abrogates his authority, ceding it to Paulina. She is the one who directs the scene:

> Music! awake her! strike!
> 'Tis time; descend; be stone no more; approach;
> Strike all that look upon with marvel. Come;
> I'll fill your grave up. Stir; nay, come away;
> Bequeath to death your numbness. . . .
> Start not . . .
> Do not shun her . . .
> Nay, present your hand.
>
> (5.3.98–102, 104, 105, 107)

She resorts to imperatives throughout this speech. Leontes, on the other hand, gives the scene to Paulina and becomes part of the audience rather than remaining the central authority figure:

> What you can make her do,
> I am content to look on; what to speak,
> I am content to hear.
>
> (5.3.91–93)

Perhaps even more importantly, Leontes seems to come to an acceptance of the body as something ruled by time and mortality—not merely by his political authority. At first he objects to the statue because "Hermione was not so much wrinkled, nothing / So aged as this seems." But Paulina's words, that this is "As she liv'd now" are accepted by Leontes, who in accepting them is recognizing the sway of time and mortality. The statue also draws from him two important statements. First he says:

> Would I were dead but that methinks already—
> What was he that did make it? See, my lord,
> Would you not deem it breath'd? and that those veins
> Did verily bear blood?
>
> (5.3.62–65)

Here Leontes would rather accept his own death than not believe what he is beginning to believe, that what is done can be undone (in *Macbeth,* of course, as Lady Macbeth says, "what is done cannot be undone"). He then states:

> *Leon.* O sweet Paulina,
> Make me to think so twenty years together!
> No settled sense of the world can match
> The pleasure of that madness.
>
> (5.3.70–73)

Leontes is ready to sacrifice his sanity in order to believe in Hermione's return. With this new respect for the representation of Hermione's body, the imagery of ghostly resurrection gives way. She is no shrieking ghost here, and the vision of that undead spirit dissipates as Leontes discovers that Hermione is warm. The domination of his subjects through violence gives way to a desire to revere the human body: Perdita kneels to its representation; Leontes wishes to kiss it. And Paulina warns:

> Do not shun her
> Until you see her die again, for then
> You kill her double.
>
> (5.3.105–7)

The idea of the body as something both precious and fragile is reaffirmed, as is the finality of death. The state returns to normal. Leontes' submission to his own mortality and his new appreciation of his wife as physical being heralds the life-affirming final resurrection of the play—just as Macbeth's denial of mortality leaves him striking out blindly at the forces of life.

These plays, then, explore radical contradictions in the metaphors through which the state attempts to bolster its authority. In *Measure for Measure,* the politics of execution clearly show the limits of state power. The excesses of execution or of violence done for political reasons in other plays (I have used *Macbeth* and *The Winter's Tale* as examples) also show how the state can maim itself by trying to inscribe its power on the body natural. Even Duncan's textbook execution of Cawdor, accomplished with the thane's full cooperation, is not exempt from this: Cawdor's treason seems to be resurrected in Macbeth at the moment Cawdor dies—one might even think of Macbeth as a ghost of Cawdor.

To Leontes, in *The Winter's Tale,* resistance to state authority is a result of the autonomy of the female reproductive body, and the king imagines a crime that gives him new control over Hermione—he feels a need to legitimize his power through the suppression of that body. But *The Winter's Tale* finally moves away from authority maintained through execution or control of bodies and to a moment when the body is revered as a work of art. The statue of Hermione forces a reevaluation of the relationship between body politic (with Leontes as its head) and the body natural. Ironically, it is when Hermione's body is presented as something overtly representational, as a signifier for the power of the artist, that Leontes moves away from a vision of the body as a symbol to be manipulated. While Macbeth, to the end, hacks away at the young bodies of Scotland that embody regeneration, fertility, and new life, Leontes finally allows the regeneration of the procreative body he originally condemned. His revised view of the body as metaphor seems to allow the state to bloom, for in so doing, he not only transforms a ghost into a living being and art into life, but a dead commonwealth of winter into a living body politic of spring.

NOTES

This essay originally appeared, in a slightly different form, in *Shakespeare Quarterly,* (Fall 1989).

1. Edward Hall, *Henry VIII,* ed. by C. Whibley (London, 1904), vol. I, 225, cites this as the sentence read to the Duke of Norfolk. For the sentence read to Raleigh, see Carrie Harris, *State Trials,* (Chicago: Callaghan and Company, 1899), 116. These ignominious sentences were frequently reduced to the more dignified ones of decapitation for those of high estate.

2. James I, *The Trew Law of Free Monarchies* (1598), in *The Political Works of James I,* reprinted from the edition of 1616, ed. Charles Howard McHwain (Cambridge, Mass.: Harvard University Press, 1918), 29. Cited in *Shakespeare's Ghost Writers,* Marjorie Garber, (New York and London: Methuen, 1987), 100.

3. All quotations are taken from *The Riverside Shakespeare,* G. Blakemore Evans, ed., (Boston: Houghton Mifflin Co., 1974).

4. Michel Foucault, *Discipline and Punish,* tr. Alan Sheridan, (New York: Vintage Books, 1979), 47, writes of the ways the spectacle of the scaffold and mutilation of the criminal body reinforce and reconstitute state power.

5. For a discussion of this phenomenon, see Pieter Spierenburg, 13, in *The Spectacle of Suffering* (Cambridge: Cambridge University Press, 1984).

6. Foucault, ibid., writes that "A body effaced, reduced to dust and thrown to the winds, a body destroyed piece by piece by the infinite power of the sovereign constituted not only the ideal, but the real limit of punishment," 50. Titus pushes at this limit in his annihilation of Chiron and Demetrius.

7. Both J. A. Sharpe in "Last Dying Speeches", *Past and Present* 107 (May, 1985), 144–67, and L. B. Smith in "English Treason Trials and Confessions in the Sixteenth Century", *Journal of the History of Ideas* 15 (1954), 471-98, testify to the astonishing number of condemned men and women who carefully played by the rules of execution and went much further than simply consenting to their own deaths. Smith, 476, writes that "those about to suffer announced that they were content to accept the penalties which the law required."

8. Carrie Harris, op. cit., 126.

9. See Pieter Spierenburg, 56, op. cit., for a discussion of the fate of suicides.

10. Steven Mullaney, 151, in *The Place of the Stage* (Chicago: University of Chicago Press, 1988), writes that "in his global unconsciousness and radical inaccessibility, Barnardine represents the limits of even the Duke's power."

11. Stephen Greenblatt, 141–42, in *Shakespearean Negotiations* (Berkeley: University of California Press, 1988), notes that "the magnificent emblems of indifference are the drunken Barnardine and the irrepressible Lucio: if they are any indication, the duke's strategy has not changed the structure of feeling or behavior in Vienna in the slightest degree."

12. Robert N. Watson, "False Immortality in *Measure for Measure* (forthcoming in *Shakespeare Quarterly*), intriguingly suggests that "Barnardine may represent the body, the stupid force of heartbeat, survival instinct, [and] physical appetite, that is unwilling to die in the condemned Everyman, and is finally spared."

13. Jonathan Dollimore, in "Transgression and Surveillance in *Measure for Measure,* in *Political Shakespeare,* eds. Jonathan Dollimore and Alan Sinfield (Ithaca and London: Cornell University Press, 1985), writes that "whatever subversive identity the sexual offenders in this play possess is a construction put upon them by the authority which wants to control them," 73. The Duke may indeed exaggerate this "subversive identity," but in a play so deeply concerned with the issue of the subjection of the body to the power of the state, minor sexual rebellions of the body become highly magnified.

14. The conspirators were brought to the scaffold more than once and forced to confront the idea of their deaths before being told the sentence had been commuted. Stephen Greenblatt, op. cit., cites this and explores the ways in which "public maimings and executions were designed to arouse fear and to set the stage for the royal pardons that would demonstrate that the prince's justice was tempered with mercy", 137.

15. See, however, Karin S. Coddon, 490–500, in "'Unreal Mockery': Unreason and the Problem of Spectacle in *Macbeth*", *ELH,* vol. 56, no. 3 (fall, 1989), for a discussion of ambiguity associated even with Cawdor's execution.

16. The Thane of Cawdor follows a pattern of behavior that is absolutely typical of traitors on the scaffold (even of "traitors" innocent of the crimes of which they were accused). For an exploration of this phenomenon, see L. B. Smith, op. cit., 471–98, and J. A. Sharpe, op. cit., 144–67.

17. Stephen Mullaney, op. cit., 118, writes that "when the body bleeds, treason has been effaced; execution is treason's epilogue, spoken by the law." This would,

of course, be the ideal—an interpretation fostered by figures of authority. The rest of *Macbeth,* however, undermines the kind of complacency Cawdor's death might generate.

18. In this sense, I agree with Alan Sinfield's anti-Jamesian reading of *Macbeth* in "*Macbeth*: History, Ideology, and Intellectuals" in *Critical Quarterly,* i–11 (1986): 63–77.

19. James L. Calderwood, "*If it Were Done": Macbeth and Tragic Action* (Amherst: University of Massachusetts Press, 1986), writes that "only men in battle, who bathe in their own and their enemies' blood, are able to partake, bodily and symbolically, in the divinity of the state," 84. At this moment, Macbeth's violence and the wounds he bathes in (presumably both his own and those he inflicts) show him to be an integral member of the body politic.

20. Leonard Tennenhouse, in *Power on Display* (New York: Methuen, 1986), writes that "usually, the scene of punishment inscribes the crime upon the body of the criminal, but here the situation is completely reversed. It is Macbeth's ambition that is written on Duncan's body," 129.

21. Leonard Tennenhouse, ibid., notes the ways in which Macbeth "uses the techniques of ritual punishment to stage this Jacobean scene upon Duncan's body," 129. Soon after the murder, however, the "techniques of ritual punishment" begin to work against Macbeth.

22. Robert N. Watson, in *Shakespeare and the Hazards of Ambition* (Cambridge, Mass.: Harvard University Press, 1984), 83–141, sees Macbeth's imagistic fragmentation as a kind of foolish wish fulfillment.

23. His fate is not unlike that of the traitor Gowrie, killed after attempting the murder of James I. Stephen Mullaney, op. cit., 116, describes how the body was "transported to Edinburgh, presented to Parliament in a spectral session, duly found guilty of treason, and then hanged, drawn and quartered, and exhibited—on poles fixed at Edinburgh, Perth, Dundee, and Stirling." Here again the state attempted to exact its due, although the criminal had escaped into death.

24. In an analysis of violence towards women in Jacobean drama, Leonard Tennenhouse, op. cit., 121, writes that "like the criminal's assault on the law, a wife's infidelity to her husband *is* an assault on the Crown. The punishment of unchaste aristocratic women therefore displays the truth of the subject's relation to the state. It displays the dissymmetry of this relationship as it imprints the crime on the subject's body, in this way demonstrating the state's absolute power over that body."

25. Christopher Pye, in *The Regal Phantasm* (London: Routledge, 1990), writes that "atrocity" and force on the scaffold "can be seen to convey the inescapability of regal authority . . . The criminal who is executed in the place and with the instruments of his initial transgression is made . . . the author of his own punishment," 112. Here, however, Paulina, by ironically ascribing to herself the authorship of her punishment and by insisting on its extreme nature, utterly undermines Leontes' power to do the same.

26. C. L. Barber, 127, in *Shakespeare's Festive Comedy* (Princeton: Princeton University Press, 1959), describes the sheep-shearing in terms of the festivals (such as those of misrule) that influence Shakespeare's comedies.

The Unheimlich Maneuver:
Antithetical Ways of Power in Shakespeare

> Be chok'd with such another emphasis!
> —*Antony and Cleopatra* 1.5.68

Back in 1977, at the time of Elvis Presley's unexpected death, there circulated a story the strict truth of which is not really pertinent here. It seems an agent or P.R. man—some sort of industry flack on the spot in Memphis, in any case—decided to give a West Coast colleague early intelligence of what would prove to be one of the biggest entertainment stories of the decade. Soberly he placed the call, and when his counterpart on the Coast picked up, announced with funereal simplicity, "Elvis is dead." There was a pause as the agent absorbed the news, then a succinct reply, which it might well be hasty to call irreverent: "Good career move," he said and hung up.

In one obvious sense, being dead is about as marginal as one gets: You can't be any poorer than dead, as the young protagonist of a Flannery O'Connor story observes. But in another sense, hardly confined to the precincts of literature, though regularly recognized there, the dead not only continue to influence the living, their power to do so may actually exceed anything they possessed in life. Freud speculated that the father of the primal horde achieved something like full control over his perpetually aggrieved sons only after they had slain and eaten him. The phenomenon of "deferred obedience" was so powerful in this case, Freud thought, that it determined the basic structure of human civilization forever more.[1] Macbeth, whose murder of Duncan is reminiscent of the primal crime that occupied Freud, has a remarkable moment of anguish when he seems actually to envy his victim:

197

> Better be with the dead,
> Whom we, to gain our peace, have sent to peace,
> Than on the torture of the mind to lie
> In restless ecstasy. Duncan is in his grave;
> After life's fitful fever he sleeps well.
> Treason has done his worst; nor steel, nor poison,
> Malice domestic, foreign levy, nothing,
> Can touch him further.
>
> $(3.2.19–26)^2$

One way, it would seem, to achieve the invulnerability that Macbeth otherwise finds so elusive, to be "Whole as the marble, founded as the rock" (3.4.21), is to have encountered and passed the very worst. And a few lines later on, with the advent of Banquo's ghost, he will discover that there is an active side to this invulnerability as well, that the man does not exactly die when his brains are out, for he rises "With twenty mortal murthers on [his] crown" to "push us from our stools" (11.80–81). We are reminded by this frequent insistence of the dead, particularly in Shakespeare's tragic worlds, that while it is perfectly possible, sometimes even easy, to murder a man, it is far harder to murder his memory. If the immortal soul is, at bottom, as Freud suggested, no more than a projection of its owner's capacity to be remembered, we do well to bear in mind that it is no *less* than that either.[3]

I pause over some examples by way of suggesting that power in Shakespeare's dramatic worlds often devolves from some rather unlikely sources, and that influence has a way of emanating from those who seem least equipped to exercise it. And this in turn suggests the opposite, that those who wield the most impressive shows of power are altogether likely to harbor fatal weaknesses. Positions of relative strength and relative weakness have an uncanny tendency to veer about into their opposites, and, as with the celebrated lady in Hamlet's production of "The Murder of Gonzago," who, according to Gertrude, protests too much, we learn to be just as suspicious of the emphatic in matters of power as we are in matters of rhetorical hyperbole.

The remarkable currency of the ideas of Michel Foucault may have somewhat obscured the antithetical ways of power in Shakespeare's work. Foucault, interested as he was in the transition from the monarchical display of absolute power in the public spectacle of dreadful punishment, on the one hand, to more "enlightened" forms of reformist penal practice, on the other, had little to remark about the way the appalling punishment meted out to the would-be regicide Robert François Damiens, for instance, famously described at the beginning of *Discipline and Punish,* might suggest not the absolute character of Louis' dispensation concerning the bodies and the lives of his subjects but, on the contrary, its provisionality and contingency.[4] Only within this carefully orchestrated pageant of cruelty can the king's power be made to seem infinite and irresistible, and even in the midst of this sanguinary procedure we may be reminded that on at least one prominent occasion, when Damiens actually attacked the king and succeeded in wounding him, royal power was far from absolute. Indeed, from the perspective of Damiens' crime the whole spectacle of his punishment may come to seem an absurd and frenetic attempt at prophylaxis after the fact, an odd case of too *much* too late.

Elaine Scarry's account of the ways torture confers authority on the torturing regime seems to me to come closer to Shakespeare's sense of the antithetical meanings of overemphasized assertions. In torture, according to Scarry, "physical pain is so incontestably real that it seems to confer its quality of 'incontestable reality' on the power that has brought it into being." And yet, Scarry adds, it is "precisely because the reality of that power is so highly contestable, the regime so unstable, that torture is being used" in the first place.[5]

Perhaps *The Tempest* is as good a place as any to begin a consideration of Shakespeare's antithetical sense of the ways of power, and not only because the play is quite evidently concerned with matters of ascendancy, shaping, containment, and control, but also because it again and again recurs to the paradoxes and contradictions in which ascendant shapers and controllers find themselves embroiled. There is a curious effect in *The Tempest* that seems to ensure that promotions will become merely a new form of subjection or slavery: thus, Antonio's bid to become Duke of Milan entails his subjection to the King of Naples and opens his dukedom to most ignoble stooping. Similarly, Caliban's freedom from Prospero comes at the price of groveling before the drunken Stephano, a foot-licking existence that is not self-evidently preferable to the bondage he thinks he has escaped. And, while I don't want to suggest that Prospero's regime on the enchanted island is based on the kind of dreadful torture of which Elaine Scarry's work treats, his at-least draconian way of dealing with Caliban (and occasionally Ariel) certainly qualifies as coercive, and can surely be seen as hinting at an underlying uncertainty about the true nature and extent of his power. Perhaps no other Shakespearean character is quite so emphatic as Prospero about the power he wields, or quite so lavish with threats to those who stand out against him.

Certainly the prospect of pinches and cramps is something that Caliban, at any rate, takes very seriously indeed. And yet, *The Tempest* contains a scattering of details that are peculiar at a minimum and perhaps downright contradictory. As Prospero soliloquizes at the beginning of the fifth act about his feats in controlling the thunder, calling forth the winds, setting roaring war "'twixt the green sea and the azur'd vault" (5.1.43), we may just possibly remember that a mere thirty lines previously we have heard Ariel telling him of the King and his entourage, all of whom are being held prisoner "In the line-grove which weather-fends your cell" (5.1.10). What need, we may want to ask, could a man with the power to set the wild waters in a roar, and allay them too, possibly have for a homely and utilitarian windbreak? We may be reminded of yet another contradiction observed by Freud in *Totem and Taboo,* this time "that the ruler is believed to exercise great authority over the forces of Nature, but that he has to be most carefully protected against the threat of danger—as though his own power, which can do so much cannot do this."[6]

Or to take an example from the other end of the play: Many have noticed Prospero's nervous and, in the circumstances, unnecessary parenthetical remark during his long expositional speech in the second scene. Miranda, who is understandably dumbfounded by the revelations concerning her father's status, asks in bewilderment, "Sir, are not you my father?" (1.2.55). Since the question calls for nothing more than quiet reassurance, Prospero's reply is given a prominence he presumably does not intend: "Thy mother was a piece of virtue, and / She said thou wast my daughter" (1.2.56–57). There is, to be sure, nothing in general surprising about male insecurity concerning paternity in Shakespeare's plays, though one might still assume in the present instance that a powerful magician who enjoys a reputation for omniscience would by this time have worked out a way of overcoming the doubt that nags at so many ordinary Shakespearean males. But this bit of cynicism, which implies, of course, mistrust of the female sex as a whole, is the more striking by its proximity to Prospero's insistence on his guileless *lack* of suspicion where his brother has been concerned, the "confidence sans bound" (1.2.97) he says he has accorded Antonio and that has produced such bitter return. Perhaps we will be justified in reading Prospero's worldly-wise implication concerning the frailty of women as a rather feeble *ex post facto* attempt to compensate for what has been after all his considerable naïveté concerning the undependability of *men.* In trotting out the hoary matter of cuckoldry and female infidelity, Prospero may hope to draw attention away from his own quite-evident lapses and perhaps from the capacity of men in general for faithlessness and betrayal.

This is scarcely the only instance in *The Tempest* where an attempt to compensate for or deny a vulnerability only ends up in calling attention to it. But it is of particular interest because it seems to be of a piece with a more general displacement of blame away from the self. For Prospero's strangely febrile and agitated, not to say vehement account of his brother's perfidy has come to suggest to many commmentators his deep recognition of his own wish to retreat from political responsibilities into a sequestered world of arcane study. As he revealingly words the matter concerning the kindness of old Gonzalo at the time of the usurpation, "He furnish'd me / From mine own library with volumes that / I prize above my dukedom" (1.2.166–68: the present tense in the final clause is telling). It is as if whatever blame attaches to Prospero's own self-indulgent wishes were being passed on to the conveniently vicious Antonio, so that what has in fact been an abdication may be reinterpreted retrospectively as a usurpation.

What we begin to glimpse in these expository moments of the play's second scene is what will prove to be a preoccupation with strategies, conscious or unconscious, of delegation and substitution, a preoccupation, to be sure, not altogether surprising in a man committed to controlling, shaping, and harmonizing the behavior of others in a manner that has reminded virtually all students of *The Tempest* at one time or another of the activity of the playwright, director, or impresario. And yet, the instances touched on above suggest that substitution and delegation are processes not entirely under Prospero's control or fully available to his conscious self; that his evident delight in moments of achieved theatricality, his high praise, for instance, of the way his spirits execute the spectacle of the disappearing banquet (3.3.83ff.), masks deeper misgivings about the extent and purpose of the power he wields; and that the whole business, whether explicitly theatrical or not, of consolidating one's own position by coercing, or attempting to coerce, the actions of others is headed for partial success at the very best.

It is, of course, mightily tempting to treat Prospero as a kind of playwright or director and in so doing to conflate him with his creator, whether as mouthpiece for a farewell to dramatic art, or, more recently, in what might be called a "neoconflationist" move, as a means of ratifying the kind of colonialist-imperialist orthodoxy beyond the horizon of which, so it is argued, neither *The Tempest* nor its playwright is capable of seeing.[7] But the life of drama is in dialogic exchange, not monologic pronouncement on the part of characters who have been awarded the status of author's agent by critical fiat. If the author's commitment to the dramatic medium is genuine, as I believe Shakespeare's was, he will certainly forgo opportunities to speak *in propria persona,* choosing, rather, to let his play arise from the collision of subjectivities within it, each with a distinct and distinctly partial "take" on the dramatic world in which it finds itself embedded. A playwright *creates* his characters, to be sure; but that does not necessarily mean that he simply *coincides* with any one of them. But *The Tempest* is a drama, not a masque, though it assuredly contains one. And surely we can insist on its truly dramatic character because we can sense that Prospero is to some extent making claims, staking out a position, bringing his partial take to bear on other partial takes, speaking a "piece" that on occasion fails to coincide with the whole. That Prospero would *like* the play to be a sort of spectacle or tableau should in no way interfere with our recognition of what it really *is*.[8]

The Tempest circles around but never really answers the question that is posed twice in its first dozen lines: "Where's the master?" (1.1.9–10, 12). The immediate object of inquiry is, of course, the captain of the foundering ship, who speaks a very few words at the outset, only to disappear after four lines, the first of a series of delegations and substitutions the play dramatizes. But the reiterated question initiates a search for an authoritative center, a search that is repeatedly frustrated in this first scene, as we turn to the captain, who fails to reappear, then to the king, for whose name the waves care not at all, and finally to the councillor, old Gonzalo, who despite the best of intentions is unable to use his authority to work the peace of the present. Indeed, the response to Antonio's repetition of the crucial question ("Where is the master, bos'n?"), the Boatswain's "Do you not hear him?" (1.1.12–13), suggests that the master in question may be at this stage the storm itself, rather than the captain with his whistle, mentioned in the sixth line of this scene. The Boatswain's wry question (for of course they hear "him": they can scarcely hear anything else above the roar of wind and wave) simply asserts the hopelessness of the situation, the fact that the ship and its passengers are wholly at the disposal of the storm.

In spite of this unsettling implication (perhaps because of it), when we make the abrupt transition from the turbulent first scene to the tranquil second, we eagerly seize the assumption that we have at length found the master and will be henceforth in his capable hands.[9] The assumption will undoubtedly be bolstered by the magisterial way Prospero assures his daughter that all she (and we) have witnessed has been "safely ordered" by a provision in his art (1.2.33–34). But I wonder if it can really survive the curious question Prospero puts to his chief sprite concerning the passengers on the ship after Miranda has been charmed (or bored?) asleep, curious because it sorts so oddly with the man who a couple of hundred lines before has been so self-confident and reassuring: "But are they, Ariel, safe?" (1.2.217). I have been trying to suggest that this assumption about who the master is and where he is to be found is considerably eroded in the course of the play, so that by the end we may wonder just what has been accomplished by all the powerful magic so often and so emphatically referred to. As a project for moral reform, Prospero's scheme seems at best spotty. The truly hard cases, Antonio and Sebastian, remain just that, sullenly unrepentant, more than willing to shift attention toward the obviously deficient Caliban and his coconspirators. The good Gonzalo has merely been along for the ride, and, though Alonso does repent and is forgiven, one feels about Prospero's scheme in this case somewhat the way one feels about Don Pedro's scheme in *Much Ado about Nothing* to get Beatrice and Benedick to fall in love: It is preaching to those who are on the verge of conversion in any case. In one sense, Prospero's renunciation of his magic seems a very small sacrifice indeed.

James L. Calderwood has remarked Shakespeare's apparent fascination with "abdication and truancy," "from the saintly Henry VI sitting on his molehill during the battle of Towton to Prospero breaking his staff and drowning his book." "Perhaps we may sense in these depictions of royal withdrawal," Calderwood observes, "an impulse on Shakespeare's part to abandon, not necessarily London for the rusticity of Stratford, but his own responsibility as playwright exercising authority over his theatrical subjects."[10] But in the present context I would like to wonder whether these abdications figure so much the playwright's weariness with exercising authority over his theatrical subjects, as if to exercise such authority were merely fatiguing rather than wholly problematic, as they do his tacit admission that his authority is always limited, always short of having full effect, and, as in the case of Prospero, sometimes hard pressed to show much effect at all. Shakespearean abdications are frequently more complex than Calderwood here allows, and, if in some instances, Richard II's, for instance, abdication seems little more than a euphemism for usurpation, in others, like Prospero's, usurpation will come to seem, as already noted, merely the exterior form of an *a priori* abdication. The ancient analogy between God and his creation, on the one hand, and the author and his poem on the other, encounters some serious rubs in the case of drama, not the least of them the fact that, having brought his internal vision as near perfection as he can, the dramatist is then obliged to turn it over for its final incarnation to a disparate group of actors, a plurality of bodies conjoined with souls containing desires, wishes, and hopes quite different, it may be, from those of the playwright.[11] I speculate, in any case, that what must often be the violent contrast between what we may call for heuristic purposes the playwright's moment of inner satisfaction with his creation and the later process in which his creation is given an alien body may have much to do with the antithetical ways of power in Shakespeare's plays, the fact that, as on so many occasions, to assert power is at once to call it into question.

For delegating your own problems and concerns to others, whether you are a deposed duke possessed of magical power or a playwright confronting the necessities of getting your work before an audience, turns out to be fraught with difficulties and unwanted implications. The difficulties, at least, are obvious and have to do with the possibility of sheer recalcitrance on the part of the delegates. If Prospero has enlisted the putatively frail and faithless female sex to restore his badly battered faith in his own shrewdness, the presence of a patent female paragon, his own daughter, for instance, may cause uneasiness even as it is welcomed. And perhaps Prospero's overemphatic and needlessly repeated warning to Ferdinand concerning the containment of a passion Ferdinand otherwise shows no signs of possessing (4.1.14–23, 51–54) bespeaks Prospero's need, in manifest default of a sexually incontinent woman, for *some* fellow creature (Caliban will shortly reappear to relieve Ferdinand of this duty) to whom he can impute an unruliness that will make his own irascible temper seem like collected tranquillity. The trouble is, of course, that when Ferdinand protests that the "white cold virgin snow about my heart / Abates the ardor of my liver" (4.1.55–56), we readily believe him.

Perhaps Antonio is an even bigger problem, simply because he starkly refuses to confess and repent his own usurpation and thus lay to rest the possibility of seeing Prospero's downfall as a kind of self-indulgent abdication. And just here, the difficulties of delegation being abundantly clear, the unwanted implications become prominent as well. For what Antonio's refusal reveals is not simply brute, inertial resistance on the part of Prospero's human subjects, but his covert dependence on them as well, the fact that, for all

his imaginative autonomy, he is obliged to rely on the good will—
it is not too much to say the *free* will—of those whose behavior
he would otherwise dictate. *The Tempest* openly confesses through
its extraordinary Epilogue the playwright's and the actor's dependence on members of the audience to assent to and complete the
dramatic illusion, to fall into a consensus that what has just taken
place has had coherence and substance and is thus worthy of the
applause they are asked to accord it.[12] But perhaps in Prospero's
dependence on the very subjects he seems to manipulate, the playwright's dependence on the actor is revealed as well, of whom he
might well say, as Prospero says of Caliban (a striking revelation
that magical powers apparently do not extend to common domestic
chores), "But as 'tis, / We cannot miss him" (1.2.310–11).

I am reminded at this juncture of a moment in *The Franklin's
Tale,* and wonder if Shakespeare might have been reminded as well.
The smitten Aurelius has applied to the clerk of Orleans for magical
help in gaining the favors of Dorigen, and the clerk has treated him,
by way of recommending his expensive services, to a spectacular
display of his powers in the form of sumptuous aristocratic visions,
scenes of hunting and hawking, jousting and dancing. But evening
draws on, and homelier considerations intrude:

> And whan this maister that this magyk wroughte
> Saugh it was tyme, he clapte his handes two,
> And farewel! Al oure revel was ago.
> And yet remoeved they nevere out of the hous,
> Whil they saugh al this sighte merveillous,
> But in his studie, ther as his bookes be,
> They seten stille, and no wight but they thre.
>   To hym this maister called his squier,
> And seyd him thus: "Is redy oure soper?
> Almoost an houre it is, I undertake,
> Sith I yow bad oure soper for to make."[13]

He cannot miss him: Surely we are justified in detecting here the
hand of the bourgeois, practical Franklin himself tugging at the
sleeve of sovereign fantasy, reminding us, anyway, if not the aristocratic Aurelius, that belief in magic comes rather more easily to
those whose privilege has long accustomed them to having their
own way than to those who have been obliged to sustain themselves through compromise and accommodation. Imagination, the
Franklin's brief episode reminds us, however lofty or imperious,
is dependent on the body and those who provide for it. To forget
that chastening perspective is to indulge in the untrammeled fanta-

sies of Shakespeare's Stephano, who blandly imagines a pliable Miranda cheerfully married to the man who has murdered her father, the happy couple inhabiting a "brave kingdom," where they will have their music for nothing (3.2.106–7, 144–45). Stephano will, of course, return to his own body by way of the horsepond.

It is not hard to believe that some part of William Shakespeare, who sprang, after all, from the provincial middle class, would have felt akin to Chaucer's Franklin. And I speculate that the same part was keenly aware of the material underpinnings of the theatrical enterprise, alive to the humiliations potentially in store for his own sovereign imagination, when obliged to cede absolute control and condescend to the flesh of dramatic production. Hamlet's charge to the players comes immediately to mind, not only because it is delivered *de haut en bas* and with undisguised distaste for the clumsiness and sweat of actual theater, but also because it shows the prescriber so painfully aware of the kinds of things that *can* go wrong once actors are given their head. And surely we are made to doubt the very efficacy of dramatic prescription when we realize that Hamlet's classicizing precepts seem utterly inadequate to contain the energies of the larger play (*The Tragedy of Hamlet, Prince of Denmark*) in which they and their preceptor are embedded. Indeed, Hamlet's warning against digressions (3.2.38–45) itself constitutes a digression within this larger play.

More generally, what might be called a reserved and skeptical attitude about mediations of all kinds may be related to the playwright's necessity of surrendering his work to strange flesh and spirit. We might consider Viola's difficulties with disguise in *Twelfth Night* in this context, the curious way that her disguise once adopted begins to commit its user to meanings and stances beyond her will, of inverting the relationship so that user becomes used, her intention cancelled by the independent logic of the means she has chosen to effect it. As Viola has said to the captain, perhaps with a good deal more truth than she is immediately aware of, "Conceal me what I am, and be my aid / For such disguise as haply shall become / The form of my intent" (1.2.53–55). She means, of course, a disguise that will *befit* her intention, but can't quite help speaking of a disguise that will become her intention in the sense that it will *turn into* or *displace* it.

Viola's plight reminds us of the uncanny way means tend to acquire meanings of their own, not excluding that ultimate mediation, language itself. Perhaps it is some stifled intuition of this phenomenon that drives Malvolio in the same play to adopt his stilted idiom, so full of doublets and overly precise inkhorn terms. It is

as if he were trying against the odds to make the treacherous linguistic medium quibble-proof, to protect it against the efforts of
interlocutors to divert or appropriate his meanings. And against
the backdrop of this radical insight in Shakespeare's last romantic
comedy, the effort of the lords in the earlier *Love's Labor's Lost*
to protect themselves from experience, in effect, by retreating into
the signifier and fetishizing it, seems naive indeed. Their witty control over signs all unwittingly thrusts into prominence the fact that
they have no control over experience whatever. It would be nice
if, as Moth jokingly suggests (1.2.35–54), one could compress a
three-years duration into one hour by studying "three years" rather
than studying three years (a witty example of what the logicians
call the "use/mention fallacy"), but the clock is still ticking here
just as surely as is Malvolio's watch in the later play, and nothing
can finally forestall the embassy of Marcade.

I would suggest that in the case of the lords in *Love's Labor's
Lost,* as in the case of Hamlet's charge to the players, we have a
situation that reminds us of the playwright's reluctance to surrender himself to the means and meanings of others, playwright, Hamlet, and lords, that is, preferring to linger in the antechamber of
the sign and not risk the vagaries of the signified. And I would
further suggest that in the case of Malvolio we have something like
the playwright's attempt to undo that surrender after the fact, to
shadow from within his fiction his regret at having delivered it up
in the first place. To try to make your dramatic fiction proof against
the wills of those who present it is surely an exercise in futility,
and just here antithetical ways of power seem to yield to a kind of
activity that seems openly to confess its impotence.

Though it is as well not to overlook the facts of the matter.
Shakespeare, unlike the University Wits who sneered at him, per-
vaded the process of theatrical production from beginning to end,
and was almost certainly an actor at one time or another in the
very plays that he had himself conceived. In a sense, he could
continue to exercise a measure of control from within the dramatic
fiction, though compared to the pre-incarnational playwright
whose command of his fictive world is nearly absolute, that control
must have been radically curtailed, and certainly effected, when
effected at all, far more by bargain and compromise than by simple
fiat. I would propose in this context to see the ghost of Hamlet's
father as a shadow of the playwright's desire to control the shape
of his dramatic fiction from within its embodiment in production,
to undo after the fact the playwright's necessary surrender to those
means, very much including the actors, that have meanings of

their own. Nobody has ever doubted the imperative and directorial character of this ghost ("Pity me not," "List, list, O, list!" "Revenge his foul and most unnatural murther," "Taint not thy mind," "Leave her to heaven"). What the ghost prescribes is, in effect, a brief and efficient revenge tragedy, and what he gets, perhaps precisely because he does prescribe so finally and flat-footedly, is surely one of the least-efficient dramas, in terms of executive dispatch, ever mounted on a stage. Young Hamlet obviously has ideas very different from his father's about the way *Hamlet* should proceed.

To the extent that the playwright-within-the-play behaves as if he were still the playwright at his desk, he appears as a ghost, a figure bearing all the forms of power without any of its substance. But we have Nicholas Rowe's say-so, and the question of its authority I will leave open, that the part of the ghost in *Hamlet* was played by none other than Shakespeare himself.[14] If so, we have a literal instance of the playwright contriving to reenter his play after he has surrendered control of it to those charged with its production.[15] And yet, he reenters it only in embracing, so to speak, the humility and uncertainty of the flesh. One wonders if, in consenting to dwindle into an actor, Shakespeare was recapitulating a gesture of renunciation required of his hero as well, who discovers, among other things in the course of his experience, that his deep plots may pall as well as another's. Shakespeare's reentry into the fiction he had otherwise relinquished, this time as an actor in the part of a ghostly and largely ineffectual preceptor, may have produced a powerful effect almost in spite of itself.

NOTES

1. See the fourth essay of *Totem and Taboo* in *The Standard Edition of the Complete Psychological Works of Sigmund Freud,* ed. James Strachey, trans. James Strachey et al., 24 vols. (London: Hogarth Press and the Institute of Psychoanalysis, 1953–1974), vol. 13, 100–61 and 143 in particular.

2. This and subsequent quotations from the works of Shakespeare are taken from *The Riverside Shakespeare,* ed. G. Blakemore Evans et al. (Boston: Houghton Mifflin, 1974).

3. Freud broaches this topic in the third essay of *Totem and Taboo, Standard Edition,* 13:94.

4. Michel Foucault, *Discipline and Punish: The Birth of the Prison* (1975), tr. Alan Sheridan (New York: Random House, 1979), 3–6.

5. Elaine Scarry, *The Body in Pain: The Making and Unmaking of the World* (New York: Oxford University Press, 1985), 27.

6. *Standard Edition* 13:48.

7. For a succinct presentation of the neoconflationist position, see Francis Barker and Peter Hulme, "Nymphs and Reapers Heavily Vanish: The Discursive

Con-Texts of *The Tempest*," in *Alternative Shakespeares,* ed John Drakakis (London: Methuen, 1989), 191–205. And for a measured, thoughtful, and sensible dissent from neo-conflationism, see Meredith Anne Skura, "Discourse and the Individual: The Case of Colonialism in *The Tempest,*" *Shakespeare Quarterly* 40, no. 1 (spring 1989): 42–69.

8. In speculating that Prospero would prefer the experience that he orchestrates to take the form of a plotless and wholly predictable spectacle rather than something we might be disposed to call a true drama, I follow Harry Berger, Jr., who remarks in what is still, after twenty-five years, one of the best essays on *The Tempest,* "[Prospero's] ingenuous pleasure tends to make him sacrifice plot to spectacle, and drama to theater." See "Miraculous Harp: A Reading of Shakespeare's *Tempest,*" *Shakespeare Studies* 5 (1969): 253–83. The current quotation occurs on p. 257 of this essay.

9. David Sundelson remarks, "*The Tempest* answers the question almost as soon as it is posed . . . for the first scene's brevity matches the ferocity of its threats. The movement from this scene to the next is from nightmare to waking relief, from a plunge toward death to the comfort of a father's reassurance." I would like to suggest that what Sundelson usefully calls "paternal narcissism" in this play nevertheless has distinct limits. See "So Rare a Wonder'd Father: Prospero's *Tempest,*" in *Representing Shakespeare: New Psychoanalytic Essays,* ed. Murray M. Schwartz and Coppélia Kahn (Baltimore: Johns Hopkins University Press, 1980), 34.

10. *Shakespeare and the Denial of Death* (Amherst: University of Massachusetts Press, 1987), 146–47.

11. An observation of Jonas Barish's is pertinent: "Artists dream of creating something permanent, fixed, and exempt from the ravages of time, well-wrought urns and mosaic saints. Inert matter they can force to do their bidding; they can impose their shaping wills on it, stamp it with their signatures. But how subdue human beings in the same way, who have wills of their own? How control a medium recalcitrant not with the brute heaviness of inanimate matter but with the wild rebelliousness of flesh and blood?" See *The Antitheatrical Prejudice* (Berkeley: University of California Press, 1981), 343.

12. For a fascinating account of the complex relations between actor and audience richly informed by psychoanalytic perspectives, see Meredith Anne Skura's recent *Shakespeare the Actor and the Purposes of Playing* (Chicago: University of Chicago Press, 1993).

13. *Canterbury Tales,* V (F) 1202–12. I quote the text of *The Riverside Chaucer,* ed. Larry D. Benson et al. (Boston: Houghton Mifflin, 1987).

14. "Though I have inquired, I could never meet with any farther account of him in this way [as an actor], than that the top of his performance was the Ghost in his own *Hamlet.*" See "Some Account of the Life of William Shakespeare," the preface to Rowe's 1709 edition of the plays.

15. Marjorie Garber notes the further and even less certain tradition, apparently founded by William Oldys toward the middle of the eighteenth century, that Shakespeare took the part of old Adam in *As You Like It,* the figure, of course, who warns Orlando of his danger and urges him to flee. She sees both parts as "appropriate to a playwright's role, giving his protagonist motive for action, so that the casting acts as a kind of metadramatic shadow or reflection of the relationship between author, actor, and plot." See *Shakespeare's Ghost Writers: Literature as Uncanny Causality* (New York: Methuen, 1987), 12.

Contributors

Kathryn Barbour received her Ph.D. in 1989 from SUNY Binghamton and is currently an Associate Professor at Cazenovia College. Her area of special interest is Renaissance and Restoration dramatic manuscripts—for her dissertation she located and prepared an edition of an unpublished late 17th century comedy. She is at work on another play from the same period: an anonymous feminist comedy.

Susanne Collier is an Associate Professor at California State University at Northridge. She has published reviews and analyses of Royal Shakespeare Company productions. Her bibliography of recent criticism of the works of James I appeared in ELR in 1994. Her current work is an analysis of the fictions of Shakespeare's life. She is the vice-President of the Renaisance Conference of Southern/California.

Sara Eaton is an Associate Professor in the Department of English at North Central College. Her recent publications include "Defacing the Feminine in Renaissance Tragedy," *The Matter of Difference: Materialist Feminist Criticism of Shakespeare*, ed. Valerie Wayne (Harvester and Cornell, 1991), 181–98; "Beatrice-Joanna and the Rhetoric of Love in *The Changeling*," *Theatre Journal* 36 (1984): 371–82; reprinted in *Staging the Renaissance: Studies in Elizabethan and Jacobean Drama*, eds. David Scott Kastan and Peter Stallybrass (Routledge, 1991); "A Woman of Letters: Lavinia in *Titus Andronicus*", *Shakespearean Tragedy and Gender*, eds. Shirley Nelson Garner and Madelon Sprengnether, (Indiana University Press, 1996).

Ann Rosalind Jones, Professor of Comparative Literature at Smith College, the author of articles on feminist theory, Renaissance writers (Sidney, Nashe, Webster) and gender ideology, recently published *The Currency of Eros: Women's Love Lyric in Europe. 1540–162-* (1990).

GILLIAN MURRAY KENDALL is an Associate Professor of English at Smith College. She has written mostly on Shakespeare and is currently at work on a book-length study of the body as political palimpsest in non-Shakespearean Renaissance tragedy.

ARTHUR L. LITTLE, JR. is Associate Professor of English at UCLA. He is currently at work on a book entitled *Sacrificial Altarings:* Virginity, Race, and Pornography in Shakespeare and Early Modern Culture, forthcoming from Stanford University Press.

RONALD R. MACDONALD, Professor of English Language and Literature at Smith College, is the author of *The Burial-Places of Memory: Epic Underworlds in Vergil, Dante, and Milton* (1987) and *William Shakespeare: The Comedies,* 1992, a volume in Twayne's English Authors series.

DAVID McCANDLESS currently teaches at the University of California at Berkeley. He has published essays on Shakespeare in several journals, including *Shakespeare Quarterly,* and is the author of *Gender and Performance in Shakespeare's Problem Comedies* forthcoming in 1997 from Indiana University Press. In addition to teaching and writing about Shakespeare's plays, he also directs them, having recently staged productions of *All's Well That Ends Well, Measure for Measure,* and *The Two Gentlemen of Verona.*

ROBERT N. WATSON, Professor of English at UCLA, is the author of numerous articles as well as *Shakespeare and the Hazards of Ambition* (Cambridge: Harvard University Press, 1984), *Ben Jonson's Parodic Strategy: Literary Imperialism in the Comedies* (Cambridge: Harvard University Press, 1987), and, most recently, *The Rest is Silence: Death as Annihilation in the English Renaissance* (Berkeley: University of California Press, 1994).

Index

Numbers in boldface refer to illustrations.